Modernism from the

Writing Wales in En

G000154940

CREW

CREW series of Critical and Scholarly Studies
General Editor: Professor M. Wynn Thomas (CREW, University of Wales, Swansea)

This *CREW* series is dedicated to Emyr Humphreys, a major figure in the literary culture of modern Wales, a founding patron of the *Centre for Research into the English Literature and Language of Wales*, and, along with Gillian Clarke and Seamus Heaney, one of *CREW*'s Honorary Associates. Grateful thanks are extended to Richard Dynevor for making this series possible.

Other titles in the series
Stephen Knight, *A Hundred Years of Fiction* (978–0–7083–1846–1)

Barbara Prys-Williams, *Twentieth-century Autobiography* (978–0–7083–1891–1)

Kirsti Bohata, *Postcolonialism Revisited* (978–0–7083–1892–8)

Modernism from the Margins

The 1930s Poetry of Louis MacNeice and Dylan Thomas

Writing Wales in English

CHRISTOPHER WIGGINTON

UNIVERSITY OF WALES PRESS
CARDIFF
2007

British Library Cataloguing-in-Publication Data
A catalogue record for this book is available from the British Library

ISBN 978-0-7083-1927-7

THE ASSOCIATION FOR
WELSH WRITING IN ENGLISH
CYMDEITHAS LLÊN SAESNEG CYMRU
Recommended text

Published with the financial assistance of the Welsh Books Council

Printed in Wales by Gwasg Dinefwr, Llandybïe

CONTENTS

GENERAL EDITOR'S PREFACE

The aim of this series is to produce a body of scholarly and critical work that reflects the richness and variety of the English-language literature of modern Wales. Drawing upon the expertise both of established specialists and of younger scholars, it will seek to take advantage of the concepts, models and discourses current in the best contemporary studies to promote a better understanding of the literature's significance, viewed not only as an expression of Welsh culture but also as an instance of modern literatures in English worldwide. In addition, it will seek to make available the scholarly materials (such as bibliographies) necessary for this kind of advanced, informed study.

M. Wynn Thomas,
Director, CREW (*Centre for Research into the English Language and Literature of Wales*)
University of Wales, Swansea

ACKNOWLEDGEMENTS

In completing this book I owe a considerable debt of thanks to my friend John Goodby for offering generous encouragement, critical insight and personal support over the whole duration of this project.

For their help and support during the development and completion of this book I would like to thank the following friends and colleagues: in particular Richard Chamberlain, Gareth Downes, and Steven Vine for, respectively, pastoral, parabolic and monstrous discussions; and in general Lynn Dobbs, Victor Golightly, Medwin Hughes, Lian John, Marcus Leaning, Kevin Matherick, Steve Norris, Linden Peach, Rob Penhallurick, Harri Roberts, Berthold Schoene, Catrin Thomas, M. Wynn Thomas, Jeni Williams, Dave Woolley and Paul Wright.

Finally, thanks to my parents and brother for their patience and support over the years.

ABBREVIATIONS

References to works by Louis MacNeice and Dylan Thomas are included within the main body of the text. The following abbreviations are used followed by the appropriate page number(s):

CPLM   Louis MacNeice, *Collected Poems*, ed. E. R. Dodds
         (London: Faber & Faber, 1979)
TSAF   Louis MacNeice, *The Strings Are False: An Unfinished
         Autobiography*, ed. E. R. Dodds (London: Faber & Faber, 1996)
CPDT   Dylan Thomas, *Collected Poems 1934–1953*, eds. Walford
         Davies and Ralph Maud (London: Dent, 1988)
CLDT   Dylan Thomas, *The Collected Letters*, ed. Paul Ferris
         (London: Dent, 1985)
UMW   Dylan Thomas, *Under Milk Wood*, ed. Walford Davies and
         Ralph Maud (London: Dent, 1995)

All other references are contained in numbered chapter endnotes.

Introduction

'Night-bound doubles':
Louis MacNeice, Dylan Thomas
and the 1930s

To return to the problems of the young poets of the 1930s: in changing social
and political circumstances they were faced with forging their own poetry and
poetics from their dual inheritance . . . What is fascinating, however, is the
way poets from differing class and educational backgrounds reacted differently
to their shared aesthetic inheritance, and thus produced differing varieties of
hybrid which expressed distinct ideological nuances.

Adrian Caesar, *Dividing Lines: Poetry, Class
and Ideology in the 1930s*[1]

I see my night-bound double, slumped apart
On a conveyor belt that, decades high
In emptiness, can neither stop nor start

But first moves on for ever till we die.
It is too late for questions; on this belt
We cannot answer what we are or why.

Louis MacNeice, *Autumn Sequel*[2]

In Canto XX of *Autumn Sequel* Louis MacNeice refers to the recently buried
Dylan Thomas (figured throughout the poem as 'Gwilym') as his 'night-
bound double'. Whilst this phrase is revealing of a kinship in morose
personality, it is also, more importantly, a notice of what separates MacNeice
and Thomas, offering 'Gwilym' up as a poetic 'other' to Louis, and vice
versa. Indeed, though *Autumn Sequel* reflects back panoramically upon a
poetic map of Britain in the 1930s and after, it is upon 'the bulbous Taliessin
[*sic*]' that the poem focuses most acutely (*CPLM*, 404). There are, of course,
biographical links to be made between Thomas and MacNeice. They were

born less than a decade apart, Thomas in Swansea on 27 October 1914, MacNeice in Belfast on 12 September 1907. Both worked and lived in London for a substantial part of their lives. During their time in London, both worked for the BBC, and they met through this connection. Both might be thought of as refuseniks in the Spanish Civil War. Both were at the periphery of radical politics and neither was a fully paid-up member of the Communist Party. Neither fought in the Second World War. Both suffered premature death caused partly by drink. There are also crucial differences, though, which cannot be overlooked. MacNeice was the son of a minister, Thomas of a schoolmaster. While Thomas's father wanted him to have an 'English' upbringing – organizing elocution lessons to erase his Welsh accent – MacNeice had a formal English education which culminated at Oxford University, from where he went on to teach classics, first at Birmingham University, and later at Bedford College, University of London.

Both Thomas and MacNeice emerged as poets in the early 1930s, a period of economic turmoil, social radicalism and the supercession of High Modernism by new literary styles. The *New Signatures* (1932) and *New Country* (1933) anthologies edited by Michael Roberts, and collections by poets represented in them – William Empson, William Plomer, Bernard Spencer, John Lehmann, Cecil Day Lewis, Stephen Spender – rapidly established a formally non-experimental, discursive, politically left poetic norm. Significantly, neither Thomas nor MacNeice appeared in either volume. And it is to their shared difference as 1930s poets that this book hopes to attend.

MacNeice and, in particular, Thomas continue to be marginal figures in literary histories of the 1930s, as is attested by recent critical work on the period. In their introduction to *Rewriting the Thirties: Modernism and After* (1997) Keith Williams and Steven Matthews write:

> Our reason for putting this anthology together is that we thought it long overdue to challenge the persistent aftermyth of the thirties as a homogeneous anti-modernist decade. Outdated cultural maps of the time sustain a damagingly restricted canon centred on a narrow genealogy of polarised relations between aesthetics and politics, or between difficulty and accessibility.[3]

Yet, in the whole collection of essays, Thomas is mentioned only twice, MacNeice less than a handful of times. If this seems like special pleading, the collection's underachievement in the task it sets itself may also be apparent in its failure to consider women writers of the period adequately, confining them effectively to one chapter, entitled 'Alien experiences'. In so doing, *Rewriting the Thirties: Modernism and After* is representative of critical studies of the literature of the pre-war decade. Lately, however, this particular imbalance has begun to be addressed. Janet Montefiore's revisionary *Men and Women Writers of the 1930s: The Dangerous Flood of History*, for example – in many regards a response to questions raised by the same author about the critical orthodoxy of accounts of the 1930s in *Feminism and Poetry: Language, Experience, Identity in Women's Writing* – addresses the critical neglect of writers such as Storm Jameson, Rebecca West and Sylvia Townsend Warner. Unfortunately, Thomas's near-total omission from, and MacNeice's partial marginalization in, critical accounts of the 1930s have yet to be rectified.

What this suggests is that literary histories of the 1930s have not changed substantially since Samuel Hynes's 1976 characterization of the decade as that of the 'Auden Generation'.[4] As Adrian Caesar, one of the few critics willing to question the validity of so totalizing an association, observes, 'Since about 1975, critics and literary historians have often agreed to define Auden by the use of the words 'the 1930s' or vice versa.'[5] Notwithstanding A. T. Tolley's *The Poetry of the Thirties* (which Caesar's canny 'about' may anyway excuse), which assigns a chapter to Dylan Thomas, the persistence of this metonymic association is easy to trace.[6] Bernard Bergonzi, in *Reading the Thirties: Texts and Contexts* (1978), for example, argues that the term 'Thirties' 'largely corresponds to what Samuel Hynes . . . calls the Auden Generation', and even Valentine Cunningham's *British Writers of the Thirties* (1986), an attempt to provide an exhaustive account of the period, does very little to challenge its own assessment that 'the Auden generation remains canonical'.[7]

Why this should actually be the case is, though, far from clear. Hynes, Bergonzi and Cunningham each fails to account adequately for the primacy of Auden in their respective study. As Caesar points outs, Bergonzi fails to offer any reasons why those writers outside of his purview 'belong on different maps . . . to be sought on different expeditions', whereas Hynes bluntly rationalizes the nature of his study in the following terms:

English literature has been middle-class as long as there has been a middle class, and the generation of the 'thirties was not different in this respect from its predecessors; most of the writers I deal with here came from professional families, and were educated at public schools and at Oxford and Cambridge. Virtually no writing of literary importance came out of the working class during that decade.[8]

This is representative not only of the huge investment of 'literary value' in Auden, but also of his ideological function. As Peter McDonald writes, 'Few better examples could be found of the "hidden agenda" of much apparently "literary" criticism, whereby games of evaluation are played in order to strengthen what is in fact an extra-literary orthodoxy . . . the English myth of the 1930s.'[9] The evaluative 'games' of *British Writers of the Thirties* may be very different, but Cunningham's grounds for the centrality of the Auden group are equally nebulous. He asserts that 'the influence of Auden on his time was extreme' and that 'Auden and his group were regarded by very many of their contemporaries as the central figures'. He fails, however, to provide any detail about how this 'influence' manifested itself.[10]

This associative justification mirrors Stephen Spender's account of Auden's presence in the 1930s:

> What we had . . . in common was in part Auden's influence, in part also not so much our relationship to one another as to what had gone before us. The writing of the 1920s had been characterised variously by despair, cynicism, self-conscious aestheticism, and by the prevalence of French influences. Although it was perhaps symptomatic of the political post-war era, it was consciously anti-political. . . . Perhaps, after all, the qualities which distinguished us from the writers of the previous decade lay not in ourselves, but in the events to which we reacted. These were unemployment, economic crisis, nascent fascism, approaching war . . .[11]

In this account Spender, like Cunningham, refers to the influence of Auden on the poetry of the period, but also, significantly, to a shared reaction against the perceived lack of political engagement by Modernism. Today, this would appear a curious distortion; how could Ezra Pound, Wyndham Lewis, D. H. Lawrence, 'the writing of the 1920s', seem 'consciously anti-political'? That said, this shift is endorsed not only by most accounts of the 1930s, but also by historians of Modernism. Thus, Bradbury and McFarlane argue that after 1930 'certain elements of Modernism seem to be reallocated, as history increasingly came back in for intellectuals, as, with the loss of purpose and social cohesion, and the accelerating pace of technological change, modernity was a visible scene open to simple report'.[12]

However, critics such as Alan Wilde have questioned the nature and extent of a 1930s break with, or shift away from, Modernism:

> No movement terminates abruptly, least of all modernism, and crisis, in any case, is not termination, in literary periods any more than in drama. So it is hardly surprising that modernism continues on – not only in isolated pockets,

as it does today – but, at least until the Second World War, as a definable (if increasingly unstable) movement with its own special characteristics, most notably in England in the nineteen thirties among the members of the Auden Group. The fact is that the major preoccupations of the earlier decade are still visible in the late modernism of its successor, and the writers of the thirties reveal themselves to be, if anything, still more self-conscious, yet more aware of the rift between self and world than their elders. But differences there are . . .[13]

Indeed, Modernism, in the wake of recent work by Peter Nicholls, Marjorie Perloff and others, is currently being rethought as a plural, multi-stranded phenomenon, rather than the monolithic movement it was often regarded as before the 1980s and 1990s.[14] This book attempts to engage with the 'differences' Wilde notes by following this recent re-imagining. Crucial to this process is a re-examination of the responses to High Modernism in the work of its 1930s successors in Britain. It is in the light of this new appraisal that the work of Dylan Thomas and Louis MacNeice can be seen as key to any understanding of the development away from the disruptive radical procedures of Eliot, Joyce and others.

As studies of British literary Modernism have noted, it was largely a non-English phenomenon.[15] Of those writers generally designated 'Modernist' – Joseph Conrad, Henry James, Ezra Pound, T. S. Eliot, W. B. Yeats, James Joyce, Wyndham Lewis, Ford Madox Ford, Katherine Mansfield, D. H. Lawrence and Virginia Woolf – only two, Lawrence and Woolf, were English by birth and upbringing. To cite them in support of claims for Modernism as an English phenomenon would therefore be to reveal the contradictions of such a formulation. Lawrence and Woolf were figures marginal, in many ways, to a metropolitan English centre, one a working-class Nottingham writer and the other a woman. Two of the other four canonical authors of High Modernism – Eliot and Pound – were American, while another two, Yeats and Joyce, were Irish.

In this connection, the Irish and Welsh contexts of MacNeice and Thomas are studied in depth in this book. Whilst the relationships of Ireland and Wales to their poetries have been tackled in criticism (in Thomas's case from the 1950s onwards, in MacNeice's since the late 1980s), these studies have been done at the expense of a consideration of the Modernism of their poetry. The explicit anti-Modernism of the critical approaches of Peter McDonald and, in particular, Edna Longley to Louis MacNeice, is matched by an implicit resistance to the Modernist engagements of Thomas's early work in critics' concentration on his work after 1940.[16] In neither case is their mediation of national identity theorized. By contrast, parts of this book follow work undertaken in the last decade on Ireland's 'post-colonial' situation. (Theoretical accounts of Wales and Welsh writing in English have emerged only very recently.)

That said, post-colonial readings of Ireland and Wales must be performed sensitively, as a consideration of the applications of such readings to Ireland suggests. Ireland's case is not that of, say, India, and to see the colonial history of Ireland as such is not only to diminish the impact of colonization in countries like India, but also to fail to understand the historical specificity of Ireland's location within a colonial framework. Yet, to see Ireland placed alongside, or as part of, the Third World in critical study is not uncommon. Edward Said, for one, regards Ireland, with areas of South America, Africa and Asia, as a site of colonial contention, positioning 'bog dwellers' as counterparts to 'innumerable niggers, . . . babus and wogs', whilst Fredric Jameson emphasizes Ireland's Third World status by characterizing Joyce's Dublin, for example, in one of the Field Day pamphlets, as an 'under-developed village'.[17] And in so doing they highlight Ireland's role, and thus the role of Irish literature, in colonial history and present Ireland as a Third World nation, a poor 'other' to England, part of the 'cultural domain' of a developing world, set in opposition to the First World of European Modernism. (To see the anglophone literature of Wales located within a similar geography is not uncommon either. For example, Tony Conran writes that 'Anglo-Welsh poetry differs from other poetry in the English language . . . First it has, in its background, a different civilization – it is like English poetry written by Irishmen or Indians. Second, it shares its territory with another linguistic community which regards its tongue as the right and natural language of the country – a claim which Anglo-Welsh writers often accept, and which even if they dispute, they cannot ignore. In this respect, Anglo-Welsh poetry is like English written by Nigerians or Maoris.'[18])

For many, however, to argue along these lines, to discuss Ireland's 'backwardness' and Third World status, is to ignore blatantly the historical and economic fact that Ireland was, and is, a relatively wealthy member of the First World. (It should be noted here, though, that at points Said's essay does seem to acknowledge the complex relationship between Ireland and Britain, as he writes that 'it is true the connections are closer between England and Ireland than between England and India'; and of the complexity of Yeats's own position Said remarks, 'he belongs . . . to the Protestant Ascendancy whose Irish loyalties . . . were confused'.[19]) Liam Kennedy, for example, writes that any comparative analysis of Ireland and African and Asian post-colonial nations has been flawed, stating that attempts 'to place Ireland in a Third World perspective turned out to be a largely empty enterprise'.[20] Kennedy explains that even if Ireland has been a nation less wealthy than Britain or France, it is wrong to think of it as underdeveloped. Average incomes in Ireland, Kennedy points out, even half a 'century earlier in time than in the case of African and Asian countries, belonged to a different economic league. That league was a West European one, with Ireland enjoying much the same average living standards as countries like Spain, Norway, Finland, Italy'.[21]

Through his rigid historical empiricism, however, Kennedy, to an extent, fails to take into account the complex ways in which the relationship between ideology and culture has been processed through Ireland's colonial history. It is primarily to this that Luke Gibbons addresses his argument in the introduction to *Transformations in Irish Culture*, asserting that 'Ireland is a First World country with a Third World memory'. Distinguishing between fact and ideology, and in so doing following the pioneering work of Raymond Williams, he argues that ideology and culture often take material form, that 'Culture transforms what it works on: it does not produce *ex nihilo*', and that 'Cultural representations do not simply come after the event, "reflecting" experience or embellishing it with aesthetic form, but significantly alter and shape the ways we make sense of our lives'. Gibbons writes of the problems of the idealist aesthetic of the 'autonomy of art', as well as of problems with the opposing approach,

> adopted by the dominant methodologies in historical research and the social sciences, which relegates questions of culture to the margins of social process. [In these terms] culture is, at best, a mere reflex of more manageable, 'objective' realities . . . or, at worst, a smokescreen, concealing economic and political truths through myth and other rhetorical excesses. Either way, cultural representations are at one remove from society, and hence are in no position to act as agents of historical change, or to help us understand social process.[22]

And, crucially for Gibbons, there is therefore a large gap between Ireland's economic and imaginative perceptions of itself. Even this account, though, whilst providing a useful corrective to crude empiricism, may be too simplistic, as to model Ireland as a country with a First World economy, in a similar fashion to Liam Kennedy, is not without its attendant complications.[23] Indeed, Stephen Slemon suggests a way out of the problematic construction of Ireland as a Third World country by offering instead the term 'Second-World', a semi-periphery in the terms of post-colonial theory. To refuse Ireland's status as Third World, though, is not to deny the legitimacy of claims for it as a country scarred by the exercise of British colonial power.

Instead, Ireland might be positioned between the colonial and the post-
colonial, as nations affected by the huge hegemonic sway of imperial and
colonial ideologies. In so doing, however, it is important to bear in mind
the important distinction to be made between imperialism and colonialism.
According to Declan Kiberd, for example, imperialism,

> is a term used to describe the seizure of land from its owners and their
> consequent subjugation by military force and cultural programming: the latter
> involves the description, mapping and ecological transformation of the occupied
> territory. 'Colonialism' more specifically involves the planting of settlers in
> the land thus seized, for the purpose of expropriating its wealth and for the
> occupiers' trade and culture.[24]

Rather than seeing MacNeice and Thomas as cases of 'Celtic' excess (and
thereby mirroring Auden-dominated accounts of the 1930s), or defining them
narrowly as 'Anglo-Welsh' or 'Anglo-Irish' writers (as in traditional
criticism of Thomas and more recent work on MacNeice), this book sees
their work as operating in dialectical and contradictory positions in relation
to discursive political norms. It argues that Thomas's work offers a critique
of the artistic rationalism and reflectionism of the 1930s, through an
insistence on the materiality of language and the inseparability of writing
and the body. MacNeice, it contends, makes explicit the contradictions
of myth-reliant High Modernism by refusing totalizing systems throughout
the contemporary and specific political and personal micro-narratives of
his work.

Taking issue with received critical opinion, chapter 1 argues that
MacNeice's Modernism is not solely to be found in his first collection of
poems, *Blind Fireworks* (1929), but continues throughout his work of the
1930s. His poetry of that period, it details, engages in complex ways with
the work of other Modernist writers. Such negotiations are traced through
close readings of a range of his poems of the 1930s, including 'Birmingham',
'An Eclogue for Christmas' and 'Snow'. The chapter acknowledges that in
each of these poems, as in most of his poetry of the 1930s, MacNeice resists
High Modernism's investments in the overarching symbol and formal frag-
mentation. It argues, though, that in the poetry's concern with the integrity
of self, its simultaneous distrust of, and fascination with, surface and percep-
tion, and its suspicion of both total systems and the process of representation,
it displays an equally valid Modernism, closely attuned to the historical and
political upheavals of the period from which it emerges.

Following on from this discussion, the second chapter argues for a recon-
sideration of Thomas's early work. Its focus is on his poetry's interest in

the body and identity formation, both of which are read in the light of various theoretical perspectives. It begins with an account of the Modernist language of his 1930s poetry, discussing the density of poetic devices, wordplay, and patterning by which Thomas mimicked something of the spatial dislocations of High Modernist poetry within formally conservative verse-structures. It then moves on to a detailed account of Thomas's surrealist engagements. In doing so it compares and contrasts Thomas's and Eliot's appropriation of the Metaphysical poets, arguing that in staging the body rather than the 'mind of Europe', Thomas's poetry challenges the impulse to transcend in High Modernism.

Chapter 3 locates MacNeice within an Irish context. It charts the history of his exclusion from an 'Irish' 'canon' and his recent recuperation by critics and poets from Ireland, among them Edna and Michael Longley, and Paul Muldoon. Further, it examines representations of Ireland and Irish identity in the poetry, arguing that in contrast to the variousness and indeterminacy of the work discussed in chapter 1, MacNeice's poetry on Ireland leans towards stasis and petrifaction. Underlying this, the chapter argues, is a characteristic tendency of Irish writing of the period to view tradition as betrayal, which in turn, and paradoxically, results in poetic representation of the splintering of the self. This Modernist refusal to locate an originary moment of selfhood in any identifiably rooted or concrete terms is traced through the poetry's interest in childhood and motherhood. The problematic of a MacNeicean self-definition (and that of the critical definition/location of MacNeice) is not read as simply that of an Irish national alienated abroad. It is regarded, instead, in terms of a hybridity that challenges those post-colonial models of Ireland that work in crudely oppositional terms.

The disturbing qualities of Thomas's Modernism are discussed in chapter 4, which reflects upon and examines the ways in which he was dismissed by critics of the time as a shallow showman offering an adolescent poetry of excess. This 'monstering' of Thomas is considered alongside the poetry's interest in the monstrous. His surrealism is discussed once more, on this occasion in relation to his timely use of the Gothic. In this way, Thomas's miscegenatory Modernism is read in the light of recent theoretical work on monstrosity and the avant-garde. The chapter argues that Thomas's poetry of the 1930s has the disruptive quality of an event that is not immediately translatable into a meaning that can be mastered. These radical and sub-versive elements of his work are discussed in the context of a mainstream 1930s response to the historical crisis that encouraged a reaction against experimentalism.

Chapter 5 begins with a consideration of the politics of MacNeice's work. Challenging both the dismissal of him as an apolitical poet and the converse recovery of him as a liberal humanist, the chapter identifies and details the unstable political pragmatism of his work of the 1930s. This instability is traced through *Autumn Journal*. The chapter argues that *Autumn Journal*, like MacNeice's poetry concerning Ireland, departs from accounting for the self in terms of surface, flux and perception. Rather than concretizing the self, though, the poem interrogates it to the point of dissolution. Through the performativity of its voices, texts and positions, *Autumn Journal* later moves away from an interrogation of the self and towards an account of the subject within history. This shift from a High Modernist search for potential autonomy towards a resigned postmodern recognition of limited agency is historicized. Throughout, the book problematizes an easy division between Modernism and postmodernism.

Chapter 6 addresses Wales's relationship to Dylan Thomas and his work. Following on from chapter 4, it is noted that the 'monstering' of Thomas was not confined to an English critical tradition, but also occurred within Wales. Engaging with more recent work on both Thomas and Welsh writing in English generally, the chapter reads this response in the light of Homi K. Bhabha's theorizing of mimicry and hybridity. It also emphasizes the liminal and hybrid qualities of Thomas's poetry, and regards its complex negotiations of 'Welshness' and identity in terms of a Welsh writing in English tradition of the Gothic and grotesque. This account is historicized and used to complicate the recent reading of Modernism as a wholly positive assertion of national identity.

The book concludes by briefly tracing the Modernist elements of MacNeice's and Thomas's poetry of the 1940s and after.

1

'Poised on the edge of absence': Louis MacNeice, Modernism and the 1930s

I doubt that the Auden Generation would, in the long run, have made substantively different decisions or expressed substantively different attitudes had events been otherwise. In retrospect at least, modernism appears to have been sliding toward a state of exhaustion and impasse. Jogged from the heights their elders held, defensively and with a kind of aesthetic bravado, the writers of the thirties, and particularly the decade's ironists, found themselves more bewildered than heartened by their frequently superficial involvements: troubled by the detachments that, as they recognized, still afflicted them but uneasy in their demand for participation in a world whispering, beneath the shrill slogans and hopeful therapies, of disaster beyond the reach of politics and psychology and of disorder not to be stabilized by the symmetries of art. The chief paradox of the decade – the inevitable but unintended subversion of depth through a relentless attention to surface, undertaken in an attempt to change both self and world by rendering language transparent – this paradox marks the effective end of modernism and of the attitudes that made absolute irony possible.

Alan Wilde, *Horizons of Assent: Modernism, Postmodernism and the Ironic Imagination*[1]

Descending out of the grey
Clouds elephant trunk
Twitches away
Hat:
THAT
Was *not* what I expected,
A
Misdirected
Joke it seems to me;
'What about a levitation?' I had said,

Preening head for halo,
All alert, combed, sanctified,
I thank Thee, Lord, I am not like other men
WHEN
Descending out of the grey
Clouds elephant trunk . . . .
(and so *ad nauseam*)

Louis MacNeice, *'Elephant Trunk'* [2]

On 11 October 1925 the teenage Louis MacNeice delivered a paper entitled 'The mailed fist of common-sense and how to avoid it' to the Literary Society of his school. John Hilton remembers it as 'an amazing conglomeration of dreams, fables, parables, allegories, theories . . . [and] . . . quotations', and MacNeice offers excerpts from the paper in *Modern Poetry*:

> Common Sense is like Jargon: it can only say a thing in one way. Sense is good in prose and Nonsense in poetry . . . [section break] . . . But you must not think that good things are only to be found in Xanadu or in past history. The dwellers in Xanadu never saw a van going down the street and piled with petrol tins in beautiful reds and yellows and greens . . . it is the narrowly scientific spirit, the common sense spirit, the reduction of everything to formulae, that is the fly in the ointment.[3]

During the course of the paper, MacNeice went on to criticize Romanticism generally, and Wordsworth's poetry in particular, as 'the stuff of personal dreams made sufficiently impersonal to be palatable to others than oneself', and proclaimed that 'The business of the poets is to produce rabbits out of apparent vacancy . . . They supply the missing pieces to our jigsaws. They delve into our brains and fish up the king of salmon from beneath the weeds of convention.'[4] This seemingly adolescent anti-rationalism and anti-Romanticism was soon to manifest itself in the Modernist aestheticism of MacNeice's first collection of poems, *Blind Fireworks* (1929). According to MacNeice, the collection was founded on 'an esoteric mythology', and was called *Blind Fireworks* because the poems therein 'are artificial and yet random; go quickly through their antics against an important background, and fall and go out quickly'. Full of circular narratives, references to T. S. Eliot, Friedrich Nietzsche and Pythagoras, the collection expressed concerns with time, surface and sensory perception, through its imagery of clocks, marble, bells, ears and eyes.[5]

Perhaps unsurprisingly, given these origins, *Blind Fireworks* is often seen by MacNeice's critics as an immature irrelevance, a necessary first step maybe, but certainly one in the wrong direction. On the rare occasions that it has been deemed worthy of even limited critical attention, *Blind Fireworks* is read as the sole example of the young MacNeice's juvenile flirtation with Modernism. Edna Longley, for example, refers to the 'hothouse solipsism' and 'uncontrolled flamboyance' of the collection, Robyn Marsack to its 'wistful sensuousness' and 'abdication of control over the words', and Peter McDonald to the 'somewhat cavalier manifestos of flux' to be found in the early work generally.[6] It is with no small measure of relief that all three critics move quickly on to what they regard as the anti-Modernist terra firma of MacNeice's writing of the 1930s and after. Each also suggests that in MacNeice's criticism of this period can be found confirmation of his rejection of Modernism.

Superficially, this case isn't a difficult one to make. In his criticism MacNeice refuses the 'closed circle of exalted moments' which restricts Eliot and James Joyce, refers to Eliot's poems as 'studies from a corner' and comments that 'his [Eliot's] world view is defeatist and he sees mankind through the eyes of a pedant', remarks that are repeated more than once.[7] Ezra Pound and Wyndham Lewis, too, attract adverse commentary. MacNeice announces, for example, that 'Pound's bits of history and culture are so diverse and so particular as to fail to arouse many echoes', whilst 'Wyndham Lewis is basically a pessimist, thinking of human beings as doomed animals or determinist machines'.[8] However, apart from the fact that care needs to be taken in judging a writer's poetry by his or her criticism – the criticism can often serve as a blind, cover or red herring with regard to the poetry (as in Eliot's own notes to and comments on *The Waste Land*) – this is a one-sided assessment. Elsewhere, MacNeice writes approvingly that Eliot's 'verse was carefully fragmented to match the world as he perceived it' and praises Eliot for incorporating into poetry for the first time 'the contemporary world (and its implications of history)', its 'boredom and . . . glory'.[9] In the same vein, he observes Eliotically that:

> Pound takes the whole of history as stock for his soup and cuts backwards and forwards from one country or one century to another, adding plenty of the smell of cooking and the noise of the typewriter to make it clear that all these elements combine for him in a living and contemporary whole.[10]

MacNeice's ventriloquizing of Eliot in order to endorse Pound is revealing of his complex, ambivalent critical attitude to Modernist aestheticism, and his critical work should not, therefore, be taken simply to endorse a rejection of Modernist practice in his poetry of the 1930s. Take, for example, a

statement made in *The Poetry of W. B. Yeats* on the influence of Yeats and
Eliot on his generation of poets:

> We admired him [Yeats] too for his form. Eliot in 1921 had argued that, as
> the modern world is so complex, the poet must become 'more allusive, more
> indirect, in order to force, to dislocate if necessary, language into his meaning.'
> A Chaotic World, that is, could only be dealt with by the methods of *The
> Waste Land*. Yeats went back to an earlier tradition and suggested by his
> example, that, given a chaotic world, the poet is entitled, if he wishes, to
> eliminate some of the chaos, to select and systematise. Treatment of form and
> subject here went hand in hand; Yeats's formalising activity began when he
> thought about the world; as he thought it into a regular pattern, he naturally
> cast his verse in regular patterns also.[11]

Here MacNeice does not dissociate the Modernist project of rendering in
artistic terms the chaos of the modern world from that of the poetry that
followed, but suggests, rather, that, in the 1930s, Yeats's refurbishment of
well-made form seemed more useful tactically than Eliot's High Modernist
aesthetic of fragmentation. Peter McDonald writes that, as distinct from
MacNeice's poetry of the 1920s, 'much of his writing [of the 1930s] turns
on the very issue of how far the self is able to marginalize the other into
mere "context" and how far it is the context, the other, which gives meaning
to the self'.[12] I would agree. Whilst McDonald, though, takes this to mark
a shift away from Modernist poetry after *Blind Fireworks*, I would see it,
instead, as showing that MacNeice's poetry of the 1930s continues in an
utterly Modernist mode. Not only does it display a simultaneous distrust
of and fascination with representing surface and perception, it also offers
a complex engagement with other Modernist writers.

MODERNIST DIALOGUES

'An Eclogue for Christmas', for example, can be read as MacNeice's
dialogue with Yeats and Eliot in poetic form, and can allow for a slightly
different reading of the relationships between MacNeice's earliest work and
that of the 1930s from the one given by Longley, McDonald et al. MacNeice
notes that while he was at Marlborough he became obsessed by the Sitwells
and wrote various poems indebted to their fascination with the 'child-cult',
'fantasies' and 'Russian Ballet colouring'.[13] These include the following
poem, described by Jon Stallworthy as a 'harlequin motley':

> The pleasure boats have paddled all the day, holiday;
> Pay your penny, go away, come again on Saturday,
> The boats will be repainted and their pennons will be gay,
> The yellow fruit umbrellas in remote Kinsay
>   Will catch the yellow sun-rays . . .[14]

In 'The mailed fist of common-sense and how to avoid it' MacNeice also wrote approvingly of the ways in which 'The Sitwells place things in new positions. By expressing something in terms of something quite different they succeed in describing what we had previously thought indescribable'; and in *Modern Poetry* he noted how 'Their little jazz fantasies seemed to me extremely exciting. They were in tune with the "childlike" painting of Matisse and the sentimental harlequins of Picasso's blue period.'[15] By the 1930s, however, he seems to have become 'jazz-weary', as he puts it in 'An Eclogue for Christmas':

> A. Jazz-weary of years of drums and Hawaiian guitar,
> Pivoting on the parquet I seem to have moved far
> From bombs and mud and gas, have stuttered on my feet
> Clinched to the streamlined and butter-smooth trulls of the élite,
> The lights irritating and gyrating and rotating in gauze –
> Pomade-dazzle, a slick beauty of gewgaws –
> I who was Harlequin in the childhood of the century,
> Posed by Picasso beside an endless opaque sea,
> Have seen myself sifted and splintered in broken facets,
> Tentative pencillings, endless liabilities, no assets,
> Abstractions scalpelled with a palette-knife
> Without reference to this particular life.
> And so it has gone on; I have not been allowed to be
> Myself in flesh or face, but abstracting and dissecting me
> They have made of me pure form, a symbol or a pastiche,
> Stylised profile, anything but soul and flesh:
> And that is why I turn this jaded music on
> To forswear thought and become an automaton.
>   (*CPLM*, 33)

Critics tend to read this passage as confirmation of MacNeice's wholesale dismissal of the abstraction of Modernism. Longley, for example, paraphrases this section in the following manner:

> aestheticism, and Modernism which partly descends from it, have denied and fragmented what MacNeice values as human wholeness. The speaker

significantly prefers the fleshy particularities to abstraction, symbolism and pure form. Similarly in *Modern Poetry* MacNeice advocates a 'concrete poet' responding as a whole 'to concrete living.'[16]

Read in this way, 'An Eclogue for Christmas' would express MacNeice's disavowal of the abstraction and dissection of the self into a 'pure form, a symbol or a pastiche/Stylised profile' – into 'anything but soul and flesh' – as a result of writing that is 'without reference to this particular life'. Phrased differently, MacNeice here rejects Modernism as partly responsible for (and symptomatic of) the alienation of the self under capitalism, along the lines of Lukács's 1930s attack on Modernist expressionism's profligate re-enforcement of capitalist alienation, charging aestheticism and capitalism with being simultaneously accountable for the fragmentation and automatonization of the self.[17] Certainly this seems to be the sentiment of speaker A:

> A. The jaded calendar revolves,
>   Its nuts need oil, carbon chokes the valves,
>   The excess sugar of a diabetic culture
>   Rotting the nerve of life and literature;
>   Therefore when we bring out the old tinsel and frills
>   To announce that Christ is born among the barbarous hills
>   I turn to you whom a morose routine
>   Saves from the mad vertigo of being what has been.
> B. Analogue of me, you are wrong to turn to me,
>   My country will not yield you any sanctuary,
>   There is no pinpoint in any of the ordnance maps
>   To save you when your towns and town-bred thoughts collapse,
>   . . .

(CPLM, 33)

However, either to adopt Longley's stance ('MacNeice values . . . human wholeness) or to characterize the poem as representative of a type of MacNeicean Lukácsism, is to mistake the voice of speaker A for that of MacNeice himself. In fact, speaker A is a version of the disguised metropolitan aristocrat of the classical eclogue, a patronizing urbanite insisting on the fortunate ignorance of the country dweller, whose 'morose routine' allows him to evade the heady stimuli of city life. As speaker B remarks, though, they are analogues of each other, bound together by a shared awareness of the impossibility of 'sanctuary' in their time.

But they are also bound together by the formal conventions of the eclogue, defined by M. H. Abrams as 'an elaborately conventional poem expressing an urban poet's nostalgic image of the peace and simplicity of the life of shepherds and other rural folk in an idealized setting'. Also relevant is J. A. Cuddon's description of it as a

> short poem – or part of a longer one – and often a pastoral in the form of a dialogue or soliloquy. The term was first applied to Virgil's pastorals or bucolic poems. Thereafter it describes the traditional pastoral idyll that Theocritus, and Sicilian poets wrote. The form was revived by Dante, Petrarch and Boccaccio and was particularly popular during the 15th and 16th c[enturies].[18]

What these definitions miss, however, is the political potential of the pastoral eclogue. Spenser's eclogues in *The Shepheardes Calender*, for example, work allegorically and submerge their engagement with the politics of Elizabethan Britain. As Louis A. Montrose argues, 'symbolic mediation of social relationships was a central function of Elizabethan pastoral forms', and 'social relationships are, intrinsically, relationships of power'.[19] Annabel Patterson refers, also, to the disguised political elements of Virgil's eclogues: '[the] Virgilian pastoral referred to something other than itself, and specifically to the historical circumstances in which it was produced – the last phases of civil war between Brutus and Cassius, representing the old republic, and Antony and Octavian, agents and heirs of Caesarian centrism.'[20] And in 'An Eclogue for Christmas' MacNeice activates the politics of allegory belonging to classical eclogue by forcing the reality of a gentrified countryside up to the surface of the poem:

> B. The country gentry cannot change, they will die in their shoes
> From angry circumstance and moral self-abuse,
> Dying with a paltry fizzle they will prove their lives to be
> An ever-diluted drug, a spiritual tautology.
> They cannot live once their idols are turned out,
> None of them can endure, for how could they, possibly, without
> The flotsam of private property, pekinese and polyanthus,
> The good things which in the end turn to poison and pus,
> Without the bandy chairs and the sugar in the silver tongs
> And the inter-ripple and resonance of years of dinner-gongs?
>
> (*CPLM*, 35)

MacNeice's version of the pastoral, then, participates in, rather than recoils from, the growing strain of 1930s political writing, exposing the inaccuracy of Stephen Spender's ambiguous claim that in the 1930s a pastoral poetry wasn't political:

The sense of political doom, pending unemployment, Fascism, and the
overwhelming threat of war, was by now so universal that even to ignore these
things was in itself a political attitude. Just as the pacifist is political in refusing
to participate in war, so the writer who refuses to recognise the political nature
of our age must to some extent be refusing to deal with an experience in which
he himself is involved. But why should he not refuse? No reason, except that
the consciousness of excluded events would probably affect the scale of his
writing. A pastoral poem in 1936 was not just a pastoral poem: it was also a
non-political poem. A poem that rejected the modern consciousness of politics
as a universal fate.[21]

MacNeice's poetic radicalization of the pastoral is analogous to Empson's
contemporaneous characterization of it, in *Some Versions of Pastoral*
(1935), as a mode of ambiguity and conflict. For Empson, 'the pastoral
process' amounts to 'putting the complex into the simple' and, as both
Christopher Norris and Paul Alpers observe, is characterized by double irony,
double plot, artificiality, self-consciousness and conflict. Quoting Frank
Kermode, Norris writes, for example, that for Empson,

> the mood of Pastoral is, in itself an implicit denial of the very possibility of
> 'complete solutions', and that 'the Pastoral ironist is a figure set about by all
> manner of conflicting pressures and demands, among them the claim of political
> commitment as against the more 'complex', self-occupied pleasures of a rich
> imaginative life.[22]

In this way, then, Empson saw the pastoral mode as unstable and as con-
taining the potential for utopian development. Indeed, its fundamental generic
instability meant that the 1930s writer could make the pastoral the vehicle
through which Modernism's dependency upon the misplaced idealism of a
metropolitan consciousness could be foregrounded. It is in this spirit that
MacNeice's exploitation of pastoral's ambivalence deconstructs not only
the binary terms of the debate around Modernism's valorization of the city
over the country, but also the assumed distance between High Modernism's
formal innovation and social commentary.[23]

SURFACE AND PERCEPTION

The tension between the aesthetic and the political is articulated most
comprehensively in 'Birmingham'. The poem, like much of MacNeice's
work of the period, displays a Modernist awareness of the circularity of

life, in terms of antinomies that continually threaten to collapse into each other.[24] His use of this strategy might be read alongside Eliot's, whose Sweeney asserts that 'Death or life or life or death/Death is life and life is death'.[25] As Anthony Burgess argues, in *A Mouthful of Air*:

> The poet's awareness of the circularity of life, in which things can be expressed in terms of their opposites, sometimes leads him [Eliot] into an aesthetic in which anything can be expressed as anything. If life can be death, it can also, and perhaps more reasonably, be a bowl of cherries, an automobile, a Force 9 wind, or a black dog. Take it further: life is a unity, and hence all aspects of life are relevant to each other. Draw . . . an arbitrary string of words, and they can all be made to stand in a tenable relation. Perspex, keyboard, cognac, magenta, spider, yogurt, eyes, forge, epilogue – these images, expressed as words, can be forced into a coherent pattern: 'The spider forges its perspex keyboard, eyes the magenta yogurt and its cognac epilogue.'[26]

'Birmingham' offers the most striking example of MacNeice's own version of this Modernist manoeuvre, its 'Cubical scent-bottles artificial legs arctic foxes and electric mops', flowing strangely into one another by means of assonance and consonance and without the demarcation of punctuation, illustrating MacNeice's fascination with sensory impressions:

> Smoke from the train-gulf hid by hoardings blunders upward, the brakes
>   of cars
> Pipe as the policeman pivoting round raises his flat hand, bars
> With his figure of a monolith Pharaoh the queue of fidgety machines
> (Chromium dogs on the bonnet, faces behind the triplex screens).
> Behind him the streets run away between the proud glass of shops,
> Cubical scent-bottles artificial legs arctic foxes and electric mops,
> [. . .]
>
> On the shining lines the trams like vast sarcophagi move
> Into the sky, plum after sunset, merging to duck's egg, barred with mauve
> Zeppelin clouds, and Pentecost-like the cars' headlights bud
> Out from sideroads and the traffic signals, crème-de-menthe or bull's blood,
> Tell one to stop, the engine gently breathing,
> [. . .]
>
>   (*CPLM*, 17, 18)[27]

In another way, too, this passage's fascination with what is referred to in 'Snow' as 'the drunkenness of things being various' (CPLM, 30), harks back to an earlier Modernist moment, since it also possesses its Futurist charge. MacNeice's weaving together of seemingly incongruous images gives way to a Futurist sense of the speed, change, flux and machinery of the city, and in the lines quoted above, his normal discursiveness is disturbed by the poem's register of spatial displacement. As Cuddon writes, both the Italian and Russian Futurists 'advocated a complete break with tradition and aimed at new forms, new subjects and new styles in keeping with a mechanistic age. They extolled dynamism, the machine (and machinery in general), speed (there was a speed cult) and the splendour of war and patriotism.' However, whilst both the Italian and the Russian Futurists privileged the liberatory power of Modernist language to shatter comfortable bourgeois modes of perception, the Russians, unlike the Italians, were wary of the alienating potential of industrial society, and also refused either to celebrate uncritically the technological acceleration of life or to glorify war.[28] Accordingly, as René Wellek argues, Futurism shares with Russian Formalism a valorization of the strange over the familiar, and several of MacNeice's images seem to work through defamiliarization, as defined by Victor Shklovsky:

> And art exists that one may recover the sensation of life; it exists to make one feel things, to make the stone *stony*. The purpose of art is to improve the sensation of things as they are perceived, and not as they are known. The technique of art is to make objects 'unfamiliar', to make forms difficult, to increase the difficulty of length and perception, because the process of perception is an aesthetic end in itself and must be prolonged.[29]

The literary language of the poem certainly defamiliarizes its objects and perceptions. The traffic lights ('crème-de-menthe or bull's blood'), the cars ('fidgety machines'), the trams ('vast sarcophagi') and the traffic policeman ('monolith Pharaoh') are all 'made strange'. However, whilst this process certainly redeems these images from the automatism of perception, there is also a sense that the Futurist frame of the poem in which they are placed is an ironic one, as the aesthetic dimension of 'Birmingham' jars against its political dimension. Throughout, in fact, MacNeice refuses to celebrate uncritically the city's abstract shapes, colours and movements, even as he is fascinated by them. (Interestingly, in 'Experiences with images', MacNeice accounts for this fascination in biographical/psychological terms: 'I also had certain early contacts with both mental illness and mental deficiency . . . I should add that our house was well lit by oil lamps (not enough of them) and so was full of shadows . . . These circumstances between them must have supplied me with many images of fear, anxiety, loneliness or monotony (to be used very often quite out of a personal context). They may also explain – by reaction – what I now think an excessive preoccupation in my earlier work with things dazzling, high coloured, quick moving, hedonistic or up-to-date.'[30]) Note, in particular, the final two lines of the poem:

> Splayed outwards through the suburbs houses, houses for rest
> Seducingly rigged by the builder, half-timbered houses with lips pressed
> So tightly and eyes staring at the traffic through bleary haws
> And only a six-inch grip of the racing earth in their concrete claws;
> In these houses men as in a dream pursue the Platonic Forms
> With wireless and cairn terriers and gadgets approximating to the fickle
>   norms
> And endeavour to find God and score one over the neighbour
> By climbing tentatively upward on jerry-built beauty and sweated labour.
> [. . .]
>
>   [. . .] to go on
> To where like black pipes of organs in the frayed and fading zone
> Of the West the factory chimneys on sullen sentry will all night wait
> To call, in the harsh morning, sleep-stupid faces through the daily gate.
>
> (CPLM, 18)

MacNeice sets up a dialectic between the sensory impressions of the poem and a critical attitude suggestive of a socialist politics. He attends to the commodified surfaces of city existence, but refuses to condemn the masses' involvement in them in the manner of the majority of the High Modernists. Instead, he writes that they exist under sedation, 'sleep-stupid' and in thrall to the 'ticketed gewgaws', in a state of false consciousness from which there is the possibility of waking to a new state of existence. Therefore, whilst MacNeice registers the damage that an industrial and commercial city like Birmingham can do to the human spirit, it is not dismissed, like the London of T. S. Eliot's *The Waste Land*, as a city of the dead. MacNeice's 'Birmingham' is more a dormant city, walked by the somnambulant rather than the phantasmal (and, indeed, he contrasted his approach to the city with that of Eliot, in *Modern Poetry*: 'living in a large industrial city, Birmingham, I recognized that the squalor of Eliot was a romanticized squalor because treated, on the whole, rather bookishly as *décor*. The 'short square fingers stuffing pipes' were not brute romantic objects abstracted into a picture by Picasso, but were living fingers attached to concrete people – were even, in a sense, my fingers.'[31]) In this way, 'Birmingham' articulates the ideological dimension of aesthetic seduction, in the Marxist sense, the state of false consciousness predicated upon the purportedly shallow pleasures of urban existence in the 1930s.

His treatment of subject matter in terms of spatial displacement rather than depth, witnessed in the aesthetic rather than cultural accretion of 'Birmingham' (and in the poem's shuttling between centre, suburbs and slums), led to MacNeice being compared unfavourably to his contemporaries. The early work's attention to surfaces was equated negatively with superficiality and facility, particularly in comparison to the work of Auden. To Geoffrey Grigson, for example, MacNeice's work of the late 1920s and early 1930s could be summed up in the following terms:

> Compared with Auden . . . all of MacNeice's fireworks and icicles were alien. Ixion, Pythagoras, Persephone, Orestes, de Sade, Origen – were mixed up in poems of a blatant cleverness. Still, cleverness it was, words were courted; and there in these juvenilia were stretched to tautness criss-crossing wires of form with this spangled acrobat performing on them; and the cleverness . . . grew and strengthened itself into a capable and convincing rhetoric, beholden to much, yet chiefly to MacNeice himself. The wires were still silvery and still glittered. The icicles, the ice-cream, the pink and white, the lace and the froth and the fireworks were still there, but underneath the game was the drop, the space, and the knowledge.[32]

The description of MacNeice as a 'spangled acrobat' is itself enamoured of the attractions of the poems and skilfully adapts MacNeice's own images of surface. However, when Grigson discusses more positively the development of MacNeice's work through the 1930s, he misses the point of its groundless performativity. This is because he insists on reading it in terms of a humanist existential evolution. In this manner, the 'game' of MacNeice's style is redeemed from irresponsibility by the 'criss-crossing wires of form' and the recognition of risk. But this is to discount the extent to which all poetry is 'game', and MacNeice's recognition of this in his dwelling on surfaces. Further, by a metaphorical sleight of hand, Grigson overcomes MacNeice's 'alien' eclecticism, in order to disguise him as an Audenesque purveyor of knowledge. The heroic circus tightrope-walker performing without a safety net may not be quite as elevated as the 'hawk . . . or the helmeted airman', but he is 'capable and convincing', nonetheless.[33] The radical superficiality of MacNeice's style has been appropriated and depoliticized.

Grigson's use of lists, in the passage quoted above, mimics MacNeice's own. In 1930s poetry generally, lists function metonymically to disperse the totalizing charm of the High Modernist investment in the symbol. They operate metonymically, rather than metaphorically; that is, in order to represent discursively a contingent snapshot of a given historical formation, as opposed to summing up a civilization.[34] Granted this, however, lists operate differently within the work of MacNeice and Auden. Auden's lists are centripetal, orientating their items towards a culturally diagnostic central consciousness:

> Yesterday the assessment of insurance by cards,
> The divination of water; yesterday the invention
> Of cartwheels and clocks, the taming of Horses.

> Yesterday the bustling world of the navigators.
> Yesterday the abolition of fairies and giants,
> The fortress like a motionless eagle eyeing the valley.
> The chapel built in the forest;
> Yesterday the carving of angels and alarming gargoyles.

> The trial of heretics among the columns of stone;
> Yesterday the theological feuds in the taverns
> And the miraculous cure at the fountain;
> Yesterday the Sabbath of witches; but to-day the struggle.[35]

MacNeice's lists, on the other hand, are centrifugal, dispersing by a principle of flux meaning outwards and onto the surface:

> With writings on the walls –
>   Hammer and sickle, Boicot, Viva, Muerra;
> With café-au-lait brimming the waterfalls,
>   With sherry, shellfish, omelettes.
> With fretted stone the Moor
>   Had chiselled for effects of sun and shadow;
> With shadows of the poor,
>   The begging cripples and the children begging.
> The churches full of saints
>   Tortured on racks of marble –
> The old complaints
>   Covered with gilt and dimly lit with candles.
> With powerful or banal
>   Monuments of riches or repression
> And the Escorial
>   Cold for ever within like the heart of Philip.
> With ranks of dominoes
>   Deployed on café tables the whole of Sunday;
> With cabarets that call the tourist, shows

Of thighs and eyes and nipples.
With slovenly soldiers, nuns,
And peeling posters from the last elections
Promising bread or guns
Or an amnesty or another
Order or else [. . .]

(*CPLM*, 110–11)

Both passages, from Auden's 'Spain 1937' and section VI of MacNeice's *Autumn Journal* (1938) (discussed in depth in chapter 5), are concerned with the volatile politics of Spain in the 1930s. Despite its seemingly arbitrary choice of items and campness of register, Auden's list works sequentially and ironically, pulling the reader inwards and downwards towards a moral centre of gravity. By contrast, MacNeice's list is less controlled and more provisional (note the repetitions of 'with' and 'or'). It surfaces MacNeice's attraction to the sensory and the physical, and puts a greater onus on the reader to construct both meaning and judgement. Put another way, the list of 'Spain 1937' is ironic in a stable way, whereas that of *Autumn Journal* is ironic in an unstable way, as MacNeice fails to distinguish between his and the residents' fascination. (The same contrast could also be drawn between the 'phonograph, [. . .] radio [. . .] car and [. . .] frigidaire' of Auden's 'The Unknown Citizen' and the 'Cubical scent-bottles artificial legs arctic foxes and electric mops' of MacNeice's 'Birmingham'.[36])

FLUX AND TOTALITY

Crucial to the surface momentum of MacNeice's poetry is his interest in the philosophy of flux. He admits to being 'swept away by Heraclitus, by the thesis that everything is flux and fire is the primary principle' whilst at Marlborough, and several of MacNeice's poems of the 1930s are concerned with the imposition of aesthetic patterns on the flux of the experience and consciousness of the self (*TSAF*, 96).[37] In 'Nature Morte', for example, the sense of representation as an ordering force gives way to the 'multiplication of lives' of the 'printed word' whilst in 'August', 'the living curve' of experience cannot follow modern representation, and is yet 'breathlessly the same' as it (*CPLM*, 21, 23). The principle of flux is, of course, a central concern of High Modernism. In the *Cantos* of Ezra Pound, for example, it connects the classical myths, esoteric references, literary allusions and ancient legends of the poem. In Canto II, it combines Browning's *Sordello*, Pound's idea of Sordello, Sordello himself, the Chinese Emperor So-Shu, Eleanor of Aquitaine, Helen of Troy, the legend of Tyro and Poseidon and that of Acoetes and Bacchus, and links the texts of Homer's *Iliad* and *Odyssey*, Browning's *Sordello* and Ovid's *Metamorphoses*.[38] As Hugh Kenner points out, Canto II is about 'the artist's struggle to bring form (Browning's *Sordello* and Pound's *Cantos*) out of flux (the Sordello documents, the sea)'.[39] Indeed, Pound's emphasis in Canto II is on the potential of transformation itself, of So-Shu's churning of the sea from liquid into solid, and of the 'void air taking pelt', both examples of what he referred to in a letter as the '"magic moment" or moment of metamorphosis, bust thru from quotidien into "divine or permanent world" Gods, etc.'.[40]

In the same way, though, that MacNeice's poetry challenges the High Modernist use of the great overarching symbol (in the *Cantos* Artemis' appearance – 'the Gods etc.' 'bust[ing] thru') in which is manifest the fate of all civilization, so, too, does it refuse the potential of flux to offer new epiphanic unities. In the place of sweeping classical allusion and prospective total systems are the transitory moments of 'The Brandy Glass' and 'The Sunlight on the Garden'. Even then, the briefest of moments of fixity are problematized. In 'The Brandy Glass', 'The moment cradled like a brandy glass' is invaded by a sense of choking and restriction, whilst the beauty of the moment of 'The Sunlight on the Garden' is dependent upon an awareness that 'it hardens and grows cold' and that 'We cannot cage the minute/ Within its nets of gold' (*CPLM*, 84).

The potential of both surface and flux to suggest and erase depth simultaneously is a constant concern of MacNeice's poetry. The world in 'Snow', 'is crazier and more of it than we think', and throughout the poem MacNeice exposes its simultaneously 'collateral and incompatible' nature by means of juxtaposition:

The room was suddenly rich and the great bay-window was
Spawning snow and pink roses against it
Soundlessly collateral and incompatible:
World is suddener than we fancy it.

World is crazier and more of it than we think,
Incorrigibly plural. I peel and portion
A tangerine and spit the pips and feel
The drunkenness of things being various.

And the fire flames with a bubbling sound for world
Is more spiteful and gay than one supposes –

On the tongue on the eyes on the ears in the palms of one's hands –
There is more than glass between the snow and the huge roses.

(CPLM, 30)

As Longley notes, 'suddenness' and 'fancy' are versions of flux and pattern, and in the poem sensory impressions are distorted and reassemble, as its images and perceptions shift from 'room' to 'bay-window' to 'snow' to 'pink roses' to 'tangerine and [. . .] pips' to 'fire flames' to 'tongue [. . .] eyes [. . .] ears [. . .] hands' and then return to the 'glass between the snow and the huge roses'.[41]

The invasions and distortions of perception in MacNeice's poetry work also to emphasize the fallacy of a totalizing world-view. In his poetry generally MacNeice is sceptical of any system that would claim for itself a position of absolute knowledge or authority, including Marxism. In the poem 'The Individualist Speaks', for example, MacNeice distances himself from all who would herald a new dawn; 'But I will escape, with my dog, on the far side of the Fair' (CPLM, 22). He assumes a similar position in 'To a Communist':

> Your thoughts make shape like snow; in one night only
> The gawky earth grows breasts,
> Snow's unity engrosses
> Particular pettiness of stones and grasses.
> But before you proclaim the millennium, my dear,
> Consult the barometer –
> This poise is perfect but maintained
> For one day only.

(CPLM, 22)

In reading this, it is worth bearing in mind MacNeice's comment that 'there is no such thing as a snow-white cause' (TSAF, 197). Indeed, the appeal of surfaces is that they often erase difference, and here it is the 'unity' of both snow and communism that 'engrosses' (a term which refers to fattening or making gross as much as it does to the absorbing of attention). The penultimate line, 'this poise is perfect', is similarly critical of the potential superficiality of communism's appeal to the predominantly upper middle-class writers of the time, referring, as it does, to aesthetic poise as much as anything else.[42] Accordingly, there is also a sense in which the poem is self-critical, less in its uncanny forward glance towards 'Snow' than in the acute awareness of the superficiality of surfaces, which culminates in its devastating final line.

What the poem is written out of, and looks forward to, in its repetitions of evanescence ('in one night only', 'For one day only'), is the topsy-turviness and opportunism of left-wing politics at the time. The shift in Comintern policy in 1934, aimed at bypassing the damaging antagonism between reformists and revolutionaries, away from a mechanistic vision of capitalism collapsing under the weight of its contradictions and towards Popular Frontism, allowed for immediate changes in party line. Arguably, it led to a terroristic reactionism in France and Spain and to support of the already established pro-Nazi Dr Dollfuss in Austria.[43] (In Spain and Italy this even led to the pursuance of alignment with the official Fascist Party, albeit a course of action followed in the belief that radical change could occur from within, that the political tools used to exploit the workers could actually be exploited by them. In fact, some accounts of the period lay a large share of the blame for the rise of Hitler on the Comintern.[44])

MacNeice's 1930s Modernism has, then, a definite historical and political depth. This is heightened by a political stance on poetry, which presents itself in the language he uses to represent the demotic experience. The flux and change predicated by MacNeice's feeling for the 'drunkeness of things being various' is marked normally by the use of conventional grammar as, for the poet, syntax implicates itself in the perception of reality. The aesthetic and thematic conditions of his poetry are, then, shackled to a political decision that poetry should be accessible and democratic.

Accordingly, MacNeice's poetry draws attention to the interdependency of the terms *depth* and *surface* – two of the most common words to be found in MacNeice's work of the 1930s are 'barometer' and 'gewgaw' – and illustrates that the meaning of one term is, in fact, generated by its relation to the other. This poetic foregrounding and disturbance of the relationship between surface and depth can also disturb any taxonomy that would classify Modernism in crude oppositional terms, whether it be of the type offered ironically by Ihab Hassan (Modernism vs. postmodernism, with the former a model of depth and the latter of surface) or of that offered by Longley and McDonald (Modernism vs. poetic realism, with the former a model of depthless experimentalism and the latter of rational engagement).[45] As I argue in chapter 3, this complication of the terms of debate extends to MacNeice's engagement with Ireland and Irish identity. Similarly, in chapter 5, I argue that his attempt to find an adequate language with which to register the historical, aesthetic and political complexities of the 'living' self in the early and mid 1930s extends to a post-mortem examination of selfhood at the end of the decade.

2

'Our modern formula/of death to sense and dissolution': Dylan Thomas, Modernism and surrealism in the 1930s

My object is . . . to 'get things straight'. Out of the inevitable conflict of images
– inevitable, because of the creative, recreative, destructive, and contradictory
nature of the motivating centre, the womb of war – I try to make that momentary
peace which is a poem. I do not want a poem of mine to be, nor can it be, a
circular piece of experience placed neatly outside the living stream of time
from which it came; a poem of mine is, or should be, a watertight section of
the stream that is flowing all ways; all warring images within it should be
reconciled for that small stop of time . . . In my earlier poems . . . images
were left dangling over the formal limits . . . the warring stream ran on over
the insecure barriers, the fullstop armistice was pulled and twisted raggedly
on into a conflicting series of dots and dashes.

CLDT, 282

And from the first declension of the flesh
I learnt man's tongue, to twist the shapes of thoughts
Into the stony idiom of the brain,
To shade and knit anew the patch of words
Left by the dead who, in their moonless acre,
Need no word's warmth.
The root of tongues ends in a spentout cancer,
That but a name, where maggots have their X.

CPDT, 22

In one of the more bizarre asides in 'The function of criticism', T. S. Eliot
observed that:

the possessors of the inner voice ride ten in a compartment to a football match at Swansea, listening to the inner voice which breathes the eternal message of vanity, fear and lust. It is a voice to which, for convenience, we may give a name . . . and the name I suggest is Whiggery.[1]

The claim is both evidence of Eliot's rightward progression in the 1920s and a coincidental seizing on the birthplace of Dylan Thomas as a location for both irredeemable provincialism and political insubordination. For Eliot, having the Vetch Field (or perhaps St Helens) rather than Little Gidding as a destination is a sure sign of the plebeian 'inner voice', Swansea equalling Dissent, industry, philistinism and also internal British difference and conflict; a would-be insider's put-down to distract from Eliot's self-fashioning as Anglican, classicist and monarchist. However, the slur can equally be said to furnish a starting-point for a consideration of Thomas's poetry and its relationship to Modernist precursors, like Eliot himself. Whilst Thomas's work was, as I will argue, close to *The Waste Land* and Eliot's essays on the Metaphysicals and Renaissance dramatists, his work also acts as a surreal form of bodily punishment for High Modernist condescension, embodying as it does the fear expressed in *Sweeney Agonistes* that life is no more than 'birth and copulation and death'.[2]

THOMAS, MODERNISM AND LANGUAGE

Any discussion of Thomas's relationship to Modernism must begin with a discussion of his use of language. Thomas was well aware of its centrality, commenting in his 'Poetic manifesto' that 'I use everything and anything to make my poems work . . . puns, portmanteau words, paradox, allusion, paronomasia, paragram, catachresis, slang, assonantal rhymes, vowel rhymes, sprung rhythm'.[3] The 1930s poetry displays not just the systematic foregrounding of the 'device' as a vehicle of estrangement, but also a belief that poetry should work *out of* words, not *towards* them. At its most extreme, this produces his attempts to mimic non-referential poems, such as those whose antecedents lie among the Russian *zaum* poets, the Dadaists and the Gertrude Stein of *Tender Buttons*. One point of such exercises is to prove that no writing can completely escape meaning-construction at the hands of a sufficiently determined (or self-deluded) reader. Only two of Thomas's poems, 'How soon the servant sun' and 'Now' go so far, and they show the parodic aspect of his poetic practice, foreshadowing in their extremism the shift away from Modernism in his poetry of the 1940s (discussed in the Conclusion to this book). However, even when not testing limits, Thomas is utterly Modernist in his insistence on the materiality and autonomy of language. As J. Hillis Miller points out, for Thomas 'words were not signs of something external to themselves, but the substance of poetry, in the same way that marble is the substance of sculpture'.[4] And as I will argue later in this chapter, it was in this connection that Thomas insisted he be read *literally*, as, for example, his objection to Edith Sitwell's well-intentioned explication of the first sonnet of 'Altarwise by owl-light' suggests: 'She doesn't take the literal meaning: that a world-devouring ghost-creature bit out the horror of tomorrow from a gentleman's loins. . . . This poem is a particular incident in a particular adventure, not a general, elliptical deprecation of this "horrible, crazy, speedy life"' (*CLDT*, 301).

It can be argued that, in its relationship to the constraints of the poetry's conservative forms, Thomas's 'everything' and 'anything' approach to Modernist practice represents an internalized, imploded Modernism. The plethora of devices replicates the effect of Modernist techniques such as collage, creating textual instability and epistemological uncertainty. In other words, the parodic element which helps constitute Modernist writing is foregrounded in his poetry. Rhyme schemes and stanza patterns are deployed, whose elaborate ingenuity is in excess of expressive requirement. 'I, in my intricate image', for example, is in three sections of six six-line stanzas (seventy-two lines), each of which contains four end-rhyme variations on 'l' or 'l's, with the two other lines linked by a different rhyme. 'I see the boys of summer' follows an $11 - 7 - 10 - 8 - 8 - 10$ syllabic pattern through nine stanzas, with only one lapse. Further, throughout Thomas's work, syntax is sabotaged, to the extent that its peculiar version of standard grammar becomes at least as hard to construe as Modernist fragmentariness, usually through parataxis, hypertaxis and the deferral of main verbs:

> Hold hard, these ancient minutes in the cuckoo's month,
> Under the lank, fourth folly on Glamorgan's hill,
> As the green blooms ride upward, to the drive of time
>
> (*CPDT*, 44)

Walford Davies unpacks the poem in the following terms:

> In these lines we are bound to hear *Hold hard these ancient minutes* as a main clause, even though the commas show that the real main clause is 'Hold hard . . . to the drive of time.' And before we've grasped as much, we will also have heard (as a complete syntactic unit, despite the comma) *As the green*

blooms ride upward to the drive of time . . . Similar ghost-effects of syntax occur too often in Thomas to be mere accidents. He seems bent on accommodating them.[5]

Indeed, this is a straightforward case. In 'When, like a running grave' there are no fewer than thirty-five subordinate clauses (some as short as a single word) in an opening sentence that stretches for twenty-five lines over five five-line verses.

Such procedures raise the issue of narrative. Virtually all of Thomas's poems are organized around a powerful narrative drive, a seemingly irresistible unfolding of event. Narrative is vital because it provides both an armature, to which the many devices the poem requires can be attached, and a motivation for their deployment. Defending his poetry in a letter to Glyn Jones of March, 1934, Thomas argued that

> all good modern poetry is bound to be obscure. Remember Eliot: 'The chief use of the "meaning" of a poem, in the ordinary sense, may be to satisfy one habit of the reader, to keep his mind diverted and quiet, while the poem does its work upon him.'
>
> (*CLDT*, p. 97)

Meaning, then (as Thomas also made clear in 'Answers to an inquiry'), refers to narrative. The echo is of 'Tradition and the individual talent', in which Eliot likens the phenomenal text of the poem to a bone used by a burglar to distract a guard-dog before he goes about his business; the lived materiality of the poem (as in *The Waste Land*) acting as a 'cover' for, and authentication of, the operations of the ghostly discourse of the mythologies framing it.[6] The narrative of *The Waste Land* is famously discontinuous, yet its very discontinuity produces a meta-narrative that is aided and abetted by Eliot's knowing annotations. Conversely, in Thomas's poetry, the local narrative of the poem appears to offer immediate coherence, unity and closure, but is frequently empty, or banal. As Neil Corcoran remarks:

> The effect can seem like being insistently told, in some baffling way, some extremely simple things that we already know perfectly well, and in a form whose cadences and circularities are suspiciously consolatory. The Thomas visions, as a result, can appear much less than real discoveries, and they constantly run the risk of bathos.[7]

The discursive meaning-content of Thomas's poetry is usually associated with the interrelatedness of the human and cosmic, and the inextricability of processes of decay and growth. More to the point is that the drive towards unification (of body, spirit, cosmos) leads directly to a language-use in which the materiality and autonomy of the signifier are a given. (This is the point that Corcoran seems to miss, that the bathos to which he refers is insignificant beside the life of the poem at the level of language-event.) Thomas grants images almost the same degree of literalness and autonomy, such that poems are not only *not* sustained by external reference, but they seem to be generated by the self-evolving dynamic of images, in narratives whose linguistic events frequently exceed any abstractable sense. Thomas's description of his writing process alludes to this:

> I let, perhaps, an image be 'made' emotionally in me and then apply to it what intellectual and critical force I possess – let it breed another, let that image contradict the first, make, of the third image bred out of the other two together, a fourth contradictory image, and let them all, within my own imposed formal limits, conflict.

> (*CLDT*, 281)

This kind of poem is entirely, or almost entirely, interiorized, moving solely by means of irreducibly literal images that, as Walford Davies observes, 'nevertheless seem to have the kind of air of significance about them that tempts us (unhelpfully) to unpack the poem like a suitcase'.[8]

One image 'breed[s] another' in a poem like 'Where once the waters of your face':

> Where once the waters of your face
> Spun to my screws, your dry ghost blows,
> The dead turns up its eye;
> Where once the mermen through your ice
> Pushed up their hair, the dry wind steers
> Through salt and root and roe.

> Where once your green knots sank their splice
> Into the tided cord, there goes
> The green unraveller,
> His scissors oiled, his knife hung loose
> To cut the channels at their source
> And lay the wet fruits low.

> Invisible, your clocking tides
> Break on the lovebeds of the weeds;
> The weed of love's left dry;
> There round about your stones the shades

> Of children go who, from their voids,
> Cry to the dolphined sea.
>
> Dry as a tomb, your coloured lids
> Shall not be latched while magic glides
> Sage on the earth and sky;
> There shall be corals in your beds,
> There shall be serpents in your tides,
> Till all our sea-faiths die.
>
> (*CPDT*, 14–15)

Here the initial mention of 'waters' is elaborated in a series of *implicit* metaphors. That is, the vehicle (the figurative part of the metaphor) – 'mermen', 'channels', 'wet fruits', 'corals' – is not related back to its tenor (what is being referred to): sexual desire, psychic depths, the amniotic 'waters' of the embryo. M. H. Abrams explains these aspects of metaphor, when found in their simplest form, as follows:

> In a widely adopted usage, I. A. Richards introduced the name *tenor* for the subject that the metaphor is applied to . . . and the name *vehicle* for the metaphorical term itself . . . In an implicit metaphor, the tenor is not itself specified, but only implied; thus, if one were to say, in commenting about a death, 'That reed was too frail to survive the storm of its sorrows,' the situational and verbal context of the term 'reed' indicates that it is the vehicle for an unspecified tenor, a human being, while 'storm' is the vehicle for an aspect of a specified tenor, 'sorrows.'[9]

As Walford Davies remarks, however, Thomas's narrative is one that 'just never *had* a real-world equivalent that could stand as referent in the first place'.[10] The narrative advances, but the poem has been turned inside out; or, to use a different image, it is as if we are viewing the back of a tapestry. Paradoxically, the high degree of control that the poems display is offset by the arbitrary power of individual words and images over their development.

THOMAS'S MODERN BODY

There is a social dimension to this. The emphasis on verbal autonomy entails a weakening of the relationship between signifiers and signifieds, raising linguistic arbitrariness above ostensible message-content.[11] According to Saussure, all meanings attached to signifiers are arbitrary, since meaning is generated, not by homologies between signifiers and signifieds, but through the system of differential relationships between signifiers themselves.[12] To enable social discourse to occur, however, the bonds between signifier and signified are habitually agreed to be stable. Yet, as Saussure points out, for the individual subject the bond never ceases to be an arbitrary one. The putative stability of social meanings inevitably becomes naturalized, and it is this fossilization of the signifier–signified bond which Thomas's writing subverts. This destabilization of the relationship between signifier and signified could well be taken to indicate the operation of the semiotic, the infantile, pre-gendered, inchoate energy which, according to Julia Kristeva, is repressed by our induction into the symbolic order of social injunctions which marshal signifiers with their signifieds.[13] (This, too can be linked with Thomas's privileging of the semiotic over the symbolic. In Kristevan psychoanalytic theory the child, either biologically male or female, inhabits the semiotic 'chora' before gaining access to the symbolic order; moving from a per-lingual and boundless state to a position of domination and judgement afforded by entry and incorporation into the structures of language. As Elizabeth A. Grosz writes, "'The semiotic . . . precedes all unities, binary oppositional structures and hierarchical forms of organization", and emerges in adult discourse, and especially in poetic discourse, in the form of disruptive, irrational, subversive speech patterns that defy the symbolic.'[14]) As Stewart Crehan argues, a poem like 'From love's first fever' is about the ways in which, through the process of language acquisition, we are *interpellated* as human subjects, accepting an inherited system of agreed linguistic meanings.[15] The radical implications of Thomas's poetic practice have thus been overlooked by critics who seek (and fail) to find a social dimension to the poetry, because they look for evidence only at the level of overt 'reference' or 'allusion'.[16]

An interesting comparison might be drawn between Thomas's privileging of the semiotic in his use of language and Eliot's rejection of the sonority, musicality and artistry of language in his critical work. As Maud Ellmann points out:

In Kristevan terms, [in *The Waste Land*] the semiotic overpowers the symbolic. It is this severance of sound from sense that Eliot calls the 'dissociation of sensibility', and regards as the linguistic fall of man. Milton is his prime culprit, because his poetry obeys the witchery of music rather than the laws of sense, forsaking meaning for mellifluence. The pleasure, Eliot complains, 'arises from the noises': from a language which refuses to efface itself, delighting in the 'mazes' of its own sonority.[17]

Similarly, too, Ellmann complains about the predominance of allusion-hunting in criticism of *The Waste Land*, suggesting that 'commentators have been so busy tracking its allusions down that they have overlooked its broken images in search of the totality it might have been'.[18] Instead, she offers a complex reading of the text in the light of Kristeva's sophistication of Freud. To Ellmann, '*The Waste Land* is one of the most abject texts in English literature', and what it attempts to abject is 'the waste land' of the body.[19] As she points out, though, the text cannot do so and is locked in a cycle of continuously returning the bodily horrors that it tries to repress. One of these horrors is the bodily materiality of language:

> [For Eliot] Milton's poetry neglects the *meaning* of the language for its *art*. Eliot's arguments imply that all these 'heresies' begin with the fetishism of the signifier – of the written or acoustic tissues of the word – where literary pleasure overwhelms the stern demands of sense, replacing sound for meaning, form for content, rite for faith. Yet although Eliot accuses Milton of dividing sound from sense and bequeathing a fallen language to posterity, his own techniques of theft and bricolage entail the same displacements. In fact, the abjection of *The Waste Land* arises out of the displacements which haunt it from within: the mutual contaminations of the past and present, of the dead letter and the living voice. Eliot's quotations demonstrate how written signs are necessarily displaceable, orphaned from their origins and meanings. Moreover, *The Waste Land* shows a Miltonic and perverse delight in the semiotic side of language, in the asemantic echolalias of words. Beneath the meaningful connections of the text a parodic underlanguage opens forth, based on the contagion between sounds.[20]

Eliot's attempt to remove the abject body from his work was not, of course, confined to *The Waste Land*, but can also be found in his writing on the metaphysical poets. The Metaphysical was essential to Eliot's construction of a Modernism that was antithetical to Romanticism, but his reclamation of Donne, at the expense of Milton and Spenser, was carried out by ignoring the bodily aspects and linguistic materiality present also in Donne's work. It is these aspects of Metaphysical poetry that Thomas wants to foreground:

> What you call ugly in my poetry is, in reality, nothing but the strong stressing of the physical. Nearly all my images, coming, as they do from my solid and fluid world of flesh and blood, are set out in terms of their progenitors . . . Only by association is the refuse of the body more to be abhorred than the body itself . . . I fail to see how the emphasizing of the body can, in any way, be regarded as hideous. The greatest description I know of our 'earthiness' is

to be found in John Donne's Devotions, where he describes a man as earth of
the earth, his body earth, his hair a wild shrub growing out of the land. All
thoughts and actions emanate from the body. Therefore the description of a
thought or action – however abstruse it may be – can be beaten home by
bringing it onto a physical level. Every idea, intuitive or intellectual, can be
imaged and translated in terms of the body, its flesh, skin, blood, sinews, veins,
glands, organs, cells, or senses.

(*CLDT*, 38–9)

Indeed, if it might be said that Eliot attempts to abject abjection in order
to stage 'the mind of Europe', Thomas, it might equally be said, foregrounds
abjection in his early work in order to reclaim the body as a site of
subversion.[21]

According to Kristeva, the abject is 'what disturbs identity, system, order.
What does not respect borders, positions, rules. The in-between, the ambig-
uous, the composite.'[22] Likewise, Thomas's early poems chart not the
achievement of stable identity but a realization of its impossibility. 'Before
I knocked', for example, refuses to naturalize gendered attributes and thus
equate biology with destiny. Instead, it allows for a mediation of Freud's
notion that sexuality is not inborn but constructed after birth, socially and
culturally. (According to Freud, we are born biologically female or male,
but without corresponding a priori feminine or masculine gender-identities.[23])
Strangely, though, within the poem Thomas's Freudian undermining of
essentialism occurs inside the body and before birth:

> Before I knocked and flesh let enter,
> With liquid hands tapped on the womb,
> I who was shapeless as the water
> That shaped the Jordan near my home
> Was brother to Mnetha's daughter
> And sister to the fathering worm.

(*CPDT*, 11)

One of the first experiences of the subject in Thomas's poem is of
bisexuality: he/she is both 'brother to Mnetha's daughter/And sister to the
fathering worm'. Throughout, normative feminine and masculine genders
are registered as non-natural and non-inherent; the poem's subject, for
example, is as 'shapeless as the water'. Instead, the poem charts the painful
construction of gender by means of the child's interaction with the social
world, and thus accounts for the fragility and instability of identity, rather
than affording it an essential immutability. However, the Oedipal struggle
of the transformation into a gendered identity occurs before birth: it is inside

the womb that the male subject's Oedipal anxiety occurs. The second and third stanzas articulate the painful consequences of the child's first recognition of phallic authority, his father's penis:

> I who was deaf to spring and summer,
> Who knew not sun nor moon by name,
> Felt thud beneath my flesh's armour,
> As yet was in a molten form,
> The leaden stars, the rainy hammer
> Swung by my father from his dome.
>
> I knew the message of the winter,
> The darted hail, the childish snow,
> And the wind was my sister suitor;
> Wind in me leaped, the hellborn dew;
> My veins flowed with the Eastern weather;
> Ungotten I knew night and day.
>
> (CPDT, 11, 12)

Here, then, is an expression of the traumatic fears of castration to be enacted by the father as a punishment for incestuous desire for the mother. (And it is worth remembering here Kristeva's commentary on the significance of abjection prior to birth: 'The abject confronts us, on the other hand, and this time within our own personal archeology, with our earliest attempts to release the hold of the maternal entity even before existing outside of her, thanks to the autonomy of language. It is a violent, clumsy breaking away, with the constant risk of falling back under the sway of a power as securing as it is stifling.'[24]) But rather than simply capitulating under the pressure of these castration fantasies, simply accepting its conversion into the 'purely' masculine, the subject of the poem allows an enactment and articulation of these pressures at their points of crisis. This is where the challenge of the poem is to be found, in the refusal of the 'I' to repress forbidden desire and identify with the father as a figure of authority and moral law, and by so doing enter into a paternal heritage:

> I, born of flesh and ghost, was neither
> A ghost nor man, but mortal ghost.
> And I was struck down by death's feather.
> I was mortal to the last
> Long breath that carried to my father
> The message of his dying christ.
>
> (CPDT, 12)

The unborn 'I' has to die because it refuses to submit to phallic authority, it is 'struck down by death's feather'. Its final breath carries a 'message of his dying christ' to the father. Here, significantly, paternity and patriarchy are conflated, each figured as equally culpable for the betrayal of the female and the feminine:

> You who bow down at cross and altar,
> Remember me and pity Him
> Who took my flesh and bone for armour
> And doublecrossed my mother's womb.

(*CPDT*, 12)

The term 'doublecrossed' is one of plural possibilities, even within the framework of a Freudian reading. On one level it refers to betrayal, as the father 'doublecrosses' the mother because any promise of plenitude and contiguity between mother and child is denied by the assimilation of the child into patriarchy, the Law of the Father (the death, therefore, of the unborn 'I').[25] Also, by being born, the child, too, would be 'doublecrossed', betrayed in a similar fashion to its mother. In this way also, the child double-crosses the mother's body by refusing to leave. By locating the poem inside the womb, then, Thomas is not undermining his own deconstruction of essentialism, but suggesting that to be born is to be incorporated without choice into the Law of the Father, and consequently the speaker of the poem attempts to remain inside the womb. (The death that the child refers to in the penultimate stanza is, therefore, its very refusal to be born.) The term 'doublecrossed', however, also refers to the motion of double-crossing, a motion which conflates the 'I' of the poem and the poet himself, as the poet literally double-crosses his mother's womb by returning to it in his poetry.

In fact, another way of reading the site of the poem, the womb, is as a symbol of the unconscious itself, which, according to Freud, is shaped by the process of repressing polymorphous desire, and principally the incestuous desire for the mother.[26] In Freudian terms, by denying the supposed bio-logical right of paternal law, the child endeavours to reject 'the reality principle', refusing to adjust and amend its libidinous desires in order to gratify them, however circuitously, in the existent world ('The rack of dreams' is painfully twisted in the process of turning into 'a living cipher'). Similarly, the speaker of the poem refuses to internalize the authority of the father into a superego, which would then operate as an internal agency of social and moral proscription. The 'I' of the poem is born neither '[a] ghost nor man, but [a] mortal ghost'. By locating his subject in the womb,

Thomas places it beyond the domain of these codes of constraint. This permits it to exist in the unconscious, which remains dominated by primal desire and bisexual drives. Unfettered by the reality principle, the unconscious is organized by the fantastic and the imaginary, to which powerful libidinal charges become concretized. Thus, in Thomas's poetry the unconscious always remains a powerful disruptive force underlying our conscious gender-identity.

But if there is a gesture towards the elimination of anxiety in the poem, there is also a petitbourgeois bravado, a desire to exorcise uneasiness by dramatizing it. As elsewhere in Thomas's poetry, the unborn child is identified with, even as it rebels against, paternal and metaphysical authority. Whilst the Christ of the poem is the representative of the father, of the phallocentric authority of the symbolic order and the promise of plenitude, he is also the betrayed son (what Thomas called the 'castrated Saviour' of official religion), and the attempt to escape anxiety by imagining an ungendered past generates new anxiety in the actuality of the father-dominated present (*CLDT*, 54). The anxiety, it might be argued, *is* the poetry; Christ is Logos, the word, the poet-as-hero charting his narcissistic, onanistic sexual experience in 'My hero bares his nerves', where masturbation and writing figure both as an unnerving absence and as a disquieting plenitude:

> And these poor nerves so wired to the skull
> Ache on the lovelorn paper
> I hug to love with my unruly scrawl
> That utters all love hunger
> And tells the page the empty ill.
>
> (*CPDT*, 14)

Writing, the means of achieving paternal sanction for the son, and thus the way to sexual experience, breaks down, leaving the speaker trapped in a cycle of identity formation through self-abuse:

> He holds the wire from this box of nerves
> Praising the mortal error
> Of birth and death, the two sad knaves of thieves,
> And the hunger's emperor;
> He pulls the chain, the cistern moves.
>
> (*CPDT*, 14)

Either form of self-authentication disrupts itself (and it is noticeable that the poem begins in the first and ends in the third person). The paper – both writing paper and toilet paper – is 'lovelorn' because it bears the evidence of an absent presence, the unruly scrawl of ink/semen telling the narrator of the deferral of real voice or love, as opposed to his auto-affection. In his discussion of Rousseau's *Confessions* in *Of Grammatology*, Jacques Derrida comments on the dangers of this process in terms of the 'supplement', that addition which would complete self-presence but which instead reveals its incompletion and lack:

> [a] terrifying menace, the supplement has not only the power of procuring an absent presence through its image; procuring it for us by proxy [*procuration*] of the sign, it holds it at a distance and masters it. For this presence is at the same time desired and feared.[27]

Owing to its assumption of authority, Thomas's 'baring' of this 'nerve' also threatened the more understated, predominantly 'English' self-presence of the 1930s. At the time, the *New Country* poets consistently linked Thomas's work to a surrealism they regarded as at odds with their own engagé writing. To Stephen Spender it was 'just poetic stuff with no beginning nor end, shape, or intelligent or intelligible control', whilst Herbert Read, in less negative terms, wrote that Thomas's work evinced 'that transcendence of reality through the paranoiac faculty which is the avowed aim of the surrealist' (*CLDT*, 297).[28] (In a similar vein, Louis MacNeice wrote that Thomas's poems were 'apparently written on surrealist principles . . . He is like a drunk man speaking wildly but rhythmically, pouring out a series of nonsense images.'[29])

THOMAS AND SURREALISM

Given their social agendas, the *New Country* poets were incapable of grasping that Thomas's resistance to their own abstraction and discursiveness was one of his central aims. As a result they relegated his poetry to an ancillary, subaltern status; a complement to, rather than a critique of, their own. Yet, it is precisely Thomas's refusal to toe a particular poetic line that makes his poetry so significant. The idea that his own imploded Modernist poetic, though, opposed as it was to the diagnostic, hyper-rational, politically left poetic norm, can be read in surrealist terms continues to be viewed with suspicion. Paul C. Ray, for example, suggests that 'Of the major poets of our time, Dylan Thomas was the one most influenced by surrealism', but later claims that 'whereas they achieved their results by immersing them-selves in automatism, Thomas achieved his by remaining in lucid control of his materials and intentions'.[30]

Thomas attended the 1936 International Surrealist Exhibition at the New Burlington Galleries in London, an exhibition which played host to, amongst others, green-haired André Breton, Paul Éluard and Herbert Read, who delivered their lecture on 'Art and the Unconscious' while perched on the back-rest of an increasingly unstable sofa, and Salvador Dalí, who was almost asphyxiated after giving his paper clad in a diving suit, whose helmet became stuck.[31] (Thomas offered visitors cups of boiled string, asking 'weak or strong?' and later read his work at one of the evening events, along with Paul Éluard, Samuel Beckett and David Gascoyne.) Thomas's involvement in the 1936 International Surrealist Exhibition is, however, frequently dismissed as inconsequential by critics unwilling to take into account the Modernist and, more particularly, surrealist elements in his work. As Alan Young remarks, there is a 'failure of British critics generally to appreciate the modernity and seriousness of the early poems and stories of Dylan Thomas, who most successfully combined traditional and Modernist elements in his quest for a solution to serious metaphysical questions'.[32] Lurking behind such readings, which often amount to little more than a kind of bardological empiricism, are attempts to secure Thomas's canonical status by situating him in a Metaphysical or Romantic tradition. Henry I. Schvey, for example, writes of Thomas's connection to surrealism in the following terms:

> as a highly conscious artist consumed by his craft, it would be wrong to classify Dylan Thomas with the surrealist movement which advocated the breakdown of the divisions between dream and reality, between art and life. For the true surrealist, whose philosophy was bent upon the revolutionary destruction of reality, art does not exist as an artefact separate from life: life itself is a surreal work of art to be performed. For Dylan Thomas, despite all we know about his lowering drunken personality, it was the other way around – his art was his life.[33]

Criticism of this sort has dominated Thomas studies over the past thirty years or so, and even those dissenting voices keen to establish a more positive relationship between Thomas and surrealism have tended not to take into account the links between the avant-garde and the political.

The lip-service paid to surrealism by, amongst others, Paul Ferris and Walford Davies reflects not only a particular desire to subordinate the avant-garde in Thomas's work, but also a suspicion of the authenticity and validity of surrealist practice in general.[34] In fact, much of the unwillingness of critics to take surrealism seriously – either in relation to Thomas's work, or in its own right – can be traced back through comments made by the poet himself. In a letter of 1934, for example, Thomas pleaded total ignorance of the surrealism of others:

> But who is this Gascoygne [*sic*]? I saw a geometrical effort of his in one *New Verse*, and also a poem in which he boasted of the ocarina in his belly. Is he much subtler or more absurd than I imagine? It is his sheer incompetence that strikes me more than anything else.
>
> (*CLDT*, 105)

Meanwhile, in a letter written six months prior to the exhibition, Thomas wrote of his own poetry in the following terms:

> I am not, never have been, never will be, or could be for that matter, a surrealist, and for a number of reasons. I have very little idea what surrealism is; until quite recently I had never heard of it; I have never, to my knowledge, read even a paragraph of surrealist literature; my acquaintance with French is still limited to 'the pen of my aunt'; I have not read any French poetry, either in the original or in translation, since I attempted to translate Victor Hugo in a provincial Grammar School examination, and failed. All of which exposes my ignorance of contemporary poetry . . . I must confess that I read regrettably little modern poetry, and what 'fashionable poetry' I do come across appears to be more or less communist propaganda. I am not a communist.
>
> (*CLDT*, 205)

Nevertheless, just as 'I am not a communist' was disingenuous, so, too, were his claims to ignorance of surrealism. The letter was written in immediate response to one by Richard Church, then the poetry editor at Dent, whose comment that 'I look upon surrealism with abhorrence . . . I am distressed to see its pernicious effects in your work', very nearly resulted in a rejection of *18 Poems*. Little wonder, then, that Thomas wrote back dismissing surrealist influence in his work with such gusto. In correspondence with Edith Sitwell in 1934 over Church's near-rejection of his first volume, though, he writes of *18 Poems* as 'surrealist imitations', whilst in a later letter to Henry Treece, Thomas calls Church 'a cliché-riddled humbug and pie-fingering hack' (*CLDT*, 210, 273). Further, the notion that the self-styled

'Rimbaud of Cwmdonkin Drive', an avid reader of and contributor to *transition*, *Contemporary Poetry and Prose* and *New Verse*, had read no foreign or contemporary poetry was, according to Constantine Fitzgibbon, 'a downright lie; he had read it all'.[35] Even a cursory glance at Thomas's *Collected Letters*, for example, falls upon the names of Gertrude Stein, Eugene Jolas, James Joyce, Ezra Pound, T. S. Eliot, Arthur Rimbaud and e. e. cummings, and one of his best friends, Norman Cameron, was a translator of Rimbaud.

If critics have taken too literally Thomas's dismissal of his work as surrealist, they have also accepted too readily his narrow definition of surrealist practice, citing his later discussion of surrealism in his 'Poetic manifesto' of 1951 as often as his earlier dismissal of it:

> I do not mind from where the images of a poem are dragged up: drag them up, if you like, from the nethermost sea of the hidden self; but before they reach paper, they must go through all the rational processes of the intellect. The Surrealists, on the other hand, put their words down together on paper exactly as they emerge from chaos; they do not shape these words or put them in order; to them, chaos is the shape and order. This seems to me exceedingly presumptuous; the Surrealists imagine that whatever they dredge from their subconscious selves and put down in paint or in words must, essentially, be of some interest or value. I deny this. One of the arts of the poet is to make comprehensible and articulate what might emerge from the subconscious sources; one of the great main uses of the intellect is to select, from the amorphous mass of subconscious images, those that will best further his imaginative purpose, which is to write the best poem he can.[36]

It is this construction of a surrealist other to bolster his craftsman-like self which is accepted and echoed by Thomas's critics. (Thomas himself was more robust: responding to Stephen Spender's claim that his poetry was 'turned on like a tap', he wrote that '[m]y poems are formed; they are not turned on like a tap at all, they are "watertight compartments"' (*CLDT*, 297). Walford Davies dismissively concedes that 'much in the early poetry smacks of surrealism . . . like the Surrealists, Thomas thought of himself as drawing on subconscious material', but goes on to state that 'whereas the Surrealists allowed no room for the selection, control, and development of images, Thomas again seems busy with those very activities, and with everything carefully subjected to the aesthetic demands of poetic form'.[37] But, as was suggested earlier, the space between this account of surrealism ('no room for selection, control and development') and Thomas's own poetic practice ('make comprehensible and articulate what might emerge from subconscious sources') is occupied only by a very limited theory of surrealism. Too heavily weighed down by Breton's initial definition of surrealism as 'pure psychic automatism by which it is intended to express . . . the real process of thought, without any control exercised by reason', Thomas's critics fall, more often than not, into the trap identified by Theodor Adorno in 'Looking back on surrealism', of explaining away the peculiar power of surrealism by explicating the irrational by the rational, the strange by the familiar.[38]

'When, like a running grave' offers a good example of Thomas's version of surrealism in practice:

> When, like a running grave, time tracks you down,
> Your calm and cuddled is a scythe of hairs,
> Love in her gear is slowly through the house,
> Up naked stairs, a turtle in a hearse,
> Hauled to the dome
>
> (*CPDT*, 19)

Walford Davies argues that 'a running grave', 'a scythe of hairs' and 'a turtle in a hearse' cannot be read as surrealist because they are 'consciously developed' and can be forced into meaning; 'a running grave' is 'meant' to imply infection and disease, and the 'scythe of hairs' is that which scythes hairs.[39] Whilst this is reasonable in itself, the point is that the poem is not structured by an external logic, but has a logic of its own (a perfectly surreal dream-logic, so to speak) by which another, equally valid, reading might well have a scythe made from hairs, a grave running around and a turtle driving a hearse up the stairs. The point is that the images should not be read in terms of what is 'meant', but, rather, in terms of their effect, as they merge and melt, jostle and collide throughout. It is better, then, to conceptualize surrealism not by going back to psychology, but by looking at the surrealist artistic techniques of montage and collage. Read in this way, the focus would be on the ways in which surrealism produces what Adorno refers to as a 'photographic negative' of modernity by foregrounding perceptions 'as they must have been then', rather than on attempting to find the originary moment of a surrealist image.[40] That is, of course, not to say that surrealism has little to do with psychoanalysis per se: Adorno is insistent upon its indebtedness to psychological dream-theory. It is merely to point out that surrealism is a disturbing and shocking articulation of the kind of images repressed in and by the conventionally structured logic of adulthood.[41]

In 1934 Thomas defined his own poetic practice in Freudian terms which echo Breton's definition of surrealism. He declared that 'whatever is hidden should be made naked', and that his poetry would be 'the record of my individual struggle from darkness towards some measure of light, and what of the individual struggle is still to come benefits by the sight and knowledge of the faults and fewer merits in that concrete struggle'.[42] Partly in the light of such remarks, Thomas has a history of being read psychologically.[43] Such readings of Thomas are too often founded on the spurious assumption that his work can be taken as a displaced or condensed registration-form for his clinical evaluation as a psychological case-study. Recently, however, the emphasis of psychoanalytic criticism has shifted from inept attempts at psycho-biography to self-aware examinations of the ways in which psychological, linguistic and literary structures are constituted. According to Elizabeth Wright, for example, the Freudian notion of the uncanny is one method by which surrealism might be usefully conceptualized. To Wright, the surrealist image is always uncanny (*unheimlich*), 'in a constant process of construction, deconstruction and reconstruction', by which it confronts representational realism with its own death by reminding it of its inability to cope with the fact that its rationality remains irrational. She expands upon the Freudian definition so that the '*heimlich* means not only homely and familiar, but also hidden and secret. The *un-* of the *unheimlich* marks the return of the repressed material: the *unheimlich* object threatens us in some way by no longer fitting the context to which we have been accustomed.'[44]

It is this uncanny and surreal struggle between the hidden and the naked that is articulated in 'Altarwise by owl-light', the sonnet sequence that closes Thomas's second volume, *Twenty-five Poems* (1936). (Even its title effects the uncanny, as the *heimlich* 'altar light' and 'owl wise' become the *unheim-lich* 'Altarwise' and 'owl-light'.) The sequence is about the problematic entry of a child into the authorized languages of adulthood. It charts the journey of a child who finds the death of a 'castrated Christ' an enabling one, as it is then forced to be its own creator of the Word. 'Altarwise by owl-light' explores the relationship between language and reality by literally forcing the child into meaning. One of the ways in which it does so is by presenting a surreal landscape, a landscape which is not only structured by uncanny effects, but is one on which is inscribed the very process of its own structuration. In other words, the sequence both entertains a number of surreal images which work by means of the uncanny (the 'wrinkled undertaker's van' of sonnet III, for instance, or the 'bagpipe-breasted ladies' of sonnet VI), and is about the ways in which, to quote Wright, these images are constantly constructed, reconstructed and deconstructed (*CPDT*, 59, 61). Indeed, Thomas described his composite method of construction in precisely these terms (quoted, in part, earlier in the chapter):

a poem by myself needs a host of images, because its centre is a host of images. I make one image, – though 'make' is not the word, I let, perhaps, an image to be 'made' emotionally in me and then apply to it what intellectual & critical forces I possess – let it breed another, let that image contradict the first, make, of the third image bred out of the other two together, a fourth contradictory image, and let them all, within my imposed formal limits, conflict. Each image holds within it the seed of its own destruction, and my dialectical method, as I understand it, is a constant building up and breaking down of the images that came out of the central seed, which is itself destructive and constructive at the same time.

(CLDT, 281)

As has been suggested, Thomas's critics refuse to entertain the notion of him as a genuinely surrealist writer because of general statements of poetic intention such as this one, and, in particular, phrases like 'within my own formal limits'. It should be borne in mind, however, that, as Alex Callinicos has pointed out, surrealism's project was aimed at realizing Rimbaud's suggestion that 'the poet makes himself a *seer* by a long, prodigious and rational disordering of the senses'.[45] And this process of image formation through a 'rational disordering of the senses' is one of the subjects of sonnet IV:

> Button your bodice on a hump of splinters,
> My camel's eye will needle through the shroud.
> Love's a reflection of the mushroom features,
> Stills snapped by night in the bread-sided field,
> Once close-up smiling in the wall of pictures,
> Ark-lamped thrown back upon the cutting flood.

(CPDT, 60)

This sonnet contains a series of transformative images; the 'hump' of line nine changes into, and with, the 'camel' of line ten, the 'camel' then changes into the 'needle' of the biblical phrase, and finally the opening 'ark' of line ten changes into its concluding 'flood'. These surreal transformations are not ahistorical, but take place within the particular context of the early cinema – the 'stills snapped', the 'close-up', the 'wall of pictures' and the 'cutting flood' – which then provides the possibility of the photographic collage of surreal characters that follows in sonnet V:

> And from the windy West came two-gunned Gabriel,
> From Jesu's sleeve trumped up the king of spots,
> The sheath-decked jacks, queen with a shuffled heart;

> Said the fake gentleman in a suit of spades,
> Black-tongued and tipsy from salvation's bottle,
> Rose my Byzantine Adam in the night;
> For loss of blood I fell on Ishmael's plain,
> Under the milky mushrooms slew my hunger,
> A climbing sea from Asia had me down
> And Jonah's Moby snatched me by the hair;
> Cross-stroked salt Adam to the frozen angel
> Pin-legged on pole-hills with a black medusa
> By waste seas where the white bear quoted Virgil
> And sirens singing from our lady's sea-straw.
>
> (*CPDT*, 60)

Wright notes that the 'uncanny effect is brought about because we are confronted with a subjectivity now alien to us', and here, as throughout the sonnet sequence, are childlike perceptions of the type described earlier.[46] Alternatively, the poem can be read as furnishing a visual confirmation of surrealist-type images; the 'frozen angel/Pin-legged on pole-hills' could fit into any of Dalí's hallucinatory realist landscapes, as could the classically inclined bear into a Magritte ensemble. Similarly, a gunslinging Gabriel and what might be read as a card-sharping Jesus are suitably iconoclastic subjects for a surrealist collage.

Of course, other poems can be integrated in a similar way. The opening poem of *Twenty-five Poems*, for example, contains both explicit and implicit references to surrealism. In the third stanza of 'I, in my intricate image', Thomas refers to the 'man or ox, and the pictured devil' (*CPDT*, 33). Here, he is adverting to the mythical figure of the minotaur used by artists of the 1930s, and in doing so echoes the title of the French periodical, *Minotaure*, in which the surrealists attempted to extend awareness of their art outside France between 1933 and 1939.[47] In the same way, in the third stanza of the second part of the poem, Thomas writes of 'Death instrumental/Splitting the long eye open . . .' (*CPDT*, 34), which Walford Davies and Ralph Maud argue is a reference to the Salvador Dalí/Luis Buñuel surrealist film, *Un Chien Andalou*, in which a woman's eyeball is split with a razor (*CPDT*, 196).

More importantly, however, parts of the sonnet are historically representative of the 1920s and 1930s, when two of the most powerful legitimating discourses were religion and cinema. What is at work, then, is a fantastical dialectic between the mythology of the Wild West, a modern extension of the Romantic notion of the frontier of the imagination, and the Authorized

Bible. Caught somewhere in the middle of all of this is Captain Ahab, a man in pursuit, significantly, of a false purity, driven by the perverse religiosity of the puritan principle. Sonnet V is thus typical of 'Altarwise by owl-light', in that a discursive sense is to be found in the fragments rather than the whole, as meaning is confined to localized points within the poem. In this way, Thomas refuses to let any single dominant narrative emerge, instead allowing powerfully insistent (but conflicting) micro-narratives to sustain themselves across individual clauses, lines or short passages. It is for this reason that its hallucinatory, childlike images of the surreal are not merely regressive, but also subversive, as the sequence reminds the reader of the artificiality of normal representation.[48] In its refusal to be absorbed into the conventional patterns of meaning construction, the uncanny discloses the constructedness of the normative, whose repressed it returns and foregrounds.

The uncanny images of the poem are significant in another way, too. They relate to the location out of which Thomas forged his surrealism. 'Altarwise by owl-light' plays very directly with the conventions of religion in Wales, and the insistence of the poem on the creative power of language, its biblical allusions, its references to Puritanism and preaching can all be associated with Welsh Nonconformity. (Thomas's uncle was a preacher in Paraclete and, as Paul Ferris notes, Thomas commented that the Bible was one of the texts that 'first made me love language and want to work *in* it and *for* it' and that 'the great rhythms had rolled over me from the Welsh pulpits; and I read, for myself, from Job and Ecclesiastes; and the story of the New Testament is part of my life'.[49]) Nonconformity had, of course, a puritan ancestry, and its teachings followed those sixteenth-century reformers who sought to rid the Church of England of all traces of Roman Catholicism and reassert the primacy of the Bible as the only authority in matters of worship and personal conduct. Further, Nonconformity's eighteenth-century Calvinist roots emphasized a suspicion of non-textual aids to devotion. However, despite this opposition to visual art as an aid to worship, by the late nineteenth/early twentieth centuries biblical texts were being extrava-gantly embroidered and hung in prominent positions in the Welsh home. (A parody of one such home can, of course, be found in *Under Milk Wood*: 'Mrs Dai Bread Two: I see a featherbed. With three pillows on it. And a text above the bed. I can't read what it says, there's great clouds blowing. Now they have blown away. God is love, the text says' (*UMW*, 43).[50] Similarly, whilst pictorial representations were frowned upon, the chapel pulpit was embellished and adorned with the Word of God. In this way,

Nonconformity's rejection of the visual image was compensated for by its investment in the power of the word, and by the iconization of the Word of God in the absence of depictions of biblical characters and scenes. The poem's iconoclasm, then, has a specific as well as a wider context, in that it uses and abuses the language of Nonconformity to challenge the relationship between word and world in general.[51] This simultaneous use and abuse of Nonconformity parallels Thomas's appropriation of surrealism and, read in this way, the poem very obviously makes a calculated appeal to a sense of the surrealist absurd.[52] Thomas, in other words, guys and mimics the attributes of a European metropolitan style where it can be made to coincide with his own contexts and tactics of estrangement. In both embracing and rejecting surrealism and Nonconformity he creates a provincial simulacrum of surrealism ('surrealist imitations'), or what might thus be called *surregionalism*.[53]

In this light, Thomas's Modernism operates in a fashion that has similarities with that of, say, James Joyce or Samuel Beckett, two writers who, according to Terry Eagleton,

> could approach . . . traditions from the outside, estrange and appropriate them for their own ends, roam . . . across a whole span of cultures in euphoric, melancholic liberation from the Oedipal constraints of a mother tongue . . . For the subjugated subjects of empire, the individual is less the strenuously self-fashioning agent of his own historical destiny than empty, powerless, without a name; there can be little of the realists' trust in the beneficence of linear time, which is always on the side of Caesar. Languishing within a barren social reality, the colonised subject may beat the kind of retreat into fantasy and hallucination which lends itself more evidently to modernist than to realist literary practice. And if the traditional national languages are now encountering global semiotic systems, cherished cultural heritages yielding ground to avant-garde techniques which are easily portable across national frontiers, who better to speak this new non-speech than those already disinherited in their own tongue?[54]

What is significant in this passage for a reading of Thomas is Eagleton's association of the hallucinatory and the fantastical techniques of the avant-garde with marginalized locations. Eagleton argues that 'Bereft of a stable continuous cultural tradition, the colonised were forced to make it up as they went along', and this is exactly what Thomas did.[55] To the extent that surrealism had affinities with the Metaphysicals' violent yoking together of heterogeneous images (the conceit as a distant cousin of Lautréamont's chance encounter between an umbrella and a sewing machine on a dissecting table), there was also a link between surrealist practice and the climate created earlier by T. S. Eliot and Herbert Grierson. Thomas, an avid reader of John Donne, exploited such similarities to forge a semi-surrealized metaphysical mode from a marginalized and, as we shall see in the following chapters, problematic Welsh Modernism.

3

'The woven figure':
Louis MacNeice's Ireland

Post-colonial theory, a mode of thought which accepts European Imperialism as a historical fact and attempts to address nations touched by colonial enterprises, has as yet failed to adequately consider Ireland as a post-colonial nation. Undoubtedly, Ireland is a post-colonial nation (where 'post-' colonial refers to any consequence of colonial contact) with a body of literary work that may be read productively as post-colonial.

Edward Said[1]

'The Character of Ireland'? Character?
A stage convention? A historical trap?
A geographical freak? Let us dump the rubbish
Of race and talk to the point: what is a nation?

Louis MacNeice[2]

In a radio programme broadcast in early 1995, Paul Muldoon was asked about the twentieth-century corpus of influence on contemporary Irish poetry. In response, he constructed an image of a man upon a horse attended by a groom. The voice of the Ascendancy gentleman sitting in grandeur was W. B. Yeats's, Muldoon suggested, while the voice of the Irish peasant attendant upon man and beast was that of Patrick Kavanagh. Finally, there was Louis MacNeice, whose voice, Muldoon remarked enigmatically, was that of the horse.[3] Muldoon is here drawing on Yeats's 'Under Ben Bulben', in which Yeats damns the middle classes and implores 'Irish poets, learn your trade,/Sing whatever is well made . . ./Sing the peasantry, and then/Hard riding country gentlemen. . .'.[4] The comment directs attention towards one of the immediate concerns regarding MacNeice's poetry and its relationship to Ireland, that of taxonomy. As was suggested in chapter 1, it is possible to read MacNeice's poetry as a site that resists those critical projects whose aim is to categorize and thereby simplify. That he emerges as a kind of protean figure, who manages to escape the confinement and concomitant restriction of imposed ideological or critical totalizations, is equally important to grasp when considering the processes of Ireland and Irishness in MacNeice's poetry.

Indeed, to locate that poetry within a framework sensitive to Ireland's particular colonial position in the twentieth century is to tread very carefully over divided historical lines, whilst at the same time confronting, head-on, questions of national and cultural identity whose answers are bound to ideas of place and displacement. The traditional readings of MacNeice and Ireland which choose either to include or exclude his work, depending on their definition, or 'fixing', of the term 'Irish', have yet to be replaced by the type of nuanced post-colonial readings which have taken place recently in Irish literary studies. What is needed is a reading of MacNeice in the light of notions of hybridity and mimicry, one in which the metaphysical unease upon which his poetry thrives throughout the 1930s is related to the ways in which Ireland and Irishness are negotiated in his work.

POST-COLONIAL IRELAND?

As the Introduction to this book has outlined, the history of Ireland's relationship with England is such that any adequate consideration of its status as colonial is fraught with difficulty. What makes the Irish example so interesting and difficult for the post-colonial theorist is the fact that Ireland was victim, accomplice and beneficiary of British imperialism. As Declan Kiberd states in *Inventing Ireland*,

> All cases [of colonization] are complex, but it is precisely the 'mixed' nature of the experience of Irish people, as both exponents and victims of British imperialism, which makes them so representative of the underlying process. Because the Irish were the first modern people to decolonise in the twentieth century, it has seemed useful to make comparisons with other, subsequent movements, and to draw upon the more recent theories of Frantz Fanon and Ashis Nandy for a retrospective illumination. If Ireland once inspired many leaders of the 'developing' world, today the country has much to learn from them . . . My belief is that the introduction of the Irish case to the debate will complicate, extend and in some cases expose the limits of current models of postcoloniality.[5]

For Colin Graham, reviewing *Inventing Ireland*, it is this final assertion, 'My belief is that the introduction of the Irish case to the debate will complicate, extend and in some cases expose the limits of current models of postcoloniality', that is 'the most promising metacritical remark in the book'.[6] Graham is part of a growing trend in Irish studies that has recently begun to explore ways in which post-colonialism attempts to fragment and disintegrate the monologism of cultural affiliation, and to rethink notions such as mimicry and hybridity 'out of a recognition of the claustrophobic intensity of the relationship between Ireland and Britain'.[7] The sense of hybridity in post-colonial culture, that 'cultures are never unitary in themselves, nor simply dualistic in relation of Self to Other' is enabling to an understanding of Irish identity.[8] Any post-colonial reading however, would need to be a complex and historical one, avoiding the dangers pointed out by Ella Shohat and Robert Stam, who rightly argue that traditional, essentialist notions of identity should not be replaced without reservation by those of a simplistic post-colonial hybridity:

> A celebration of syncretism and hybridity per se, if not articulated with questions of historical hegemonies, risks sanctifying the fait accompli of colonial violence. For oppressed people, even artistic syncretism is not a game but a sublimated form of historical pain, which is why Jimi Hendrix played the 'Star Spangled Banner' in a dissonant mode, and why even a politically conservative performer like Ray Charles renders 'America the Beautiful' as a moan and cry. As a descriptive catch-all term, 'hybridity' fails to discriminate between diverse modalities of hybridity: colonial imposition, obligatory assimilation, political co-option, cultural mimicry and so forth.[9]

That said, eight centuries of exchange between Ireland and Britain (albeit largely one-sided) have produced complex cultural identities that manifest themselves today in Northern Ireland as problematically as they ever have in Irish–British relations. Indeed, it is because Ireland is not clear-cut as a colonial paradigm that it is important to look at the situation in terms of the relationship between Ireland and England.

According to W. J. McCormack, it is this dynamic between the metropolitan and colonial aspects of the Irish experience that is important to grasp, and consequently the only historically accurate way of thinking about Ireland is as a metropolitan colony.[10] It is within this dynamic space between England and Irelands (Northern Ireland/Republic; Anglican/Presbyterian/Roman Catholic; Nationalist/Unionist/Loyalist) that MacNeice negotiates an unlocated sense of identity in his poetry. This is not to suggest that MacNeice accepts a monolithic, unitary England (he is clearly well aware of class divisions, for example). It is merely to note, in line with the concerns of this chapter, the complexity of the Irish identities negotiated in his poetry and MacNeice's own identity as a 'woven' figure amongst them. MacNeice's work upon an Irish subject-matter articulates Modernist concerns of self and origin, place and displacement, mediated by Graham's 'claustrophobic intensity'. In this way, MacNeice can usefully be read as disruptive of Kiberd's version of post-colonialism, the essentialism of which (through its reliance on birth and residence as qualifications) automatically excludes Anglo-Irish Protestant writers.

The lack of a stable, unitary identity with which to 'fix' (and to 'fix' to) MacNeice is something of a thorny issue for some critics of his work, whilst for other critics it is precisely his lack of rootedness that attracts attention. Part of the reason for this is MacNeice's complex personal history. Born in Belfast to parents from Connemara, in the west of Ireland, MacNeice was raised in Carrickfergus and later moved to England, first to Oxford, then Birmingham and then London. To MacNeice, his life in England was always laden with a sense of alienation (from the very beginning he asso- ciated himself with outsider figures such as his fellow Marlburian, the aesthete Anthony Blunt). That MacNeice chose to live in England, however, was not due to his feeling more 'at home' there than in Ireland. In an article for *The Listener* concerning Gaelic-speaking islanders met on a trip to the Outer Hebrides, he referred to his 'sentimental reluctance to be an outsider', and articulates a double sense of alienation:

> I do not wish to visit them again because they are in decline. London also is in decline but there I feel that I am present in a family sickbed – if not indeed a family deathbed. By blood I may be nearer to a Hebridean than to a Cockney, but my whole upbringing has alienated me from that natural (some will call it primitive) culture which in the British Isles today is only found on the Celtic or backward fringes. I went to the Hebrides partly hoping to find that blood was thicker than ink – that the Celt in me would be drawn to the surface by the magnetism of his fellows. This was a sentimental and futile hope. Once, sitting by a river drinking beer with some Lewismen while one of them sang a love song in Gaelic, I felt strongly that I belonged to these people and that, for all I cared London could sink in the mud. But the conviction of alcohol does not last.[11]

It is precisely this lack of a fixed identity that led to a change in his critical fortunes and to his rehabilitation as a kind of father figure to the younger Northern Irish writers of today. The assignment of pride of place to MacNeice by Paul Muldoon in his controversial *Faber Book of Contem- porary Irish Poetry* was partly the result of the important work carried out by critics such as Edna and Michael Longley, who had been calling for his inclusion within an Irish tradition since the early 1970s. In the volume MacNeice is allocated more space than any other Irish poet, including Patrick Kavanagh. The controversy over Muldoon's anthology is due to his inclusion of only two poets born in the Republic of Ireland, Thomas Kinsella and Paul Durcan (Patrick Kavanagh is included, but was born in pre-1922 Ulster), and his exclusion of several other significant figures. Amongst those who fail to merit a place within the anthology, for example, are Muldoon himself, Austin Clarke and Eavan Boland.[12] The clue to MacNeice's inclusion and prominence within Muldoon's anthology is to be found in the prologue, an edited transcript of a discussion between MacNeice and F. R. Higgins that first appeared in *The Listener* under the title 'Tendencies in modern poetry' in 1939. Whereas the title of the article would seem to indicate a 'gentlemanly' conversation on the changes taking place in poetry in the 1930s, in actuality it was a heated debate on race and identity in modern and Modernist poetry. Higgins bemoans the lack of 'racial rhythms' in the poetry of the day and, in a passage that is not included in Muldoon's editorial reworking, he discloses the extremity of his position, misquoting Wordsworth to do so:

> MacNeice: Well, to go back to the question of racial rhythm, am I to take it that you think that today racial rhythm is more important for the poet than the international or extra-national rhythms we have mentioned?
> Higgins: Yes, I would say racial rhythms are better for the poet who exists within the rhythm than the international rhythms that are only dimly perceived or felt by those who try to interpret them.
> MacNeice: On those premises there is more likelihood of good poetry appearing among the Storm Troopers of Germany than in the cosmopolitan communities of Paris or New York.
> Higgins: In some respects I actually believe so – it is better to write out of an emotion 'remembered in tranquillity' than out of the diluted sentiment of another. Although assailed by the world's mental – as well as mechanical – standardisation, this Irish life of ours is still very conservative, most compact and indeed old fashioned. It is not so in industrial England today. Is not Ireland still lucky in the slow movements of nature's everlasting law and process? Our rural traditions, born from the ancient, yet everlasting, soil, maintain a regular rhythm in keeping with the old racial heart-beat. And that integral life in rural Ireland breeds, with viciousness, a race of individuals, or personalities – each curiously unique, a law unto himself, yet all in national character. By reason of these figures rural Ireland remains today largely free from standardisation of type and literary idea.[13]

Not only does this embarrassing moment expose the relationship of race theory to Irish cultural nationalism's concept of identity, it also points toward an Irish nationalist exclusion of MacNeice from an 'Irish' canon. (MacNeice's own use of racial terminology, such as 'blood', in the passage cited earlier does not, I would argue, show an acceptance of these terms. Rather, it suggests that these are the only terms available to the debate, that MacNeice is forced into using a language that is bound to racial discourse in order to deny it.) The attitude to MacNeice from the North was no warmer, however, and is summed up in John Hewitt's dismissal of him as a type of 'airy internationalist', one who has rejected the project of a Northern Irish identity founded upon a cultural regionalism.[14] Hewitt stipulates conditions for the Ulster writer:

> He must be a *rooted* man. He must carry the native tang of his idiom like the native dust on his sleeve; otherwise he is an airy internationalist, thistle-down, a twig on a stream . . . he must know where he comes from and where he is; otherwise how can he tell where he wishes to go?[15]

Hewitt is attempting to define an Ulster nationalism that he projects in Protestant terms which, through its response to MacNeice (widely agreed to be the writer to whom Hewitt is referring), reveals itself as exclusive and prescriptive. However, Hewitt later admitted that his casting of a regional nationalism ignored the problems of geographical sectarian division.[16]

The attacks on MacNeice, then, focus upon a supposed inauthenticity, on a lack of Irish ancestral ties and racial blood (and hence rhythm and subject matter). Such critical attacks are examples of nationalist discourses that have since been superseded by a post-nationalist displacement of binary dualisms in favour of more subtle spectrums of differentiation. For the younger Northern Irish poets these spectrums of differentiation are to be found in MacNeice's poetry, and it is his refusal to yield to a specific and particular meaning which they admire. As Gerald Dawe affirms, 'I call MacNeice the source because his poetry points to the one thing that is absent from most Irish life and literature. He is a source of alternatives, another way of seeing, another way of experiencing. MacNeice perceives, tolerates, cherishes and celebrates difference.'[17]

Similarly, Kiberd, in more disapproving mode, recognizes a celebration of difference in MacNeice's work:

> Estranged as the son of a Church of Ireland bishop from southern Catholics and northern Presbyterians, MacNeice cannily blocked the retreat to all commitments, not even managing a brief membership of the Communist Party during the 1930s. His dread of fixed positions allowed him instead to become a poet of the plural, to celebrate 'the drunkenness of things being various':

and there is about his performance a touch of the flâneur, who savours the sights and sounds of an urban setting, but with a sense that it is a setting in which he himself will never be able to settle on a role other than that of an elegist to a more courtly time.[18]

Attacked by one type of nationalist, Higgins, for being too 'modern', here MacNeice is criticized for being too regressive, accused of being a type of Elizabethan elegist and of having a colonialist's nostalgia. Bearing in mind that Kiberd seems to replace the second 'e' in Dawe's 'difference' with a Derridean 'a', though, this is a strange passage indeed, as Kiberd simultaneously grafts on to MacNeice a late twentieth-century postmodern identity that would be more suited to Muldoon or Dawe.[19] In this way, his reading of MacNeice's celebration of 'the drunkenness of things being various' exposes the limitations of a post-colonial approach that mis-understands the postmodern as an unproblematic (and, to a certain extent, apolitical) celebration of the fragmentation for which Modernism sought a ghostly paradigm. To term MacNeice a flâneur is to damn with faint praise, and to see MacNeice's work on Ireland as that of, to quote Michel Foucault's definition of the flâneur, an 'idle, strolling spectator . . . satisfied to keep his eyes open, to pay attention and build up a storehouse of memories' is simply to misread him.[20] This is not to say that a theoretical approach attuned to postmodernism and post-colonialism is inappropriate, only that such an approach must not fall back on the generalities and universal pre-sumptions that the postmodern and post-colonial strive so hard against. To keep, briefly, within Kiberd's framework, it would be better to see MacNeice as the type of figure that Baudelaire sets in opposition to the flâneur, the man of modernity:

> Away he goes, hurrying, searching . . . Be very sure that this man . . . this solitary, gifted with an active imagination, ceaselessly journeying across the great human desert – has an aim loftier than that of a mere flâneur, an aim more general, something other than the fugitive pleasure of circumstance. He is looking for that quality which you must allow me to call 'modernity' . . . He makes it his business to extract from fashion whatever element it may contain of poetry within history.[21]

The desire behind MacNeice's own search for 'poetry in history' should not be confused with the desire of the flâneur to arrest the present moment forever and release it from contingent materiality. Rather, throughout MacNeice's poetry personal and historical narratives exist simultaneously, and his own personal sense of displacement or exile is linked to, and in part symptomatic of, the wider Irish (post-)colonial experience. Thus, in 'Western Landscape', published in 1945, he writes,

> Let now the visitor, although disenfranchised
> In the constituencies of quartz and bog-oak
> And ousted from the elemental congress,
> Let me at least in token that my mother
> Earth was a rocky earth with breasts uncovered
> To suckle solitary intellects
> And limber instincts, let me, if a bastard
> Out of the West by urban civilisation
> (Which unwished father claims me – so I must take
> What I can before I go) let me who am neither Brandan
> Free of all roots nor yet a rooted peasant
> [. . .]

(*CPLM*, 257)

The events and experiences inscribed in this passage are clearly not those of the 'fugitive pleasure of circumstance'. Rather, the narrator is 'ousted from the elemental congress' and thrown into a indeterminate state where he is neither 'Free of all roots nor yet a rooted peasant'. The narrator is now a 'visitor', out of England, and 'a bastard/Out of the West by urban civilisation', displaced, too, from both the west of Ireland and the 'urban civilisation' of Belfast. The refusal throughout to resolve a Modernist concern for the originary moment in any identifiably rooted or concrete terms suggests that the problematic of a MacNeiceian self-definition is not simply that of an Irish national alienated abroad. It resides (or fails to reside) in the 'interlude' that cannot be cancelled, which he identifies in the final stanzas of a poem marking his return to Carrickfergus:

> Torn before birth from where my fathers dwelt,
> Schooled from the age of ten to a foreign voice,
> Yet neither western Ireland nor southern England
> Cancels this interlude; what chance misspelt
> May never now be righted by my choice.
>
> Whatever then my inherited or acquired
> Affinities, such remains my childhood's frame
> Like a belated rock in the red Antrim clay
> That cannot at this era change its pitch or name –
> And the pre-natal mountain is far away.

(*CPLM*, 225)

The sense of geographical exile in the first stanza, however, gives way to a different type of anxiety, in this case to something psychologically grounded, albeit ironically perhaps, the childhood frame remaining 'a belated rock in the red Antrim clay'. The concerns articulated in these two stanzas, of exile and unstable selfhood, are crucial to a reading of MacNeice's Modernism.

MACNEICE'S MOTHER IRELAND

The (non-)relationship of poet to place is at the centre of much of MacNeice's negotiation with Ireland and Irishness, and has to do with the poet's own sense of being unable to ground himself within the framework of Ireland's impacted and compromised colonial status. An Ireland bound up in identitarian politics of the sort espoused by Higgins from the Republic and Hewitt from the North was never going to be a comfortable one in which MacNeice could locate himself, a factor augmented by his own vicious sense of guilt at fluctuating between Northern and Southern Ireland and England. Bearing this in mind, it might be better to think of MacNeice as a type of baseless refugee or fugitive, one without the relative security of a place of recourse or retreat. As Michael Longley notes, 'to the Irish he has often seemed an exile, to the English a stranger'.[22] One of the results of this is that the ambiguity and difference that characterize much of MacNeice's writing as a whole are, on occasion, displaced by a capitulation to the oppositional paradigms of the past. Thus, whereas in his writing of England, in, say, 'Birmingham' (discussed in chapter 1), MacNeice resists the Modernist impulse of casting the contemporary city as the centre of corruption, in some of his writing concerned with Ireland, and in particular Belfast, he gets caught up in polarized meanings. 'Belfast', for example, written two years earlier than 'Birmingham', is wholly contemptuous of the mass urban market:

> The hard cold fire of the northerner
> Frozen into his blood from the fire in his basalt
> Glares from behind the mica of his eyes
> And the salt carrion water brings him wealth.
>
> Down there at the end of the melancholy lough
> Against the lurid sky over the stained water
> Where hammers clang murderously on the girders
> Like crucifixes the gantries stand.

> And in the marble stores rubber gloves like polyps
> Cluster; celluloid, painted ware, glaring
> Metal patents, parchment lampshades, harsh
> Attempts at buyable beauty.
>
> (*CPLM*, 17–18)

The poem could even be read as a less democratic prototype of the later 'Birmingham'. In stanza three, for example, he refers to 'harsh/Attempts at buyable beauty', and the types of images which are listed with excited fascination, almost affection, in 'Birmingham' – 'Cubical scent-bottles artificial legs arctic foxes and electric mops' – are here evoked with cold disdain; 'celluloid, painted ware, glaring/Metal patents, parchment lamp-shades' (*CPLM*, 17). This is the Belfast of 'Valediction', 'devout and profane and hard,/Built on reclaimed mud' (*CPLM*, 52); or that of *Zoo*, wherein MacNeice recalls that

> The weekend was all sunshine. I could not remember Belfast like this, and the continuous sunshine delighted but outraged me. My conception of Belfast, built up since early childhood, demanded that it should always be wet, grey, repellent and its inhabitants dour, rude and callous.[23]

(However it should be noted that MacNeice qualifies this statement by stating that '[t]his conception had already been shaken last night in the boat-train from London; a Belfast man sitting opposite me at dinner was nice to my little boy, said: "A child should live a life like an animal till it's five." This did not seem true to type. Belfast men were expected to be sadists.'[24])

Terence Brown refers to a freezing-up of MacNeice's early poetry about Ireland, citing 'Carrickfergus' as an example:

> Irish reality as both imprisonment and exclusion. Born in the oppressive space 'between the mountains and the gantries', the poet evokes a social and cultural condition characterised by frozen constraint manifested in such words and phrases as 'bottle-neck harbour', 'crystal salt', 'jams', 'slum', 'walled', 'stop his ears', 'banned forever', 'barred', 'knelt in marble'.[25]

In 'Belfast', too, the language emphasizes stasis rather than movement. The 'hard cold fire of the northerner' causes the blood to become 'frozen', the sky is 'lurid', the shops are given the status of mausoleums by the phrase 'marble stores', and in the first stanza there are references to rock formations, 'basalt' and 'mica', as well as to 'carrion', the dead and putrid body or flesh of an animal.

MacNeice's slippage into cliché and stereotype when writing of an Ireland that he sees as polarized can also be traced through his sense of the self as splintered. For this reason, W. J. McCormack groups MacNeice with Samuel Beckett, Elizabeth Bowen and Francis Stuart in a 'class of 1939'. According to McCormack, 'the whole metaphysics of identity, the self and so forth . . . subject to an intensely sceptical scrutiny' is present in their work because of the pressing question of Ireland's status in the war.[26] Underlying this in MacNeice's work is something that McCormack addresses elsewhere, an Anglo-Irish tendency to see tradition as betrayal.[27] In MacNeice's work, as in that of the other writers that McCormack mentions, however, the sense of betrayal resides not only in the specific condition of Anglo-Irishness, through a refusal to identify himself with the cultural nationalism of the Celtic Twilight – itself a Protestant attempt to resist implication within a colonial system – but also in a more general sense of the integration of the self as an act of betrayal in its own right. In his work on Ireland, MacNeice's suspicion of the integrated self has the effect of deconstructing his polarization of Ireland, thawing the freezing-up that occasionally occurs. As Peter McDonald suggests, 'If Yeats used Ireland to construct a dominant myth of the self, MacNeice undermined the self to complicate and qualify the myth of Ireland.'[28] One such myth that MacNeice is concerned to explore, if not explode, is that of Mother Ireland.

In *Autumn Journal* (discussed at length in chapter 5), MacNeice writes about the long history of the allegorical identification of Ireland with women such as Kathleen ni Hoolihan, Mother Eire, Dark Rosaleen or the Shan Van Vocht.[29]

> The shawled woman weeping at the garish altar.
> Kathleen ni Houlihan! Why
>   Must a country, like a ship or a car, be always female,
> Mother or sweetheart?
>
> (*CPLM*, 132)

In this passage, though, prompted by the return of one of the shawled women of 'Belfast', 'Kathleen ni Houlihan' is exclaimed and dismissed. Thus discharged, the mythopoetic-feminized edifice upon which Ireland constructs itself is voided of its symbolic value and denaturalized, revealed only as a construction 'like a ship or a car'. The case might be made that it is MacNeice's uncanny (in this sense literally *unheimlich*, or unhomely) hybridized, post-colonial status that allows his disruption of the masculine inscription of the nation as female. The notion of hybridity is, after all, one that allows for a revalorization, by inversion, of what had formerly been seen as negative, especially within nationalist discourse. Further, it undermines the masculine conceptualization of the nation as a fortress, seen, for example, in Seamus Heaney's final Oxford poetry lecture. In this lecture, he drew an imaginative map of Ireland as a castle consisting of five towers, the first of which, central to the construction, was 'the round tower of original insular dwelling'.[30] The other four towers were those of Edmund Spenser, W. B. Yeats, James Joyce and Louis MacNeice. Such a systematizing and exclusive model would have been anathema to MacNeice, whose writing works to complicate the masculine structuration of Ireland as passively feminine.

If the first three stanzas of 'Belfast', for example, represent and enact the monolithicism and rigidity of Northern Irish identity, the final two offer the vaguest hint of something different:

> In the porch of the chapel before the garish Virgin
> A shawled factory-woman as if shipwrecked there
> Lies a bunch of limbs glimpsed in the cave of gloom
> By us who walk in the street so buoyantly and glib.
>
> Over which country of cowled and haunted faces
> The sun goes down with a banging of Orange drums
> While the male kind murders each its woman
> To whose prayer for oblivion answers no Madonna.
>
> (*CPLM*, 17)

The history present here is one that denies religious difference, as neither the Virgin or Madonna of Catholicism, nor the Orange drums of Protestantism is able to escape the silencing as 'the male kind murders each its woman'. In the Machereyan sense, however, this is a silence that speaks, voicing the necessity of the erasure of female identity in the self-authenticating ideologies of Catholicism and Presbyterianism.[31] As Derrida puts it, 'A pure singularity can recognize another singularity only in abolishing itself or in abolishing the other as singularity.'[32] The position of the Virgin Mary in Catholicism may seem to offer a space for the articulation of female identity. Women are, though, excluded from the running of the Church, and Marian iconography ultimately leads to the cult of the Virgin, in which childbirth is associated with corruption and the female body is tainted, fallen. The use of the Virgin reinforces women's unworthiness because the Virgin, to use Derrida's term, is so perfect a 'singularity'. As Marina Warner writes of the illusory potential offered by the Virgin as a role model:

the very conditions that make the Virgin sublime are beyond the powers of women to fulfill unless they deny their sex. Accepting the Virgin as the ideal of purity implicitly demands rejecting the ordinary female condition as impure. Accepting virginity as an ideal entails contempt for sex and mother-hood . . .[33]

Similarly, although in Calvinist Presbyterianism there is a nominal adherence to freedom, that freedom remains notional for women, restricted by the Presbytery's perpetual definition of itself against siege. Further, because of the significance of the cult of the Virgin to Catholicism, Presbyterianism cannot even offer an iconography through which female identity may be negotiated. (MacNeice's religious background, Irish Anglicanism, is posi-tioned somewhere between these two.) Read in this light, by obtruding the violence required by those religious discourses that deny the voice of the female, 'Belfast' foregrounds the means of its own deconstruction. In other words, it offers up (even though it cannot exploit) a space where gender fluidity would dissolve the monolithicism of Northern Irish identities.

THE RETURN OF THE REPRESSED: FRAGMENTATION AND CHILDHOOD

Nonetheless, MacNeice does represent Ireland as a motherland. Rather than figuring the country as a transhistorical and essential location of female silence of the sort mentioned earlier, though, he writes of Ireland as, literally, the country of his mother. In the discussion of 'Carrick Revisited', I argued that the fundamental dislocation of the self to which MacNeice constantly returns is inextricably linked to childhood trauma. The persistence of this 'childhood frame' into adulthood is also, I would argue, registered throughout MacNeice's semi-autobiographical prose. In a passage in *Modern Poetry: A Personal Essay*, for example, MacNeice explicitly refers to the death of his mother, as well as to other biographical information concerning his childhood, in order to account for some of the thematic tensions of his 1930s poetry:

> Having been brought up in the North of Ireland, having a father who was a clergyman; the fact that my mother died when I was little; repression from the age of six to nine; inferiority complex on grounds of physique and class-consciousness; lack of a social life until I was grown up; late puberty; ignorance of music (which could have been a substitute for poetry); inability to ride horses or practise successfully most of the sports which satisfy a sense of rhythm; an adolescent liking for the role of the 'enfant terrible'; shyness in

the company of young women until I was twenty; a liking (now dead) for metaphysics; marriage and divorce; Birmingham; an indolent pleasure in gardens and wild landscapes . . . a liking for animals, an interest in dress.[34]

Similarly, in a passage in *Zoo*, MacNeice offers up certain reasons for his antipathy towards Northern Ireland by rehearsing the trauma of a childhood inflected with an almost biblical sense of apocalypse:

> I have always had what may be a proper dislike and disapproval of the North of Ireland, but largely, as I find on analysis, for improper – i.e. subjective – reasons. A harassed and dubious childhood under the hand of a well-meaning but barbarous mother's help from County Armagh led me to think of the North of Ireland as prison and the South as a means of escape. Many nightmares, boxes on the ears, a rasping voice of disapproval, a monotonous daily walk to a crossroads called Mile Bush, sodden haycocks, fear of hell-fire, my father's indigestion – these things, with on the other side my father's Home Rule sympathies and the music of his brogue, bred in me an almost fanatical hatred of Ulster. When I went to bed as a child I was told: 'You don't know where you'll wake up'. When I ran in the garden I was told that running was bad for the heart. Everything had its sinister aspect – milk shrinks the stomach, lemon thins the blood. Against my will I was always given sugar in my tea. The North was tyranny.[35]

Both accounts can be thought of in Freudian terms. Indeed, their very idiom and frame of reference (to repression, inferiority complexes, nightmares, barbarous parenting, etc.) recall the mainstays of Freudian psychology. Not only are we directly presented with the continuing resonance of the death of his mother for the older MacNeice, but, in the second passage above, we are also given an insight into one of the poet's surrogate mothers. This surrogate was not MacNeice's stepmother, Georgina Beatrice, but Miss MacReady who, MacNeice tells us, 'brought Hell home for [him]', drafted in as help for his ailing mother (*TSAF*, 42).[36]

However, just as the law of the mother is foregrounded in these quasi-Freudian accounts, so, too, is the law of the father: the symbolic order of the public sphere is also cited as part of the make-up of the adult MacNeice. In the above excerpt, for instance, the poet refers to an acute awareness of both class distinctions and the political climate of Northern Ireland at the beginning of the century as formative influences on his adult consciousness. Terence Brown, who cites them more specifically as generic to a Northern Irish identity, unpacks the historical circumstances:

> For all those associated with Anglo-Ireland in any way, the period (which was that of Louis MacNeice's childhood and adolescence) was one of profound

identity crisis. Anglican and propertied, Anglo-Ireland recoiled from the non-conformist populism of Ulster's vocal 'loyalty' but its members found themselves confronted in the rest of Ireland, whether they had nationalist sympathies or not, with a conception of Irish identity which excluded Protestants from full spiritual citizenship in the Irish nation.[37]

MacNeice constantly returns to his childhood in his poetry. 'Carrickfergus', for example, begins,

> I was the rector's son, born to the anglican order,
>   Banned for ever from the candles of the Irish poor;
> The Chichesters knelt in the marble at the ends of a transept
>   With ruffs around their necks, their portion sure.
>
> (CPLM, 69)

Nevertheless, it is important to grasp that this return to (rather than of) the repressed is not merely thematic but also technical, a strategy for negotiating an unprecedentedly hybridized English/Irish sense of identity. In fact, this is one of the ways in which MacNeice guards against superficiality and garrulity. The fundamental dislocation of the self, to which MacNeice so often returns, is something over which he also desperately attempts to maintain control. The ruptured self is, throughout his poetry, located in the traumas of the past that, when linked to constructions of national identity, are often constrained formally within ballad, nursery rhyme or mnemonic refrain. The last two of these forms are used in an attempt to ground the subject in the poem 'Autobiography':

> When I was five the black dreams came;
> Nothing after that was quite the same.
>
> *Come back early or never come.*
>
> The dark was talking to the dead;
> The lamp was dark beside my bed.
>
> (CPLM, 183–4)

As I shall suggest in the Conclusion, the sinister psychology of his 1930s poetic comes to be framed differently in his later work, which mobilizes allegorical and parabolic strategies that might be traced back to earlier Irish literary precedents. What marks his poetry of the 1930s is the way in which MacNeice conflates different forms in order to stave off (or at least come to terms with) the dissolution of a self constructed, inevitably, by the paradigms of the past. Within these differing, and often competing, structures a dark Freudianism and a refusal to be assimilated into traditional models of identity persist. As I have argued, most traditional readings of MacNeice stress his status as an outsider, a visitor or a tourist in Ireland. However, the definitions of MacNeice's identity as 'lack' are not confined to the early part of the twentieth century. Tom Paulin, for example, writing in 1984, termed him 'The Man from No Part'.[38] It is not 'no-space' that MacNeice inhabits, I would suggest, but, rather, a 'space in-between', a relationship which intersects and complicates facile notions of Englishness and Irishness, colonizer and colonized. This is the dilemma that MacNeice writes of in falsely authenticist terms in 'Valediction':

> I can say Ireland is hooey, Ireland is
> A gallery of fake tapestries,
> But I cannot deny my past to which my self is wed,
> The woven figure cannot undo its thread.

> *(CPLM, 52–3)*

The concept of fakery, of course, presupposes one of reality, but within MacNeice's hybrid context there is no 'real', as the experiences of Ireland are to him precisely those of fakery, mimicry and hybridity.

It is not only traditional, under-theorized readings of MacNeice that are difficult to accept, though, but also those crude post-colonial ones, such as Kiberd's, which all too easily reveal their nationalism. Within such polarized paradigms the complexity of MacNeice's Modernist relationship to Ireland is never going to be adequately accounted for. A post-colonial approach that could do so would bring in the notion of hybridity (later explored in depth in relation to Dylan Thomas in chapter 6) and stress the anomalousness of MacNeice. MacNeice's Modernist strangeness, I would argue, subverts such dominant cultural narratives. The entry of this formerly excluded subject – and his subjects – into the debate deconstructs the series of inclusions and exclusions on which that dominance is premised. Modernist hybridity can be seen, to extend Homi Bhabha's interpretation, as a counter-narrative, a critique of the canon and its exclusion of other narratives. The figure of MacNeice confounds, rather than resolves, the entrenched dualisms of the critical debates around Irish identities. To return tentatively to Muldoon's terms used at the opening of the chapter, MacNeice's position is that of the horse, a third term different in kind from that of either the aristocrat or peasant, a hybrid position that, according to Bhabha, 'has no such perspective of depth or truth to provide: it is not a third term that resolves the tension between two cultures'.[39]

4

'Here lie the beasts': Dylan Thomas's monsters, monstrous Dylan Thomas

The Monster is a Monster, is monstrous, because it escapes classification, because it scrambles codes, confounds rules, causes administrative chaos. It is this that makes it catastrophic. The Monster is not 'in itself' monstrous, there is no inherent monstrousness; monstrousness is that which is prescribed and proscribed by the facile categorizings of the social and cultural order. The Monster is all that a society refuses to name, refuses to make nameable, not just because its very heterogeneity, mobility, and power is a threat to that society but, much more importantly, it is the very flux of energy that made society possible in the first place and as such offers the terrible promise that other societies are possible, other knowledges, other histories, other sexualities.

David E. Musselwhite[1]

> The atlas-eater with a jaw for news,
> Bit out the mandrake with tomorrow's scream.
> Then, penny-eyed, that gentleman of wounds,
> Old cock from nowheres and the heaven's egg,
> With bones unbuttoned to the halfway winds,
> Hatched from the windy salvage on one leg,
> Scraped at my cradle in a walking word
> That night of time under the Christward shelter,
> I am the long world's gentleman, he said,
> And share my bed with Capricorn and Cancer.

(*CPDT*, 58)

The use of surrealism, discussed in chapter 2, was only one of the ways by which Dylan Thomas deliberately opposed what he saw as the presumptive hyper-rationality of those he regarded as the poetic establishment. If any of Thomas's early poetry, for example 'The force that through the green fuse' or 'Light breaks where no sun shines', is compared to that of Auden, the differences become obvious. They include the use of language not immediately translatable into meaning, a disconcerting combination of lack of specificity (of time, place and so on), a lack of abstraction, and the use of the grotesque, rather than irony, as a mode of critique. Thomas's first major published poem 'That sanity be kept', however, stands out as very different from both of these poems. Victor Neuburg, who wrote that it was 'perhaps the best modernist poem that as yet I've received', published it in the *Sunday Referee* on 3 September 1933:

> That sanity be kept I sit at open windows,
> Regard the sky, make unobtrusive comment on the moon,
> Sit at open windows in my shirt,
> And let the traffic pass, the signals shine,
> The engines run, the brass bands keep in tune,
> For sanity must be preserved.
>
> Thinking of death, I sit and watch the park
> Where children play in all their innocence,
> And matrons, on the littered grass,
> Absorb the daily sun
>
> The sweet suburban music from a hundred lawns
> Comes softly to my ears. The English
> Mowers mow and mow.
>
> I mark the couples walking arm in arm,
> Observe their smiles,
> Sweet invitations and inventions,
> See them lend love illustration
> By gesture and grimace.
> I watch them curiously, detect beneath the laughs
> What stands for grief, a vague bewilderment
> At things not turning right.
>
> I sit at open windows in my shirt,
> Observe, like some Jehovah of the west,
> What passes by, that sanity be kept.[2]

In this poem Thomas is very consciously parodying the English Auden school who 'mow and mow': its use of 'everyday' language; the lists of stanza one ('let the traffic pass, the signals shine,/The engines run, the brass bands keep in tune,'); the assumed role of dispassionate observer; the societal façade, and so on. In this poem, at least, Thomas ensures that sanity is kept. But, as he points out at the end, he is of the west, and in his poetry can be found a radical alternative, a monstrous poetic, an aesthetic of monstrosity.[3]

THE MODERNIST MONSTER

In two remarkable letters of 1934, to Pamela Hansford Johnson, Thomas writes of his interest in dark material. In May he refers to Neuburg's concern about the experimentalism of Thomas's work:

> Tell him [Victor Neuburg] I write of worms and corruption, because I like worms and corruption. Tell him I believe in the fundamental wickedness and worthlessness of man, and in the rot in life. Tell him I am all for cancers. And tell him, too, that I loathe poetry. I'd prefer to be an anatomist or the keeper of a morgue any day. Tell him I live exclusively on toenails and tumours. I sleep in a coffin too, and a wormy shroud is my summer suit.
>
> (*CLDT*, 134)

Meanwhile, in a letter of a month earlier Thomas contrasts his own poetry with that of his contemporaries:

> I believe in writing poetry from the flesh, and generally, from dead flesh. So many modern poets take the living flesh as their object, and, by their clever dissecting, turn it into a carcass. I prefer to take the dead flesh, and, by any positivity of faith that is in me, build up a living flesh from it.
>
> (*CLDT*, 72–3)

In this striking and suggestive image, Thomas presents his own poetry as born from a monstrous process of reproduction. As was suggested in the Introduction to this book, histories of the 1930s tend to regard the period as dominated by the 'Auden generation'. Yet, in reality, the decade might just as easily be defined in terms of the work of James Whale, the horror-film maker and an equally important figure on the cultural map of the time. In 1932 Boris Karloff played the mad butler terrorizing Wales in Whale's *The Old Dark House* – a year before Karloff's *The Mummy* went on show – and it was also the decade of their *Frankenstein* (1931) and *Bride of Frankenstein* (1935). Both *18 Poems* and *Twenty-five Poems* trail their Gothic properties, and are crammed with, to list a sample, ghosts, vampires, mummies, cadavers, references to 'Struwwelpeter', tombs, sores, flies, cataracts, carcasses, cancers, cypress lads, hanged men, mandrakes, gallows, crosses, worms and maggots. Throughout, Thomas's early poetry exudes a charnel-house atmosphere of decay and mortality and its libertarian strivings are always inextricably linked to the darker aspects it purports to reject, with the first poem of the first collection exploring the idea that the 'boys of summer' are 'in their ruin', always in the process of themselves becoming 'the dark deniers' (*CPDT*, 7).

As Fred Botting has argued, the Gothic is concerned with the transgression of boundaries and is the 'signification of a writing of excess', which shadows the progress of modernity and enlightenment with a dark counter-narrative.[4] The Gothic also fulfilled Thomas's career need to subvert what he regarded as the hyper-rationality and dogmatism of the *New Country* poets, although not necessarily in a merely irrational or ahistorical manner. As Stewart Crehan notes, 'the rich polysemy and fluidity' of the early poetry – thematic as well as linguistic – can be seen as an attempt to keep in motion the dialectic which Stalinism had stilled by the early 1930s, just as it was being erased by Hitler.[5] The Gothic operates in the same way as Thomas's early work, exploring hybrid states and forms and insisting on the inescapability of the biological bases of existence. In it, as in Thomas's poetry generally, 'ambivalence and uncertainty obscure single meaning', whilst the anxiety over boundary transgression that the Gothic feeds off was, at the local and international geopolitical levels, in line with the 1930s *Zeitgeist* and its concern with eugenics and the technology of the impending war. [6] (Thomas's specifically Welsh use of the Gothic is discussed in chapter 6.)

Thomas's poetry is full of monsters (one of his early poems begins 'Here lie the beasts'), and it is perhaps worth noting in the title of one of Thomas's most famous early poems, 'And death shall have no dominion', not only the reference to Paul's First Epistle to the Romans, but also the uncanny echo of Walton's letter in *Frankenstein* in which he discusses Victor's quest.[7] Further, it might be argued that Thomas's poetry, like Shelley's novel, can be read as recreating one of the most dominant mythical narratives of the western tradition, the Judaeo-Christian myth of the Creation and Fall. For repeatedly in Thomas's poetry, in his patching together of the dead in his poetic workshop of the flesh, we find, not Adam and Eve falling from Edenic innocence into knowledge and sin, but Thomas's nameless monsters, like Victor Frankenstein's, falling from innocence into bitter experience and wretched isolation.

One such violent display of the excessive and irrational is the poem 'How shall my animal':

> How shall my animal
> Whose wizard shape I trace in the cavernous skull,

Vessel of abscesses and exultation's shell,
Endure burial under the spelling wall,
The invoked, shrouding veil at the cap of the face,
Who should be furious,
Drunk as a vineyard snail, flailed like an octopus
Roaring, crawling, quarrel
With the outside weathers,
The natural circle of the discovered skies
Draw down to its weird eyes?

(*CPDT*, 75)

The poem is concerned with the self-defeating nature of poetic articulation, the narrator anguished by the impossibility of reconciling self and word, 'animal' and 'spelling wall'. However, in the very utterance of this despair, the 'animal' of the poem comes to assume a monstrous life of its own. The language of the poem creates a reality which, rather than confining the animal, bringing about its death, and burying it 'under the spelling wall', liberates the monster from fixity, freeing it to mutate in a series of surreal transformations from human to lion to horse to turtle and beyond. At one and the same time, then, 'How shall my animal' registers the prison-house of language and figures the means by which it can be escaped. It is to this paradoxical autonomy of the surrealist artwork that Thomas appealed in correspondence about the poem with Henry Treece:

> [The poem] is its own question and answer, its own contradiction, its own agreement . . . The aim of a poem is the mark that the poem itself makes; it's the bullet and the bullseye; the knife, the growth, and the patient. A poem moves only towards its own end, which is the last line.
>
> (*CLDT*, 297)

Further, 'How shall my animal' turns on the figure of the monster, regarded by Elza Adamowicz as 'the Surrealist figure *par excellence*'.[8] As Adamowicz points out, one of the major impulses of surrealism is the relocation of the marginalized – *objets trouvés*, discarded materials, sweeps of the pen or brush – and the monstrous is no exception. A surrealist zoo, for example, would include Max Ernst's Lop Lop, Dalí's 'Great Masturbator', Pablo Picasso's and Man Ray's Minotaurs, and Thomas's 'Atlas-eater with a jaw for news' (*CPDT*, 58).[9] Yet, in this surrealist manoeuvre, the irrational and uncomfortable monster of Thomas's poem does not escape from the ghetto only to be reconfined by the closure implicit in a centre/periphery opposition. The central position that it comes to occupy is also one which it disturbs. As Thomas wrote of his Atlas-eater, 'What is this creature?

It's the dog among the fairies, the rip and cur among the myths, the snapper at demons, the scarer of ghosts, the wizard's heel-chaser'(*CLDT*, 301).

One of the most significant positions that the monsters of surrealism and the Gothic problematize is that of masculine identity. Traditionally, surrealism, like the Gothic, indulges an aggressive masculinity, articulating it through the likes of Picasso's tauromachias or Dalí's neurotic male fantasies. It can be argued, though, that the surreal is also that which haunts the violent construction of the male. In the first book of Ernst's *Une Semaine de Bonté*, for example, the masculine iconography of warfare is examined through the revolutionary lionheaded hero. 'How shall my animal', which uses the word 'lion-head', goes further back to disturb the male (in this reading the animal might be considered as *anima*), prior to its construction as the masculine:

> How shall it magnetize,
> Towards the studded male in a bent, midnight blaze
> That melts the lionhead's heel and horseshoe of the heart,
> A brute land in the cool top of the country days
> To trot with a loud mate the haybeds of a mile,
> Love and labour and kill
> In quick, sweet, cruel light till the locked ground sprout out,
> The black, burst sea rejoice,
> The bowels turn turtle,
> Claw of the crabbed veins squeeze from each red particle
> The parched and raging voice?
>
> (*CPDT*, 75–6)[10]

The poem is concerned to interrogate the false rootedness of aggressive masculinity, of the 'studded male' (with a play on 'studied' and 'stud') trotting, loving, labouring and killing in the 'brute land'. This leads to the male animal's pregnancy in the following stanza and, in the final stanza, the birth:

> Sigh long, clay cold, lie shorn,
> Cast high, stunned on gilled stone; sly scissors ground in frost
> Clack through the thicket of strength, love hewn in pillars drops
> With carved bird, saint, and sun, the wrackspiked maiden mouth
> Lops, as a bush plumed with flames, the rant of the fierce eye,
> Clips short the gesture of breath.
> Die in red feathers when the flying heaven's cut,
> And roll with the knocked earth:
> Lie dry, rest robbed, my beast.

You have kicked from a dark den, leaped up the whinnying light,
And dug your grave in my breast.

(*CPDT*, 76)

This stanza, however, reveals the birth to be a stillbirth. Articulated in language, the animal gasps and dies – 'Cast high, stunned on gilled stone' – and the final lines make it clear that this is an internal death: 'Lie dry, rest robbed, my beast,/You have kicked from a dark den, leaped up the whinnying light,/And dug your grave in my breast.'. Read in this way, the poem exposes, as does Mary Shelley's novel, the destructive consequences of the patriarchal inscription of the male as the centre of reproduction.

Thomas's disruption of culturally central categories, like masculinity, and his poetry's transgressive miscegenation have led critics to treat both him and his writing as monstrous. His disruption of the boundaries of conventional reason is in line with the way monsters have been defined historically. Since Aristotle's *Generation of Animals*, monsters have been connected with concepts of trangression, as locations of an otherness, deviance or alterity that disturbs officially recognized accounts of reality. For Aristotle, it is upon the violation of the natural principle of resemblance that monstrosity transpires; monstrosity deviates from and transgresses the general laws of nature:

> what is the cause why sometimes the offspring is a human being yet bears no resemblance to any ancestor, sometimes it has reached such a point that in the end it no longer has the appearance of a human being at all, but that of an animal only – it belongs to the class of monstrosities, as they are called . . . A monstrosity, of course, belongs to the class of 'things contrary to Nature', although it is contrary not to Nature in her entirety but only to Nature in the generality of cases.[11]

Katherine Park and Lorraine Daston observe that, in the Renaissance, monsters were seen as prodigies, phenomena out of the course of nature; and the etymology of the word itself, which derives from two different Latin sources, suggests the way in which monsters were both revealing spectacles and divine messages. With regard to the former, 'monster' is from *monstrare*, meaning to 'show', 'display' and 'make visible' (as in 'demonstrate', 'demonstrative', 'demonstrable').[12] In the sixteenth century, therefore, monsters displayed truths that were out of the course of nature, that were somehow unauthored by God. Following this period monsters were increasingly seen as objects of spiritual significance, rather than as objects of scientific inquiry:

The treatment of monsters and attitudes towards them evolved noticeably during the sixteenth and seventeenth centuries. Characteristically, monsters appear most frequently in the context of a whole group of related natural phenomena: earthquakes, floods, volcanic eruptions, celestial apparitions, and rains of blood, stones and other miscellenea. The interpretation of this canon of phenomena underwent a series of metamorphoses in the years after 1500 . . . By the end of the seventeenth century, monsters had lost their autonomy as a subject of scientific study, dissolving their links with earthquakes and the like, and had been integrated into the medical disciplines of comparative anatomy and embryology.[13]

The other Latin root of 'monster', *monere*, from to 'warn', 'portend', 'give warning of' (compare 'admonition', 'monitor', 'monitory'), makes clear the potential for the monster's later assumption of a more ideological function.[14] As Michel Foucault states,

until the beginning of the nineteenth-century . . . madmen remained monsters – that is, etymologically, beings or things to be shown . . . Madness was shown, but on the other side of bars; if present, it was at a distance, under the eyes of a reason that no longer felt any relation to it and that would not compromise itself by too close a resemblance. Madness had become a thing to look at: no longer a monster inside oneself.'[15]

From the eighteenth century onwards, in other words, madness was considered a monstrosity to be objectified through display. This display, spectacle or 'monstering' of the mad worked, then, ideologically, satisfying the bourgeoisie by externalizing and distancing (or 'othering') the mad and irrational as freakish and foreign, and thus securing and authorizing its hold over, and monopoly of, normality and reason. And later, as Foucault explains, the figure of the monster becomes bound to that of the criminal:

[in the nineteenth-century the criminal was] nothing less than a traitor, a 'monster' . . . Between the contractual principle that expels the criminal from society and the image of the monster 'vomited' by nature, where is one to find a limit, if not . . . in the sensibility of the reasonable man who makes the law and does not commit the crime? . . . The criminal designated as the enemy of all, whom it is in the interest of all to track down, falls outside the pact, disqualifies himself as a citizen and emerges, bearing within him as it were, a wild fragment of nature: he appears as a villain, a monster, a madman, perhaps a sick and, before long, 'abnormal' individual . . . On the other hand, the need to measure, from within, the effects of the punitive power prescribes tactics of intervention over all criminals, actual or potential . . . All this leads to an objectification of criminals and crimes.[16]

Given Thomas's refusal, following his first major published poem, to main-
tain sanity, this Foucaldian or 'disciplinary' function of monstrosity is of
great importance when considering the English reaction to him in the 1930s.
Under the hyper-rational, self-serving gaze of many of his contemporaries
and critics at the time and since, Thomas was indeed *monstered*, discussed
negatively, in terms of show and display and excess and madness. As James
A. Davies notes, in English reviews of the time critics referred to Thomas's
'conjuring tricks with words' and to his 'Welsh oral trickery'.[17] W. H.
Mellors wrote that 'his Welsh non-conformist background encourages the
bardic gesture, the rapture of hell-fire', Robin Mayhead talked of Thomas's
'self-indulgent religiosity . . . pseudo-liturgical verbal juggling', and Robert
Graves claimed that 'Thomas was nothing more than a Welsh demagogic
masturbator who failed to pay his bills'.[18] (Significantly, Graves's charging
of Thomas with sexual immaturity and 'unmanliness' mirrors the notorious
assaults on Keats's poetry a century before. Just as for Byron Keats's 'shabby
genteel' class origins were linked to infantile immaturity in his poetry –
'Johnny piss-a-bed Keats' – so Thomas's class and national identity, and
through them his poetry, are impugned by Graves. As Marjorie Levinson
maintains, it was precisely those 'sensual' and improper aspects of Keats'
style – his very 'badness' and excess – which were foregrounded in his
most significant poetry.[19]) Michael Roberts saw Thomas's early poetry as
'a mere riot of noise', full of 'uncontrolled verbal associations'; Cyril
Connolly called Thomas 'a kind of mad hit-or-miss experimental scientist';
Geoffrey Grigson saw Thomas's poetry as 'psychopathological nonsense',
and in a famous essay, 'How much me your verbal acrobatics amaze', talked
about Thomas's poetry as 'inhuman and glandular. Or rather like water and
mud and fumes mixed in a volcanic mud-hole, in a young land . . . [a]
meaningless hot sprawl of mud.'[20] 'Inhuman', 'pathological', 'a mad . . .
scientist', 'self-indulgent', 'Welsh oral trickery': Thomas is figured as
deviant, freakish, transgressive, monstrous, and, to borrow a phrase from
H. G. Porteus, can be read as offering in his poetry 'an unconducted tour
of bedlam'.[21]

MONSTROSITY, THE AVANT-GARDE AND THE
POSTMODERN EVENT

Remarkably, Thomas links both of these notions of monstrosity – his own
hideous progeny (his poems and the monsters therein) and that of exhibition
and display – in a letter to Henry Treece of 1 June 1938:

Edith Sitwell's analysis [of 'Altarwise by owl-light'], in a letter to the Times, of the lines 'The atlas-eater with a jaw for news/Bit out the mandrake with tomorrow's scream', seems to me very vague and Sunday-journalish. She says the lines refer to 'the violent speed and sensation-loving, horror-loving craze of modern life'. She doesn't take the literal meaning: that a world-devouring ghost creature bit out the horror of tomorrow from a gentleman's loins. A 'jaw for news' is an obvious variation of a 'nose for news', & means that the mouth of the creature can taste already the horror that has not yet come or can sense it coming, can thrust its tongue into news that has not yet been made, can savour the enormity of the progeny before the seed stirs, can realise the crumbling of dead flesh before the opening of the womb that delivers that flesh to tomorrow. What is this creature? It's the dog among the fairies, the rip and cur among the myths, the snapper at the demons, the scarer of ghosts, the wizard's heel-chaser. This poem is a particular incident in a particular adventure, not a general, elliptical deprecation of this 'horrible, crazy, speedy life'.

You say you intend showing the book to Michael Roberts who will be 'sympathetic towards us'. You are not treading on my corns when you call Roberts a good Thinker, but I personally can do without his condescension. He commented in the London Mercury that 'it is a pity D.T. should sometimes give the impression of using a large & personal vocabulary merely to make a schoolboy exhibition'. The phrase I object to is not 'a schoolboy exhibition', for I'm not afraid of showing-off or throwing my cap in the air, but 'It's a pity'. What function has this patronising 'pity' in criticism? Do I need a critic to weep over my errors of taste? Let him point them out, tell me, if he likes, how to rectify them; but, for Christ's sake, not sympathise.

(*CLDT*, 301)

In the second paragraph quoted above, Thomas acknowledges a contemporary patronizing criticism of his work as childish showmanship, but acutely reveals that this has more to do with his perceived lack of 'taste' than genuine critical engagement. In aesthetic terms, Michel Foucault finds at work in the Modernist avant-garde of James Joyce, for example, or of Antonin Artaud, Jorge Luis Borges and Samuel Beckett, a monstrous 'counter-discourse', which challenges and refutes classical values of taste, truth, naturalness and pleasure, and instead privileges the ugly, the body and the scandalous; what Thomas referred to in a letter to Vernon Watkins of March 1938 as 'breaches of the nostalgic etiquette' (*CLDT*, 279).[22] But it is Thomas's remarks in the first paragraph quoted above that are potentially more significant for a reading of his work, in the light of recent theorizing on monstrosity and the avant-garde.

For Jacques Derrida, in *Of Grammatology*, monstrosity must be elaborated in relation to the idea of an unnameable futurity, whereby the future can only be anticipated in the form of an absolute danger. It is that which breaks absolutely with constituted normality and can only be proclaimed, *presented*, as a sort of monstrosity. For that future world and for that within it which will have put into question the values of sign, word, and writing, for that which guides our future anterior, there is as yet no exergue.[23]

Further, the monstering of Thomas can be read in the light of other work by Derrida on monstrosity:

Texts and discourses that provoke at the outset reactions of rejection, that are denounced precisely as anomalies or monstrosities are often texts that, before being in turn appropriated, assimilated, acculturated, transform the nature of the field of reception, transform the nature of social and cultural experience, historical experience. All of history has shown that each time an *event* has been produced, for example in philosophy or in poetry, it took the form of the unacceptable, or even of the intolerable, of the incomprehensible, that is, of a certain monstrosity.[24]

'Unacceptable', 'intolerable', 'incomprehensible'; all standard conservative reactions to the radical avant-garde, whose project was to 'transform the nature . . . of cultural experience' through the production of an event. As, for Jean-François Lyotard, the notion of eventhood is crucial to an understanding of the politics of the avant-garde, or postmodern, artwork, it is worth recalling here Thomas's discussion of Vernon Watkins's poetry, in a letter to Watkins of 21 March 1938: 'I can see the sensitive picking of words, but none of the strong inevitable pulling that makes a poem *an event,* a happening, an action perhaps, not a still-life or an experience put down, placed, regulated' (my emphasis) (CL, 278).

In opposition to the likes of Fredric Jameson and Terry Eagleton, who choose to see the defining characteristic of the postmodern artwork as its break with and from Modernism and history, Lyotard famously characterizes the postmodern sensibility as an 'incredulity towards metanarratives'.[25] Thriving on the process of totalization, to Lyotard, meta- or grand narratives are inevitably terroristic. As such, his work celebrates the play of heterogeneity and reviles all attempts at totalization:

We have paid a high enough price for the nostalgia of the whole and the one, for the reconciliation of the concept and the sensible, of the transparent and the communicable experience. Under the general demand for slackening and appeasement, we can hear the mutterings of the desire for a return of the terror, for the realisation of the fantasy to seize reality. The answer is: Let us wage a war on totality; let us be witnesses to the unrepresentable; let us activate the differences and save the honour of the name.[26]

However, as the final two lines above suggest, he manages to align his criticism of the meta-narrative to a political commitment, which might in turn be associated with the process of Thomas's poetry. A profoundly anti-representational argument against all forms of realism emerges in Lyotard's work as, within his writing, realism is figured as the language that has secured an authorization for itself as a consensus. (He cites Nazism and Communism as regimes of realism.) Indeed, throughout his work he calls for the mobilization of a language that will disrupt what he regards as terroristic consensual harmony. As a result, he looks toward the aesthetic of the sublime because of its point-blank refusal to conform to the conventions of a norm. However, rather than appropriating the sublime, as Jameson does, in either a Kantian or Burkean formulation, he returns to and recasts the sublime of Romanticism, shifting its emphasis from an attempt to represent the unrepresentable to a structure concerned with temporality. This is the sublime, Lyotard argues, that has found political purchase in and through the imagination of the modern avant-garde:

> The postmodern would be that which, in the moderns, puts forward the unpresentable in presentation itself; that which denies itself the solace of good forms, the consensus of a taste which would make it possible to share collectively the nostalgia for the unattainable; that which searches for new presentations, not in order to enjoy them but in order to impart a stronger sense of the unpresentable. A postmodern artist or writer is in the position of a philosopher: the works he produces are not in principle governed by preestablished rules, and they cannot be judged according to a determining judgment, by applying familiar categories to the text or to the work. Those rules and categories are working without rules in order to formulate the rules of what will have been done. Hence the fact that work and text have the characters of an event; hence also, they always come too late for their author, or, what amounts to the same thing, their being put into work, their realization always begins too soon. The postmodern would have to be understood according to the paradox of the future (post) anterior (modo).[27]

Like the sublime, the avant-garde is that which breaks the conventional rules of the game by shattering the existing map of aesthetics. Rather than periodizing postmodernism, as Jameson attempts to do, in order to locate the historical discourse of class struggle (that Jameson's announcement that the aesthetic of the modern avant-garde lies in the wake of the cultural logic of late capitalism is symptomatic of his radically different constitution of the postmodern), Lyotard frames his account of the postmodern with the same paradoxical tense that characterizes the monstrous for Derrida: the future anterior. (It is important to note that Lyotard is extremely uncomfortable with the term 'postmodernism'.) This, though, is of political significance, as the avant-garde is able to shock and break the hold of consensual reality only because it has the disruptive quality of an event that is not immediately translatable into a meaning that can be mastered. As he explains, because the post-modern artist is in search of new rules that can be formulated only after the event, the postmodern artwork can only retrospectively be constituted at a level of meaning.

I would argue that to understand Thomas's poetry of the 1930s, it is crucial to grasp this relationship between the avant-garde and the political. (Surrealism [discussed in chapter 2], for example, was, as a movement, keen to establish its political credentials. Breton yoked surrealism to Trotsky's Fourth International and stated, at the 1935 Congress of Writers for the Defence of Culture, '"Transform the World" Marx said; "change life" Rimbaud said – these two watchwords are for us one and the same', and Walter Benjamin famously declared that the aim of surrealism was 'to win the energies of intoxication for the revolution'.[28]) For to talk of Thomas politically is not simply to refer to a political poetry of the kind normally associated with the 1930s, to poems like 'The hand that signed the paper' or 'And death shall have no dominion', but is, more importantly, to understand the political nature of the avant-garde. Thus, Breton's attempt to create a 'surreality', a fusion of dream and reality, to reintegrate art and life and to resist the separation of art and social praxis, can be seen as an example of that which, for Peter Bürger, is the ultimate political manoeuvre of the avant-garde: the turning of art against itself as institution.[29] The avant-garde artwork, then, is inevitably self-critical, bound to the very processes that it attempts to critique.

As such, Thomas writes a perfectly monstrous, surreal and uncanny language that at one and the same time reveals and breaks the rules by which it is constituted. The disparate parts of Thomas's framed assemblages of dissociation both reflect and, through their assumption of autonomy and self-sufficiency, enact a schizophrenic world that disrupts the asceticism of Eliotic High Modernism. This is, as I have shown, of political significance, as Thomas's work of the 1930s is able to shock and break the consensual reality of the existing map of aesthetics because it has the monstrous disruptive quality of an event that is not immediately translatable into a meaning that can be mastered. Thomas continues to be a central and disturbing fact of the period, one that it is impossible, despite the best critical attempts, to expel or exclude.

5

'But one – meaning I':
Autumn Journal's histories
and voices

One other point: you seem to think I have a purely aesthetic approach to the world. This is crazy of you. I suppose you think that the reason I haven't got a comprehensive world-view is that I amn't interested in world-views. When I was married I did try to do without a world-view but it was a failure & I am trying to develop one but I am damned if I am going to swallow Marx or Trotsky or anyone else lock stock & barrel unless it squares with my experience or, perhaps I should say, my feelings of internal reality.

Louis MacNeice[1]

And we who have been brought up to think of 'Gallant Belgium'
    As so much blague
Are now preparing again to essay good through evil
    For the sake of Prague;
And must, we suppose, become uncritical, vindictive,
    And must, in order to beat
The enemy, model ourselves upon the enemy,
    A howling radio for our paraclete.
The night continues wet, the axe keeps falling,
    The hill grows bald and bleak
No longer one of the sights of London but maybe
    We shall have fireworks here by this day week.

(CPLM, 114)

For Samuel Hynes, *Autumn Journal* is 'the best personal expression of the "end of the thirties mood"'.[2] It is, as Hynes writes elsewhere, 'most simply, what its title says it is: a personal record of the period from August through December 1938'.[3] For Hynes, this 'mood', of which *Autumn Journal* is the best expression, is that of a 1930s poetry of empiricism and realism or reflectionism. This is, though, not quite accurate. As I have shown, MacNeice's poetry of the period is, in certain important ways, very different from the work of those poets who, for Hynes at least, represent the mainstream of the 1930s. Edna Longley is, perhaps, nearer the mark when she suggests that 'All the currents of MacNeice's writing during the 1930s flow into *Autumn Journal* and find a new dynamic there: lyrics, eclogues, prose, the Audenesque play *Out of Picture*, images, strategies, tones of voice. His entire creative kaleidoscope breaks up and reforms.'[4] This is not to say, though, that the reader must agree with Longley on what 'the currents of MacNeice's writing in the 1930s' precisely are. For Longley, what characterizes MacNeice in this period is a liberal humanism, which distances him from both his Modernist precursors and an English 1930s Marxist poetic. MacNeice is, however, as this chapter will argue, more difficult to pin down than that; inscribed within his poetry is a resistance to totalizing gestures, critical or otherwise. If anything distinguishes MacNeice's poetry of the 1930s it is, as I suggested in chapter 3, its sheer obstinate indeterminacy, contradictoriness, variousness and flux. For obvious reasons this has led critics to call into question his political commitment.

As Longley notes, MacNeice was – and continues to be – attacked from both left and right, particularly with regard to *Autumn Journal*. Julian Symons, for example, mocks the poem as 'The Bourgeois's Progress', and Hynes argues that the poet's 'self-proclaimed role of a common man was a kind of substitute for political commitment, a way of being apolitical with a good heart'.[5] The idea of MacNeice as 'apolitical with a good heart' was also the predominant one in the 1930s, an opinion which led to his exclusion from Michael Roberts's *New Signatures* (1932) and *New Country* (1933), the two anthologies of the 1930s whose remit was avowedly Marxist. Part of the reason for MacNeice's exclusion was that his pragmatic politics were deeply at odds with what he regarded as the political opportunism of the 1930s. As he writes in *The Strings are False*,

> The great danger of Marxist doctrine is that it allows and even encourages opportunism. All their talk about strategy. After a bit the Marxist, who is only human, finds it such fun practising strategy – i.e. hypocrisy, lying, graft, political pimping, tergiversation, allegedly necessary murder – that he forgets the end in the means, the evil of the means drowns the good of the end, power corrupts, the living gospel withers, Siberia fills with ghosts. Fills with the victims of idealists trying to be pragmatic – or of pragmatists pretending to ideals.

And the present master of the Kremlin, being infallible, has scrubbed the
walls to get rid of the echo of the voice of Lenin who admitted he made
mistakes.

(TSAF, 161)

D. E. S. Maxwell argues that MacNeice's poems express a sort of 'reluctant
Marxism which accepts the premises but has no enthusiasm for the con-
clusion', a commentary which seems to invert MacNeice's own terms ('he
forgets the end in the means, the evil of the means drowns the good of the
end').[6] Either way, this suggests not only that MacNeice was deeply
concerned with politics at the time, but also that he was more politically
engaged than most accounts of his work allow. (As I will argue, one way
to read *Autumn Journal* is as a desperate search for a language of polit-
ical engagement.) That MacNeice is wrestling with the political is also
apparent in the poetry immediately leading up to *Autumn Journal*. In both
'Bagpipe Music' (1937) and 'The Sunlight on the Garden' (also 1937),
perhaps MacNeice's two most anthologized pieces, this anxiety is present.
In the former, MacNeice attempts to represent the skirling, topsy-turvy chaos
of capitalist Scotland, an attempt which is ultimately in vain. As the final
two lines of the poem register, 'The glass is falling hour by hour, the glass
will fall forever/But if you break the bloody glass you won't hold up the
weather.' In the latter, there is a similar failure, as the surface elegance of
the poet's obvious delight in the lyrical pleasures of the moment is con-
tinually hardened by a knowledge of the approach of war. In fact, many of
MacNeice's poems of the period register an invasion of the sinister and
thus deny the poet the private sense of security which, on the surface, he
seems to strive for. (MacNeice's poetry of the period is rich with the sinister
chiming of church bells, noises of sirens and premonitions of political terrors.
In 'The Sunlight on the Garden', for example, nearly the entire form and
content of the poem contribute to a sense of approaching doom.)

It is this instability in MacNeice's pragmatism that *Autumn Journal*
articulates. Thus, the point to be made is not that Longley and Hynes are
wholly wrong to see an empirical and liberal humanism in *Autumn Journal*.
Nor is it that charges of political quietism cannot be levelled at MacNeice's
work. It is, rather, that both of these critical manoeuvres, because of their
very attempts at totalization, deny the performativity aspect of *Autumn
Journal*.[7] From the very beginning *Autumn Journal* undermines the security
of the liberal humanist self by pluralizing voice and subjectivity, and
problematizing its own relationship to history and truth.

This manifests itself in the uneasy status that MacNeice affords the poem in his retrospective preface of March 1939:

> In a journal or a personal letter a man writes what he feels at the moment; to attempt scientific truthfulness would be – paradoxically – dishonest. The truth of a lyric is different from the truths of science, and this poem is something half-way between the lyric and the didactic poem. In as much as it is half-way towards a didactic poem I trust that it contains some 'criticism of life' or implies some standards which are not merely personal . . . I [am not] attempting to offer what so many people now demand from poets – a final verdict or a balanced judgement. It is the nature of this poem to be neither final nor balanced. I have certain beliefs which, I hope, emerge in the course of it but which I have refused to abstract from their context. For this reason I shall probably be called a trimmer by some and a sentimentalist by others. But poetry in my opinion must be honest before anything else and I refuse to be 'objective' or clear-cut at the cost of honesty.
>
> (*CPLM*, 101)

Here he announces a definite shift away from the objectivity of his earlier poetry towards an aesthetic which is more self-aware (if only of its instability). On one level, of course, this is a reflection of MacNeice's rejection of Marxism, as the possibility of writing from a position 'outside of history' in order to reveal the 'truth' is rendered untenable.[8]

Read in this way, MacNeice's prefacing comment that 'The truth of a lyric is different from the truths of science' is less a declaration of the difference of poetry than a suggestion that scientific 'truth' may not be as certain as it would seem to be: 'to attempt scientific truthfulness would be – paradoxically – dishonest'. Thus, his subsequent claim that 'It is the nature of this poem to be neither final nor balanced' gestures towards the impossibility of finality or balance in all poetry, as much as it modestly apologizes for the inconsistencies of *Autumn Journal*.

This is the recurrent anxiety of *Autumn Journal*, as, from the outset, it foregrounds not only problems of inclusion and exclusion, but also the impossibility of objectivity and a consequent ungraspability of history as external reality. This is formal as well as thematic, and while traditional readings of *Autumn Journal* attempt to view the poem as a meta-narrative, or in Longley's case a 'synthesis', in which is contained the 1930s, it can also be read as a collection of micro-narratives, in which the impossibility of containment itself is registered. Put another way, *Autumn Journal* works by a process very similar to postmodern decentring.

VOICES AND SUBJECTIVITIES

Autumn Journal begins with one such episode:

> Close and slow, summer is ending in Hampshire,
>   Ebbing away down ramps of shaven lawn where close-clipped yew
> Insulates the lives of retired generals and admirals
>   And the spyglasses hung in the hall and the prayer-books ready in
>   the pew
> And August going out to the tin trumpets of nasturtiums
>   And the sunflowers' Salvation Army blare of brass
> And the spinster sitting in a deck-chair picking up the stitches
>   Not raising her eyes to the noise of the 'planes that pass
> Northward from Lee-on-Solent. [. . .]
>
> (*CPLM*, 101–2)

An everyday meaning of the first word, 'Close' – as hot and humid, referring in this context to the sultry and oppressive summer weather – is immediately accessible, and can be linked to MacNeice's earlier concern with sensory impressions. However, the first word also may be read as an expression of a Modernist awareness of the fragility of conventional, linear narratives, in that it foregrounds the provisionality of time and language. In this way, 'close' may refer to both a beginning and an ending, to the fact that summer is now 'closed' so that autumn can open. As well, or alternatively, 'close' may be imperative, demanding of the reader that she or he come 'close' and move towards the surface of the poem. This variation of meaning between conclusion and proximity signifies immediately the difficulty of the act of narration, and signals the inadequacy of conventional narrative techniques.

Correspondingly, 'close', read in its sense with 'and slow', also suggests the presence of a filmic narrative device (close-up), a recurrent trope throughout *Autumn Journal*. (Several other notable works of the period employ similar devices, of course. The narrative of Malcolm Lowry's *Under the Volcano* is filmic throughout, and, famously, the second paragraph of Christopher Isherwood's *Goodbye to Berlin* reads, 'I am a camera with its shutters open, quite passive, recording not thinking. Recording the man shaving at the window opposite and the woman in the kimono washing her hair. Some day, all this will have to be developed, carefully printed. Fixed.'[9]) This matrix of competing yet coterminous meanings, an extension and examination of the Modernist technique of point of view, continues throughout the poem as language is exposed as an index of plural as opposed to singular, meaning(s).

It is this threatening of secure signification that allows the poet to destabilize the assuredness of a class system which affords the retired generals and admirals of the opening passage the luxury of distancing, 'insulating', themselves from history. (Although this takes place at first by traditional means – *Autumn Journal* begins with a declining year, a declining class and a declining country – it is the threat to fixed meaning which is perhaps more critical, in that the poem is so apparently discursive and 'realistic' in its surfaces and language use.) Indeed it is their, rather than MacNeice's, detachment that stands out here, as is suggested by the 'spyglasses . . . and prayer-books', the bourgeois trappings of distant observation and genuflection as opposed to engagement. It is, moreover, the ability of the retired generals and admirals to withdraw from history, to step outside it in order to observe, that determines their very status. The old order is about to be overturned, however, signalled by the end of summer and the coming of autumn, and its ability to remain 'outside' events, the possibility of detached observation that led to its auspicious situation, is about to be lost irrevocably by the entry of the 'planes that pass' into the picture. Unsurprisingly, there is an attempt to deny or ignore their presence, an attempt which is unsuccessful because of their intrusive noise. While the spinster may not want to see the evidence in front of her, she cannot fail to hear it. This sense of voluntary isolation continues throughout the first section:

> [. . .] Macrocarpa and cypress
> And roses on a rustic trellis and mulberry trees
> And bacon and eggs in a silver dish for breakfast
> And all the inherited assets of bodily ease
> And all the inherited worries, rheumatism and taxes,
> And whether Stella will marry and what to do with Dick
> And the branch of the family that lost their money in Hatry
> And the passing of the *Morning Post* and of life's climacteric
> And the growth of vulgarity, cars that pass the gate-lodge
> And crowds undressing on the beach
> [. . .]

(CPLM, 102)

In this passage an identity founded upon class and marriage structure is threatened not only internally, as inheritances of 'assets of bodily ease' are replaced by inheritances of 'worries and taxes' and family failures, but also externally, by the entry into the narrative of those subjects formerly excluded. These subjects are represented as transgressive and excessive; 'vulgarity' grows, cars 'pass' the gate-lodge, the crowds undress, and, in the passage that follows, the cockney lovers refuse to ground their relationship in the grand, capitalized abstraction of religion and state. Individualist, hedonistic, monadic, they exist only in relation to each other:

> And the hiking cockney lovers with thoughts directed
> > Neither to God nor Nation but each to each.
> But the home is still a sanctum under the pelmets,
> > All quiet on the Family Front,
> Farmyard noises across the fields at evening
> > While the trucks of the Southern Railway dawdle . . . shunt
> Into poppy sidings for the night – night which knows no passion
> > No assault of hands or tongue
> For all is old as flint or chalk or pine-needles
> > And the rebels and the young
> Have taken the train to town or the two-seater
> > Unravelling rails or road,
> Losing the thread deliberately behind them –
> > Autumnal palinode
> And I am in the train too now and summer is going
> > South as I go north.
>
> > > > > > (*CPLM*, 102)

The fact that these lovers exist by defining themselves without reference to God or Nation, but in terms of each other, confirms the boundary between the public and private worlds of the poem as they retreat more firmly into themselves and away from duty. So, too, does the irony of some of this passage, as in, for instance, its sideways glance at Erich Maria Remarque's *All Quiet on the Western Front*, 'All quiet on the Family Front', which figures the family as a paralysed battlefield, or its revealing self-parody of the poem's title and aim as an 'Autumnal palinode'.[10] Most commentaries on the 1930s writing emphasize the division between public and private worlds as the overriding theme of the period.[11] Certainly, *Autumn Journal* registers the difference between local, or personal, history and the public and official history upon which the bourgeoisie has secured its position. The poem, though, also problematizes this division. By the end of this passage, for example, the self-reflexive entry of the narrator, or the 'I', has the effect of closing the gap between private and public worlds by suggesting the impossibility of dissociating the individual from any given history: 'And I am in the train too'.

Traditional readings of *Autumn Journal* tend to see the different and competing voices of the text as part of a nonetheless unified, albeit diffuse, consciousness. Edna Longley, for example, argues that the poem is a dramatization of the 'subdivisions of MacNeice's persona'.[12] This monologic view of the poem, though, too often fails to note adequately how the different styles and registers of the voices distinguish one from another (even though MacNeice informs the reader that 'monologue/Is the death of language' [*CPLM*, 135]. Indeed, in order to understand fully the undermining and investigation of subjectivity and the self that is taking place throughout, I would argue that it is better to read the poem as a catalogue of different voices which may be looked at separately, or dialogically, so that the subjects of the poem are not defined as the passive recipients of introjected, precast Freudian or psychoanalytic drives, but understood in terms of, to quote Lynne Pearce, their 'fully intersubjective relations'.[13] What is interesting about *Autumn Journal* is not its construction of a universal model of the subject (this is how it is normally read, as 'capturing the mood and essence of the period') but, to paraphrase Pearce, its interest in multiple subjectivities, in the differences between those subjectivities, and even the differences within a single subjectivity.[14] To read the poem otherwise is to reduce *Autumn Journal* to versified autobiography.

Throughout the first section several registers are mixed and voices heard, and this continues as it draws towards its inconclusive conclusion:

> Surbiton, and a woman gets in, painted
> 　　With dyed hair but a ladder in her stocking and eyes
> Patient beneath the calculated lashes,
> 　　Inured for ever to surprise;
> And the train's rhythm becomes the *ad nauseam* repetition
> 　　Of every tired aubade and maudlin madrigal,
> The faded airs of sexual attraction
> 　　Wandering like dead leaves along a warehouse wall:
> 'I loved my love with a platform ticket,
> 　　A jazz song,
> A handbag, a pair of
> 　　Stockings of Paris
> Sand –
> 　　I loved her long.
> I loved her between the lines and against the clock,
> 　　Not until death
> But till life did us part I loved her with paper money
> 　　And with whisky on the breath.
> I loved her with peacock's eyes and the wares of Carthage,
> 　　With glass and gloves and gold and a powder puff
> With blasphemy, camaraderie, and bravado
> 　　And lots of other stuff.

> I loved my love with the wings of angels
>   Dipped in henna, unearthly red,
> With my office hours, with flowers and sirens,
>   With my budget, my latchkey, and my daily bread.'
> And so to London and down the ever-moving
>   Stairs
> Where a warm wind blows the bodies of men together
>   And blows apart their complexes and cares.
>
> <div align="right">(<i>CPLM</i>, 103)</div>

It is not only 'the calculated lashes' that surprise here, but the song that the woman occasions. In fact, the song is not really a 'tired aubade' or a 'maudlin madrigal' at all, but a parodic account of a lover's gifts and promises that operates on several different levels. Its effect is a strange one, disrupting the easy filmic rhythm of the section just at the point when its tempo has stabilized. (Its register is very different from those that have gone before, but the number of preceding alternative registers leads the reader to expect the unexpected.) Most readings of this part of the poem envisage a chorus of men inspired to song by the presence of the woman, and overlook the fact that she may well be the singer herself, a possibility that would also disturb the flow of the passage.[15] Her voice arises in and from, and penetrates, various time-frames (the effect that MacNeice wants, of course, is for the reader and traveller to collapse into one another), gesturing toward the role of memory and the fusion of past and present, and disrupting the moment of the poem's narrative. It is also, crucially, her language (as well as the language of her song: parodic, self-parodic or mock-parodic) that is the template upon which the narrator of the end of the section is constructed. As much as the wind of the escalator of London, it is the dialogism of her voice and presence that 'blows the bodies of men together/And blows apart their complexes and cares'.

HISTORICAL TEXTS, HISTORICAL TRUTHS

There are several other crucial voices within the poem, not least the one that begins section II:

> Spider, spider, twisting tight –
>   But the watch is wary beneath the pillow –
> I am afraid in the web of night
>   When the window is fingered by the shadow of branches,
> When the lions roar beneath the hill
>   And the meter clicks and the cistern bubbles

> And the gods are absent and the men are still –
>   *Noli me tangere*, my soul is forfeit.
> [. . .]
> Glory to God in the Lowest, peace beneath the earth,
>   Dumb and deaf at the nadir;
> I wonder now whether anything is worth
>   The eyelid opening and the mind recalling.
> And I think of Persephone gone down to dark,
>   No more virgin, gone the garish meadow,
> But why must she come back, why must the snowdrop mark
>   That life goes on for ever?

(CPLM, 103–4)

On one level this is the voice of an authority grounded in learning, as the passage abounds with literary references, for example, to Blake's 'Tyger', or to Wyatt's 'Who so list to hount I knowe where is an hynde'.[16] The voice wants to undermine authority of reference, and reveals that the securing of meaning by grounding authority in a text is a self-undoing gesture. The texts mentioned are, of course, parabolic, designed to make sense of and give significance to that which is otherwise a senseless and insignificant world; they tell, for example, of loss and redemption, or of higher authority. But why, the voice demands, do these texts signify, why 'must the snow drop' mean? For this reason the speaker feels alienated from human meaning. Self-enclosed, his inward gaze falls not upon justification or presence, but on absence:

> Good-bye the Platonic sieve of the Carnal Man
>   But good-bye also Plato's philosophising;
> I have a better plan
>   To hit the target straight without circumlocution.
> If you can equate Being in its purest form
>   With denial of all appearance,
> Then let me disappear – the scent grows warm
>   For pure Not-Being, Nirvana.

(CPLM, 104)

The text which the speaker first takes on in this passage is Plato's *Gorgias*, and the passage to which it refers is the debate between Socrates and Callicles over the quality of pleasure.[17] In a similar fashion to the celebrity of the first section of *Autumn Journal*, who 'wants more/Presents, jewellery, firs, gadgets, solicitations', Callicles argues that the meaning of life is to be found in the search for pleasure, pure and simple (*CPLM*, 102). For Socrates, however, the search for pleasure cannot exist without an attendant awareness of the meaning of pain, and therefore implies an original or originary lack of pleasure. For Plato's Socrates, therefore, pleasure lies not in itself, but is, rather, to be found in the liberation from pain.

This knowledge alone, however, does not allow MacNeice's speaker to 'hit the target'. Instead, that target is met by conflating the classical and the modern, as pleasure is associated also with death, in the Freudian sense. (Nirvana is defined from the Sanskrit, as 'pure Non-being', extinction.[18]) All of this is figured in the speaker's own narrative of the spider:

> Only the spider spinning out his reams
>> Of colourless thread says Only there are always
> Interlopers, dreams,
>> Who let no dog lie nor death be final;
> Suggesting while he spins, that to-morrow will outweigh
>> To-night, that Becoming is a match for Being,
> That to-morrow is also a day,
>> That I must leave my bed and face the music.
> As all the others do who with a grin
>> Shake off sleep like a dog and hurry to desk or engine
> And the fear of life goes out as they clock in
>> And history is reasserted.
> Spider, spider, your irony is true;
>> Who am I – or I – to demand oblivion?
>
> (*CPLM*, 104)

The consistency of the spider (it is only the spider who can say 'Only') is projected onto the consciousness of the speaker. Yet the singularity of the logic of the speaker's narrative is here disturbed by the intrusion of his imagination, which reminds him of 'Interlopers, dreams'. Whilst these seem to originate only in the speaker, the lines also suggest the possibility of the agency of the spider (the spider might say instead [or as well] 'Only there are always/Interlopers, dreams'). It is this merging of the speaker and the spider that offers the possibility of a way of negotiating the nirvana principle. The spider is, in actuality, an ambivalent symbol, simultaneously positive and negative, and it ultimately allows the speaker to grasp meaning, to 'face the music'. To do so is, in fact, less to avoid reality or withdraw from the political than to acknowledge positively their potential. One of the ironies that the speaker concedes is that it is a spider, as opposed to any grand authority, that affords the possibility of meaning. The spider is, of course, material rather than textual, and it functions in a similar way to the wasp that engages Mrs Moore in E. M. Forster's *A Passage to India*.[19] More significantly, however, like William Blake's 'Tyger', the spider signifies creativity. (An early poem, 'Breaking Webs', was originally titled 'Impermanent Creativeness', and one of the many origins of the word 'text' listed in the *Oxford English Dictionary* is 'that which is woven'.[20]) Certainly, the spider's creativity is delicate and temporary (as the earlier title of 'Breaking Webs' also suggests), but, significantly, its efforts are none the less for that. It is, therefore, the process of creation, rather than the thing created that MacNeice privileges. Meaning, in other words, resides in uncertainty, in the oscillation represented by the 'I – or – I' of the speaker. Consequently, section II of *Autumn Journal* ends very differently from how it began, with affirmation and commitment:

> I must go out to-morrow as the others do
> And build the falling castle;
> Which has never fallen, thanks
> Not any formula, red tape or institution,
> Not to any creeds or banks,
> But to the human animal's endless courage.
> Spider, spider spin
> Your register and let me sleep a little,
> Not now in order to end but to begin
> The task begun so often.

(CPLM, 104)

This passage offers a kind of existential alternative to the earlier part of the section, where meaning is created in and through repetitions at a local level. 'The task begun so often', and the references throughout the section to Hades and Persephone, might recall the plight of Sisyphus, who was condemned forever to roll a boulder to the top of a mountain, only to have the rock tumble back down once it had reached its greatest potential energy. Significantly, bearing in mind the earlier discussions of this section, Sisyphus' punishment, bestowed upon him because of his cheating of death, accomplishes nothing and is seemingly meaningless.[21] However, Sisyphus is also the classical character whom Albert Camus was later to emblematize as the absurdist hero of the modern man's predicament, scornful of the gods, playing with death and ultimately thriving in his fate. Camus is most interested in the moment when Sisyphus returns to retrieve the rock:

> I see that man going back down with a heavy and yet measured step toward the torment of which he will never know the end. That hour like a breathing-

space which returns as surely as his suffering, that is the hour of his consciousness. At each of the moments when he leaves the heights and gradually sinks toward the lairs of the gods, he is superior to his fate. He is stronger than his rock.[2]

According to Camus, then, Sisyphus is able to endure in this situation out of rebellion. Thus the descent that should take place in sorrow 'can also take place in joy'. In this way, Sisyphus can master his fate and can face the absurd: 'Sisyphus teaches the higher fidelity that negates the gods and raises the rocks. This universe henceforth without a master seems to him neither sterile nor futile. The struggle itself toward the heights is enough to fill a man's heart. One must imagine Sisyphus happy.'[23] The figure in this passage, MacNeice's Sisyphean spider, operates in the same way. It is now a symbol of the possibility of 'the human animal's endless courage', gesturing towards a way out of the bind in which the speaker finds himself, which is the dilemma of the modern self.

By contrast, that the register of section II is confused and cagey suggests that it is perhaps the voice of the poet. Whilst the section is about the impossibility of a priori meaning which frees the speaker to engage in or commit to the creation of his own meaning, the insistence upon the fragility of this position means that, even here, the voice is not solipsistic. Elsewhere, MacNeice foregrounds his investment in the poem, which was written partly as a response to a personal crisis. In section IV of *Autumn Journal*, for example, he recalls the failure of his relationship with Nancy Coldstream, who left him for Michael Spender at the end of 1938.[24] Jon Stallworthy notes that the tribute to Nancy in section XIX of *Autumn Journal* ('I wish you luck and I thank you for the party') suggests that 'he was not utterly heart-broken at the party's end'.[25] Yet, in *The Strings are False* (as well as in *Autumn Journal*) MacNeice cannot even mention her by name:

I went out with – of whom I cannot write, but who was for me what is called an education – or rather illumination; so feminine that I sometimes felt like leaving the country at once; and so easily hurt that to be with her could be agony. She could be so gloomy as to black-out London and again she could be so gay that I would ask myself where I had been before I met her and was I not colour blind then. Of all the people I have known she could be the most radiant. Which is why I do not regret the hours and hours of argument and melancholy, the unanswerable lamentations of some-one who wanted to be happy in a way that was just not practical.

(*TSAF*, 171)

As I have argued, however, *Autumn Journal* confuses the private and the public, the personal and the political, throughout. Thus the shift away from the possibilities of the self as a monadic autonomous structure, existing outside of history, towards an awareness of the limitations of the subject as agent, which the poem articulates, is not confined to such passages. Analogously, the poem is about an attempt to find a critical language adequate to describe the historical moment of autumn, 1938. The section which deals with the Spanish Civil War, for example, is fraught with anxieties about representation.

> And I remember Spain
>> At Easter ripe as an egg for revolt and ruin
> Though for a tripper the rain
>> Was worse than the surly or the worried or the haunted faces
> With writings on the walls –
>> Hammer and sickle, Boicot, Viva, Muerra;
> With café-au-lait brimming the waterfalls,
>> With sherry, shellfish, omelettes,
> With fretted stone the Moor
>> Had chiselled for effects of sun and shadow

(CPLM, 110)

The gaze of the pleasure-seeker falls only on Moorish architecture, as the tourist fails to read the writing, which is not coded in an obscure language but is, literally and metaphorically, the 'writings on the walls'. The politics of this are made explicit a little later:

> And the standard of living was low
>> But that, we thought to ourselves, was not our business;
> All that the tripper wants is the *status quo*
>> Cut and dried [. . .]

(CPLM, 112)

This may be the attitude not only of the tourist, however, but also, perhaps, of the radical intelligentsia, amongst whom MacNeice includes himself, who do not as yet realize

> That Spain would soon denote
>> Our grief, our aspirations;
> Not knowing that our blunt

> Ideals would find their whetstone, that our spirit
> Would find its frontier on the Spanish front
>
> (*CPLM*, 112)

Not only does this reflect back upon MacNeice's visit to Spain in 1936, prior to the outbreak of civil war, it also looks forward to section XXIII, written as a result of MacNeice's second visit to Spain – again as a writer and not an activist – to Barcelona in December 1938, immediately before its fall to Franco.

Whilst section XXIII also expresses MacNeice's unwillingness to enter into conflict, this time he is even further removed from both the self-preening Cambridge don, who states "'There's going to be trouble shortly in this country",/And ordered anis, pudgy and debonair,/Glad to show off his mastery of the language', and the mob who strip bare the church at Algeciras (*CPLM*, 112). MacNeice is one of the 'We who play for safety', but now understands that it is 'A safety only in name' (*CPLM*, 150). The possibility of a secure grounding is disappearing:

> May God, if there is one, send
> As much courage again and greater vision
>   And resolve the antinomies in which we live
> Where man must be either safe because he is negative
>   Or free on the edge of a razor.
> Give those who are gentle strength,
>   Give those who are strong a generous imagination,
> And make their half-truth true and let the crooked
>   Footpath find its parent road at length.
> I admit that for myself I cannot straighten
>   My broken rambling track
> [. . .]
> All my heredity and my upbringing
> [. . .]
>   The price of a drawn battle.
> For never to begin
>   Anything new because we know there is nothing
> New, is an academic sophistry –
> [. . .]
>   Now I must make amends
> And try to correlate event with instinct
> [. . .]
> We who play for safety,
>   A safety only in name.

> Whereas these people contain truth, whatever
> Their nominal façade.

                                                                    (*CPLM*, 149–50)

In this passage, traditional foundations of the self are revealed as empty and inadequate, as the abstraction and colourlessness of its language, in comparison to that of section VI, indicates. MacNeice's appeals to religion ('May God') and personal history ('my heredity and my upbringing') are rendered useless, as the linear narrative of his 'track' is broken. These narratives are not, though, replaced by new grand structures, but instead by an awareness of the centrality of grand narratives to the projects of fascism, 'To maim or blind or kill . . . The stubborn heirs of freedom' (*CPLM*, 150). Indeed, throughout the poem, representations which claim for themselves status as objective truth are revealed to be in the service of the enemies of freedom.

The posters, captions, electric signs and newspaper presses of section V, for example, are components of a media which is figured throughout as complicit in the rise of totalitarian regimes, and which leaves

> [. . .] the individual, powerless, [having] to exert the
> Powers of will and choice
> And choose between enormous evils, either
> Of which depends on somebody else's voice.

                                                                    (*CPLM*, 109)

History as a narrative is also registered as corrupt in the poem, available to the highest bidder, its accounts less historical than financial (to be 'audit[ed . . .] later' (*CPLM*, 153). All of which leads MacNeice to comment at the end of *Autumn Journal* that, for his own part, 'he must make amends/And try to correlate event with instinct' (*CPLM*, 153). For MacNeice, to do so is to understand that 'truth' is not contained in language: 'in name', or 'nominal façade'. In this way, his attitude to Spain is like that of George Orwell, who in 'Looking back on the Spanish Civil War', recounts having told Arthur Koestler that 'History stopped in 1936':

> I saw great battles where there had been no fighting, and complete silence where hundreds of men had been killed. I saw troops who had fought bravely denounced as cowards and traitors, and others who had never seen a shot fired hailed as heroes of imaginary victories, and I saw newspapers in London retailing these lies and eager intellectuals building emotional superstructures over events that had never happened. I saw, in fact, history being written not in terms of what happened but of what ought to have happened according to the various party lines. [26]

From the outset, then, the poem articulates and enacts the problems of perceiving and recording history. Longley rightly picks up on the critical role that the conjunction 'and' plays in the poem from its very beginning, and writes that. 'This obvious syntactical means of being "surrounded by everything" is also a structural means of not forcing issues or pushing connections and generalisations; but rather of presenting things that coexist and letting patterns emerge.'[27] Elsewhere, she has remarked that the monosyllabic repetition of the conjunction effectuates a 'precarious synthesis' between the flow of discordant themes, images and emotions.[28] Longley, however, fails to go far enough, and MacNeice's use of the hypertactical 'and' also signifies the lack of an adequate language, and an adequate space and time, in which to express the poem's historical crises.

Longley does write elsewhere of the different possibilities of MacNeice's use of 'and':

> 'I loved her between the lines and against the clock,/Not until death/But till life did us part I loved her with paper money/And with whisky on the breath.' The zeugma dependent on 'loved' . . . co-operates with 'and' to create a more swiftly inclusive syntax than that of the 'Close and slow' start. 'And' can thus emphasise disjunction as well as harmony.[29]

This disjunctive effect of MacNeice's 'and' is important to note. In 'An Eclogue for Christmas', for example, MacNeice denies the possibility of a monadic master-structure by metonymically cataloguing varying discursive possibilities. Something similar is at work in *Autumn Journal*, and MacNeice's use of the conjunctive might be contrasted with Auden's use of the definite article, which prefaces his lists of nouns and noun phrases. There is, too, a philosophical level to *Autumn Journal* which escapes the attention of MacNeice's critics; that, in its concern with the close correspondences of the world, it explores the ways in which, to quote Maurice Merleau-Ponty, the individual is 'but a network of relationships'.[30] In this regard, the poem is a phenomenological work, deeply probing immediate experience. Indeed, throughout *Autumn Journal*, MacNeice displays that desire which Merleau-Ponty considers to be representative of phenomenological thinking, the 'will to seize the meaning of the world or of history as that meaning comes into being'.[31] Moving away from philosophical idealism by suggesting that 'the world is not what I think, but what I live through', Merleau-Ponty insists on the human subject's rootedness in the world and argues that, as opposed to some predetermined logos to be extrapolated, 'truth' is to be found only in the intricate network of relationships which connect consciousness to the world, and the world to consciousness.[32]

Certainly, *Autumn Journal* is a historical text, foregrounding its history throughout, but it is also a text about the processes of history-making and foregrounding history, and the fact that this occurs during a period of intense crisis for liberal humanism is hugely significant. It is, above all, a poem about personal and political failure, which articulates and enacts, at every stage, the virtual impossibility of freedom in a world of total systems. *Autumn Journal* can, though (like MacNeice's other work of the 1930s), be read politically, as a poem that continually questions and undermines the liberal humanist notion of the self as outside of history, and strives to find a critical position which is aware of this. In so doing, it looks forward to the post-modern (albeit with a sense of despair, far more than celebration). Accordingly, I would argue that *Autumn Journal* should be considered one of the key poetic texts of the twentieth century, a text in which the modern notion of the possibilities of the individual self, a position revived by a 1930s reaction to High Modernism, is interrogated almost to the point of extinction.

6

'Crying with hungry voices in our nest': Wales and Dylan Thomas

I am a Welshman who does not live in his own country, mainly because he still wants to eat and drink, be rigged and roofed, and no Welsh writer can hunt his bread and butter in Wales unless he pulls his forelock to the *Western Mail*, Bethesdas on Sunday, and enters public-houses by the back door, and reads Caradoc Evans only when alone, and by candlelight . . . . Regarded in England as Welsh (and a waterer of England's milk) and living in Wales as an Englishman, I am too unnational to be here at all. I should be living in a small private leper-house in Hereford or Shropshire, one foot in Wales and my vowels in England. Wearing red flannel drawers, a tall witches hat, and a coracle tiepin, and speaking English so Englishly that I sound like a literate Airedale, who has learnt his a's and e's by correspondence course, piped and shagged and tweeded, but also with a harp, the look of all Sussex in my poached eyes, and a whippet under my waistcoat. And here are Scotch writers at home, their only home, and greeted by writers of England and France, and a border case like myself!

Dylan Thomas[1]

> We have no choice, the choice was made
> Before our blood;
> And I will build my liquid world,
> And you, before the breath is cold
> And the veins are spilled and doom is turned,
> Your solid land.

Dylan Thomas[2]

As was discussed in chapter 4, Thomas was 'monstered' by the English critics of his time. This, as was noted, was a response to the perceived excess of the work and the perceived showmanship of the writer. However, it also had much to do with an 'English' response to Thomas's Welshness, as phrases such as 'Welsh oral trickery', 'bardic gesture' and 'Welsh demagogic masturbator' clearly revealed. It would, though, be quite wrong to suppose that criticism in Wales went entirely the other way, and that Thomas was the subject of rave reviews and unilateral approval. The Welsh response to Thomas was, of course, mixed; as James A. Davies points out in his meticulous and exhaustive study *A Reference Companion to Dylan Thomas*, whilst there were ardent supporters of Thomas at the time (amongst them the publisher, poet and editor of *Wales*, Keidrych Rhys, and, slightly later, the poet and critic John Ormond), the general tenor of criticism from Wales was unfavourable.[3] Early reviews in the *Western Mail* were, as Davies notes, full of criticism of the supposed surrealist obscurity and incoherence of the poetry (they were more favourable to the prose), and several major Welsh intellectual and cultural voices of the time, including Nigel Heseltine and Pennar Davies, were deeply suspicious of Thomas's work.[4] Another, T. Gwynn Jones, in an article entitled 'The modern trend in Welsh poetry', implied that Thomas was one 'of those who evidently think that 'pure poetry' need not be intelligible, at least to anyone but the author, who may even make his own vocabulary'.[5] Others, such as Bobi Jones, referred to Thomas in precisely the same way that mainstream English critics had:

> His exuberant but irresponsible concoction of verbal cleverness . . . [and] . . . undisciplined decorative flaccidity has not gone unnoticed in England . . . With all the advantages that we have in Wales of a living traditional community and literature it is incongruous that we should spy cravingly on such a decadent pretence at literature.[6]

A strand of criticism hostile to Thomas continues to the present day, with a Welsh television documentary on Thomas attempting to establish (rather unsensationally) that he was an incomprehensible, inadequate poet who was out of control and drank too much.[7]

Much of the Welsh hostility to Thomas may be traced through Saunders Lewis's contribution to the debate about Thomas in particular, and Anglo-Welsh writing in general. Lewis, the Welsh nationalist intellectual and founder of Plaid Cymru, famously remarked of Thomas that 'there is nothing hyphenated about him. He belongs to the English', whilst acknowledging magnanimously in the same essay that 'he is obviously an equipped writer'.[8] For Lewis, Thomas could not be considered an Anglo-Welsh writer because he was not 'a Welshman who writes of Wales and of Welsh life in the English language'.[9] Less well documented is that Lewis later modified his view, writing in a special 'Dylan Thomas number' of *Dock Leaves* that 'The English critics see Welsh characteristics in his work. He brought honour to Wales, and in his latter years became increasingly Welsh in his sympathies, and found his themes in Welsh society.'[10] There is a sense here, however, that Lewis's enemy's enemy is his friend (or at least compatriot), though the comment can also be read as representative of a different, more positive, strand of criticism that emerged from Wales after Thomas's death.

Among those in Wales attempting to change the suspicion with which Thomas was viewed were Raymond Garlick and Gwyn Jones. More recently, Walford Davies, James A. Davies, Tony Conran and John Ackerman have done much to redress the balance, through incisive and closely argued readings of Thomas's work. However, whilst these critics engage with Thomas's work of the 1930s and 1940s and even attempt to situate him in a Modernist tradition, their main focus in considering Thomas's relationship to Wales has been on the later work.[11] Underlying this is an implicit acceptance of Saunders Lewis's assessment of what constitutes Anglo-Welsh writing: the sense that in the later poetry Thomas is somehow more Welsh because he seems to be writing about Welsh subject-matter. Thomas himself wrote about the meanings of Wales and of Welshness in his work, in a letter to Henry Treece of June 1938, in the following terms:

> I wonder whether you've considered writing anything – perhaps only a few paragraphs – about the Welsh-ness of my poetry: – this is often being mentioned in reviews and criticisms, and I've never understood it. I mean, I've never understood this racial talk, 'his Irish talent', 'undoubtedly Scotch inspiration', apart from whiskey. Keidrych Rhys – editor of the very good little magazine 'Wales' – always has a lot to say about it. He's an ardent nationalist, and a believer in all the stuff about racial inspiration etc. If you felt like it, you might drop him a line (c/o J. F. Hendry, 20 Vernon Road, Leeds) & tell him about your book and ask him what he thinks about the Welsh in my work. Anyway you'll get back a long & interesting letter: he's the best sort of crank.
>
> (*CLDT*, 301)

Whilst here Thomas refutes the notion of any Welsh 'racial inspiration' and questions the meaning and usefulness of the term Welshness, an empirical case regarding the later work's engagement with Wales is easy to make. For example, 'Fern Hill' and 'Over Sir John's hill' refer to actual Welsh locations, and much of the later poetry makes reference to the Welsh countryside. Yet it is just as possible to undertake similar readings of the early work. References to Wales abound in the prose, certainly, but can be found also in the poetry: the 'loud hill of Wales' in 'Especially when the October wind'; 'Welsh verse' in 'A Letter to my Aunt discussing the Correct Approach to Modern Poetry'; 'the Welshing rich' in 'Our eunuch dreams'; and 'Glamorgan's hill' in 'Hold hard, these ancient minutes, to name but a few (*CPDT*, 19, 17, 44).[12] Such an approach, though, is inadequate to deal with Thomas's complex relationship to Wales. Whilst it can provide empirical evidence, it views Welshness referentially, as an unproblematic given, determined by allusion or subject matter.

It can further be argued that this has been the dominant (or perhaps even sole) critical idiom of Welsh writing in English, and that, whilst certain writers, such as Caradoc Evans, Leslie Norris and Emyr Humphreys, have attracted critical attention, the field in general has suffered from a lack of alternative critical models, particularly ones willing to engage with critical and literary theory. Recently, however, this deficit has been partially addressed, and several critics, including Jane Aaron, John Goodby, Katie Gramich, Linden Peach, Daniel Williams, Kirsti Bohata and Stephen Knight, have engaged Welsh writing in English critically with theories of gender, class and identity.[13] It is also important to note here the impact of *Welsh Writing in English: A Yearbook of Critical Essays* in encouraging new research that attempts to read Welsh writing in English in theoretical terms.[14]

Perhaps the most prominent example of this new trend is M. Wynn Thomas. Along with his notable critical contribution to Welsh literary studies in both the Welsh and English languages, M. Wynn Thomas was also responsible for shifting the terms of the debate around anglophone Welsh literature from Anglo-Welsh writing, with its potentially negative associations, to Welsh writing in English. In *Corresponding Cultures: The Two Literatures of Wales*, Thomas reads Welsh writing in English in the light of the work of Homi Bhabha, and specifically with Bhabha's theorizing of notions of hybridity in mind. He remarks that Bhabha's 'crucial point is that there is no such thing as a "pure", "uncontaminated", "self-sufficient" culture. *All* cultures are unstable compounds', and asserts elsewhere in the book that Dylan Thomas might be read as a 'specifically *Welsh* modernist'.[15]

M. Wynn Thomas is interested in claiming Bhabha's sense of hybridity as a space for cross-cultural dialogue or, more accurately, 'correspondence'. Whilst there is much in this idea, the notion of hybridity is arguably more often related in Bhabha's work to a critique of essentialist constructions of identity. As in the discussion of Louis MacNeice and Ireland in chapter 3, it is in this sense that the concept of hybridity offers most for a reconsideration of Dylan Thomas's complex relationship with Wales and the complex mediation and negotiation of Welshness in his work.

This recent post-colonial theorizing of identity can enable a rethinking of the threat that Thomas represented to the poetic establishment of the 1930s. For, as Bhabha argues in *The Location of Culture*, what disturbs the metropolitan centre most profoundly are those identities seen as sham. Thus, Bhabha states that:

Hybridity represents that ambivalent 'turn' of the discriminated subject into the terrifying, exorbitant object of paranoid classification – a disturbing questioning of the images and presences of authority, [. . . whilst . . .] the paranoid threat from the hybrid is finally uncontainable because it breaks down the symmetry and duality of self/other, inside/outside. In productivity of power, the boundaries of authority – its reality effects – are always besieged by 'the other scene' of fixations and phantoms.[16]

The whole tenor of the critical attack on Thomas from both England and Wales, as has been noted, centres on his alleged inauthenticity, on the poet as deviant. Crucially for Bhabha (as was shown in chapter 3), and for a more nuanced understanding of Thomas's relationship to Wales, hybrid writings have to be distinguished from the simple inversion of binary terms. Accordingly, the concept of hybridity also offers an alternative to a potentially crude English/Welsh opposition. As was argued in chapter 2, most, though certainly not all, critical discussions of the relationship between Thomas's work and his Welsh origins relate him in some way to a putatively 'essential' Welsh identity, mirroring those dominant discourses of Englishness they generally purport to displace. The idea of a hybrid writer – not 'a third term that resolves tension' – can confound these polarized views and the process by which they mutually confirm and entrench each other.

Bhabha's notion of hybridity derives from the work of the Indian Subaltern Studies Group, work which emphasizes the need to look at post-colonial writing in terms of its subversion of mainstream writing through an awareness of its location on the boundaries between the provincial and the outright colonial, a location which does not permit a simple ethical response ('a small private leper-house in Hereford or Shropshire, one foot in Wales and my vowels in England'). Subaltern Studies Group members, that is, see traditional nationalist responses to national subordination as totalizing, restrictive and ultimately untenable political discourses which are compromised by their tendency to mimic the repressive, essentialist structures and values of the (ex)colonial/metropolitan centre. In this way, they reject opposed positions which are part of the same discourse, each produced within a framework of identity-thinking which holds as self-evident the origin of meaning in a unitary self and, by extension (according to the imperatives of liberal ideology), in a nation-state. For Bhabha, as I have argued, hybridity is threatening only, and precisely, because it discloses the inauthenticity of identity through the display of an excess that exposes its lack of foundation. Hybridity's threat, therefore, emerges through the strategic production of fantastical and discriminatory "'identity effects" that hide "no essence, no itself".'[17]

It can be argued that this is the way in which Thomas's early poetry operates, that his interest in identity as lack, identity that hides no 'essence, no itself', is itself hybrid. This exploration of identity might be informed by Thomas's status as a writer of Wales, and, in this regard, certain interesting comparisons might be made, and certain contrasts be drawn, between Dylan Thomas's and R. S. Thomas's poetics of identity.

ESSENCE, LIMINALITY, IDENTITY

In the essay 'Community', first published in the *London Review of Books* in 1985, and later collected in *What I Came to Say*, Raymond Williams begins by distinguishing two distinct models of cultural and national identification that have operated in modern Wales:

> Two truths are told, as the alternative prologues to the action of modern Wales. The first draws on the continuity of Welsh language and literature: from the sixth century, it is said, and thus perhaps the oldest surviving poetic tradition in Europe. The second draws on the turbulent experience of industrial South Wales, over the last two centuries, and its powerful political and communal formations.[18]

According to Williams, the first version venerates origin and essence in its prescription of an authentic Welshness, and tends to operate in terms of closure and restriction, as it predicates identity as a natural given, rather than a cultural construct. The other version emerges from south Wales, and imagines identity less definitely, consequently accommodating a more fluid definition of nationality. And it is worth recalling here, whilst bearing in mind the time of its writing and to whom it is being written, a letter of October 1933 to Pamela Hansford Johnson in which Thomas remarks, with apparent Modernist condescension, upon the industrial nature of Wales:

> each town [is] a festering sore on the body of a dead country, half a mile of main street with its Prudential, its Co-Op, its Star, its cinema and pub. On the

pavements I saw nothing but hideously pretty young girls with cheap berets on their heads and paint smudged over their cheeks; thin youths with caps and stained fingers holding their cigarettes; women, all breast and bottom, hugging their purses to them and staring in at the shop windows; little colliers, diseased in mind and body as only the Welsh can be, standing in groups outside the Welfare Hall. I passed the rows of colliers' houses, hundreds of them, each with a pot of ferns in the window, a hundred jerry-built huts built by a charitable corporation for the men of the town to breed and eat in.

All Wales is like this. I have a friend who writes long and entirely unprintable verses beginning, 'What are you, Wales, but a tired old bitch?' and, 'Wales my country, Wales my cow.'

It's impossible for me to tell you how much I want to get out of it all, out of narrowness and dirtiness, out of the eternal ugliness of the Welsh people and all that belongs to them . . . I'm sick, and this bloody country's killing me.

(*CLDT*, 30)

The emphasis placed by Williams upon 'told' is, of course, crucial, because, as we have seen, concerns about the relation of language to national identity are constantly foregrounded in the dynamic debate between the 'alternative prologues'. In terms of early and mid twentieth-century Welsh literature, and, in particular, Welsh poetry in English, these 'truths' correspond generally to Tony Conran's formulation of twentieth-century Anglo-Welsh poetry as either *buchedd*ist or anti-*buchedd*ist. (Conran writes that he uses the term *buchedd* from the Welsh word meaning a 'way of life' or 'ethos', and notes his indebtedness to David Jenkins.[19]) *Buchedd*ist writers, for Conran, are those poets who write of an older, lost Wales. Predominantly, though not exclusively, lower class ('beyond the bounds of an upper class that had gone English, of an alliance between the peasantry, the respectable working class and the petty bourgeoisie') and north Walian, these writers represented a Wales that was homogeneous and unitary in its resistance to Anglicization in any form.[20] Thus, the poetry written from the *buchedd* was reflective and directly representational of the specific situation of Wales and the Welsh language (though, as Conran also notes '[t]he buchedd was of course not as homogeneous as sometimes it tried to make out'[21]).

This 'truth', articulated most exactly, according to Williams, in the work of Saunders Lewis and Emyr Humphreys, can be explored through an examination of the work of R. S. Thomas. There is, of course, a clear and discernible relationship between the nationalist ideology of Saunders Lewis and the essentialist rhetoric of R. S. Thomas's poetry, and M. Wynn Thomas argues that 'R. S. Thomas is . . . Saunders Lewis's [Anglo-]Welsh heir'.[22]

Anti-*buchedd*ism, on the other hand, was predominantly middle class and south Walian, and reacted against the totalizing and prescriptive notions of nineteenth-century Wales, in which the *buchedd* was born. Analogously, the poetry of Dylan Thomas may be heard as a voice of Williams's second 'truth'. These two 'truths' – of the *buchedd* and anti-*buchedd* – are useful to an understanding, not only of Dylan Thomas's 'difference' as a Welsh poet, but also of the debate over national identity in Wales which has been, at least in part, responsible for the marginalization of Dylan Thomas as a Welsh writer.

The poetry of R. S. Thomas is very clearly expressive of a structure of feeling akin to Williams's first description of a process of identification, and his poem 'Welsh History' is an articulation of such a prescribed inheritance. As Tony Bianchi explains, 'the reader is incorporated into the subject through the almost incantatory repetition of "we"', which consequently enfranchises him, if only temporarily, into an exclusive brotherhood of Welshness.[23] The gender-specific 'him' is due, in part, to R. S. Thomas's failure to mention women at all in his prose. Moreover, Thomas, like Seamus Heaney, at times seems reliant upon the flawed idea of the Jungian racial or mythical archetypes which are often used to justify a certain representation or under-representation of women. His is a brotherhood, however, whose membership hinges on a notion of identity and history which is both firmly rooted, and, although veiled at times by the bluff and bluster of a nation's propensity for fictionalizing, eminently discoverable:

> We were a people bred on legends,
> Warming our hands at the red past.
> The great were ashamed of our loose rags
> Clinging stubbornly to the proud tree
> Of blood and birth [. . .][24]

The phrase 'the proud tree/Of blood and birth' is one of plural possibilities, as it defines a threefold identity: racially (through 'blood and birth'), naturally (through the personification of the tree, which wears 'loose rags'), and ancestrally (through the implication of 'proud tree' as family tree). Further-more, with this last image R. S. Thomas is referring to the erroneous stereotyping of the Welsh as a nation obsessed with family pedigree by such canonically privileged writers as Shakespeare and Dickens.

Similarly, his socio-political poem 'It Hurts Him to Think' refers to the erosion of the Welsh language and the colonization of the Welsh social infrastructure, which R. S. Thomas sees as a corollary of industrialization by the English:

> [. . .] The
> industrialists came, burrowing
>   in the corpse of a nation
> for its congealed blood. I was
>   born into the squalor of
> their feeding and sucked their speech
>   in with my mother's
> infected milk, so that whatever
>   I throw up now is still theirs.[25]

The poem focuses on the naturalization of a colonizing language and the subsequent stigmatization of the indigenous language. Relishing the graphically grotesque portrayal of the English as necrophagous, R. S. Thomas figures the colonizers as, at first, ingesting the rich coalfields of Wales, and then infecting its societal, cultural and linguistic corpse. (Significantly, it is suggested that Wales was already dead before industrialization, implying, perhaps, that it was in some way responsible for its own death.) Colonization then takes on more profound and sinister proportions, as R. S. Thomas sees himself 'born into the squalor of/their feeding' (he was born in Cardiff, the great port of industrial south Wales), and he represents the colonial enterprise as corrupting the cycle of life through its infection of the mother's milk.[26] Finally, Thomas cannot resist a dig at the English language itself by presenting it as emetic.

Yet, it must be said that it is often too easy to read R. S. Thomas as unrewardingly simplistic, and there is the possibility that a very different meaning lies in the background. For example, the final line may be opened up to an alternative reading in which 'throw up' may refer to a sense of serendipity, to the creativity of the randomness of chance. Certainly, this is indicative of the ambiguous attitude towards the English language which R. S. Thomas shows throughout his work, as, on the one hand, he deeply resents it, but, on the other, he is all too aware of its creative possibilities. His writing emerges, for example, from a distinctly Wordsworthian tradition, and in 'Confessions of an Anglo-Welshman' he admits that 'Blake/Shelley and Shakespeare and the ravished Keats' have been empowering influences on his imagination.[27] All of which culminates in R. S. Thomas's final, distressing realization that, despite all of his endeavours to be recognized as a Welsh writer of specifically Welsh poetry, his work remains English, 'still theirs'.

That there may be a furtive, clandestine identity to be found in an assertion of a language which the colonizer cannot speak seems a valid suggestion.

Indeed, perhaps the replacement of the colonizer's language by the original or indigenous language of a people, once the process of colonization has been negotiated, is the theoretical ideal. But in Wales colonization may well be a 'settled' condition rather than an episode, and it has been argued that the Welsh language was eroded partly because of its diasporal immigrant and emigrant culture. Consequently, it is important to note that the way in which R. S. Thomas sees industrialization as Anglicization is very much an individual and specific reading of the Welsh-language debate, behind which lies a complex economic and cultural ideology. However, it is a side of the debate which has encountered critical opposition from historians and economists alike. Brinley Thomas, for example, has famously proposed that in actual fact industrialization was the saviour of the Welsh language:

> The Welsh language was saved by the redistribution of a growing population brought about by industrialism . . . In the sixty years, 1851–1911, there was a net loss of 388,000 people by migration out of Welsh rural areas; in the same period the Glamorgan–Monmouthshire colliery districts and the North Wales towns absorbed on balance 336,000 by inward migration. It is true that a good proportion of the latter were non-Welsh. A detailed analysis of the census figures for Glamorgan enables us to estimate that 160,000 of the migrants to that county between 1861 and 1911 came from Welsh counties. To these one would need to add the number of children and grandchildren they had after settling down in Glamorgan. If a similar analysis had been made of the inflow into the rest of the South Wales coalfield in Carmarthenshire and Monmouthshire, we could arrive at a rough estimate of the total number of people received into the industrial areas from the rest of Wales which was largely rural. [28]

R. S. Thomas, then, refuses the attempt to transcend identity politics, and takes it for granted that identity is the basis of a self which is therefore posited as an unproblematic essence.[29] Tony Bianchi goes further, and highlights similarities between R. S. Thomas's work and the views of the elitist proponents of the monolithic and exclusive English literary canon. Bianchi points out that, 'Even Saunders Lewis's criticism, replete with "principles", "standards", "learning", "tradition", "organic community" and appeals for "learned men to raise the intellectual level of the people", is frequently no more than an elegant reworking of Eliot and Leavis'.[30]

    For Dylan Thomas, on the other hand, as the discussion of 'Before I knocked' in chapter 2 suggested, identity formation is more crucial than identity description, so that whilst, as the writer Niall Griffiths has pointed out, Dylan Thomas's work is also concerned with essentialism, it is not necessarily essentialist.[31] Rather, it can be argued that what characterizes Thomas's poetry of the 1930s is, above all, its interest in problematic formations or *processes* of identity. This is far from a wholly new argument, though. Ralph Maud, in particular, has argued that Thomas's work of the period is concerned with 'process', which he defines as expressing the 'struggle between black and white', explaining that the early poems contain 'a particular kind of diction, usually accompanied by antithetical structure, giving a sense of the interplay of forces beneath the ordinary events of life'.[32] Further, Maud argues that these concerns are unique to Thomas's 1930s poetry. He notes that the characteristic words of the poetry of that period, including flesh, ghost, bone, blood, fork, bud, force, womb, vein, root, oil, wax, matter, skin, dry, damp and weather, 'disappeared by the outbreak of war'.[33] Also, Peter Barry, though in a different context, argues that Thomas's work is full of competing oppositions that fail to resolve themselves.[34] Put a different way, Thomas's early work is fascinated by liminality, a term which has recently gained critical currency in the field of literary studies and which derives from the Latin word *limen*, meaning threshold.

In various ways, all of Thomas's early poems might be said to be about thresholds and in-between states, with most of the poems in *18 Poems* and several in *Twenty-five Poems* concerned with identity formation before birth. 'In the beginning', 'When once the twilight locks', and 'I dreamed my genesis' provide the following three examples, but a longer list would also include the likes of 'Especially when the October wind', 'A process in the weather of the heart', 'All, all and all', 'My world is pyramid' and 'Do you not father me':

> In the beginning was the word, the word
> That from the solid bases of the light
> Abstracted all the letters of the void;
> And from the cloudy bases of the breath
> The word flowed up, translating to the heart
> First characters of birth and death.
>
> In the beginning was the secret brain.
> The brain was celled and soldered in the thought
> Before the pitch was forking to a sun;
> Before the veins were shaking in their sieve,
> Blood shot and scattered to the winds of light
> The ribbed original of love.

('In the beginning', CPDT, 22)

> When the galactic sea was sucked
> And all the dry seabed unlocked,
> I sent my creature scouting on the globe,
> That globe itself of hair and bone
> That, sewn to me by nerve and brain,
> Had stringed my flask of matter to his rib.
>
> My fuses timed to charge his heart,
> He blew like powder to the light
> And held a little sabbath with the sun,
> But when the stars, assuming shape,
> Drew in his eyes the straws of sleep,
> He drowned his father's magics in a dream.
>
> ('When once the twilight locks', *CPDT*, 9)

> From limbs that had the measure of the worm, shuffled
> Off from the creasing flesh, filed
> Through all the irons in the grass, metal
> Of suns in the man-melting night.
>
> Heir to the scalding veins that hold love's drop, costly
> A creature in my bones I
> Rounded my globe of heritage, journey
> In bottom gear through night-geared man.
>
> I dreamed my genesis and died again . . .
>
> ('I dreamed my genesis', *CPDT*, 26)

The same can be said, too, of those poems uncollected in either volume, such as 'Before we mothernaked fall':

> Before we mothernaked fall
> Upon the land of gold or oil,
> Between the raid and the response
> Of flesh and bones,
> Our claim is stake for once and all
> Near to the quarry or the well,
>
> Before the promises fulfill
> And the joys are pains.
>
> ('Before we mothernaked fall')[35]

As can be seen, the subjects of all of these poems are in process, strangely conscious before birth, but as yet unfixed. The space they might be said to inhabit is an in-between, or liminal, space. In turn, this may offer a way of reading Thomas's relationship to Wales. The concept of liminality can also be defined in either of the following ways: as relating to an initial stage in a trans-national process of change; or, as occupying a position on a boundary/threshold. In this way, both Thomas himself and his poetry can be read liminally: Thomas occupying, or rather transgressing, the boundaries between Wales and England *and* within Wales itself, and his work as articulating a liminal poetics, as a result. In post-colonial studies, for Edward Said, but especially for Homi Bhabha, the concept of liminality is important as a category, and is strongly related to the concept of cultural hybridity. For Bhabha, the liminal is an interstitial passage between fixed identifications, which affords the possibility of a cultural hybridity that entertains and interrogates difference by transgressing assumed or imposed hierarchy.[36]

WALES, MODERNISM AND THE GOTHIC

If consideration of Thomas's status can lead to a modification of the way in which national 'identity' operates in his work, what exactly was his relationship to Welsh Modernism? As Gareth Thomas has pointed out, in Thomas's time 'no Anglo-Welsh literary tradition that was in any way comparable to the Anglo-Irish had yet been established'.[37] Modernism in Britain was largely imported (as I noted in the Introduction), in the shapes of Henry James, Joseph Conrad, Ezra Pound, T. S. Eliot and James Joyce, and heavily Irish-influenced. Its Welsh variant has, to date, been seen solely in terms of its contribution to the definition of British (that is, English) Modernism, in the figure of David Jones. Although Jones's anomalous and belated achievement might arguably be considered writing which deals with the condition of Welshness, concentration on his High Modernism (read through his endorsement by Eliot and his Faber publication) has led critics away from Welsh Modernism. Welsh Modernism continues to be neglected, even within Wales. One reason for this has been the type of critical valor-ization of content above form already mentioned. Commentators on their Welsh writing in English may be changing their critical approach, but despite valiant attempts by the critics discussed earlier in the chapter to encourage work on new writers, those allowed within it remain largely the same; they include Emyr Humphreys, R. S. Thomas and Glyn Jones. Certainly, there is urgent and important research to be done on these writers, but there are also other writers who merit attention and whose work might be included in a study of Modernism and Wales. These would include Lynette Roberts (also published by Eliot at Faber), Goronwy Rees, Jean Rhys,

B. S. Johnson, Oliver Reynolds, John James and Iain Sinclair. Such an account need not necessarily be solely recuperative, but could work thematically or in terms of genre.

In this connection an area of Dylan Thomas's work that immediately suggests itself is the use of grotesque style and the Gothic (discussed, in part, in chapter 4), elements that can be said to arise from his displaced, hybrid location. Seen previously in purely Freudian and surrealist guise, they can also be read as Modernist. Traditionally associated with mixing and impropriety, grotesque style and the gothic played a central role in Welsh Modernism. As Tony Conran has argued:

> Modernism in Wales is most at home with the grotesque. It is there that modernism characteristically shows itself, in Saunders Lewis as much as in Caradoc Evans and Dylan Thomas. The nightmare of monstrosity underlies the middle-class rejection of the *buchedd*, the sense of being suffocated by its hypocrisy and narrowness.[38]

It is in the short stories written before 1940's *Portrait of the Artist as a Young Dog* that the Gothic and grotesque aspects in Thomas are flaunted most extensively. Many of the stories, some collected also in *The Map of Love*, centre on an imaginary Jarvis Valley Gothicized under the pressures of social crisis and literary displacement. Thomas's Jarvis Valley provides the setting for a collection of Welsh rural stereotypes; thus, its weather is always louring, its landscapes charged with apocalyptic threat and repressed sexual energy, its scattered dwellings inhabited by lost children, murderers, Bible-spouting gardeners, vivisectionists, witches, Satanists, psychopaths and decayed gentry, and haunted by the 'Holy Six', whose names anagrammatize six of the seven deadly sins. Moreover, as I suggested in chapter 4, what applies to the prose applies more variously to the poetry.

Indeed, the value of the Gothic to Thomas stemmed from its generic capability for organizing disparate stylistic and thematic elements – parodic appropriation, belated Modernism, social radicalism, sexual uncertainty and the plenitude/lack of writing itself – within the outrageous constructedness which is its hallmark. A Gothic thematics cannot 'explain' Thomas's early work, but can provide a framework for interpreting a series of Welsh and Modernist elements therein. Again, I would argue that it has been overlooked because of the lack of awareness of recent developments in criticism of those writing about Thomas.[39] The basic evidence, however, is clear enough, and possible Gothic influences – Thomas's 'serious' reading, interest in film and taste for pulp fiction – have been known for years. Thomas's devotion to the work of the Welsh horror novelist Arthur Machen, for example, has occasionally been mentioned in critical work but not really considered significant.[40] Machen, the author of what has been described as 'the most decadent book in English', *The Hill of Dreams* (1907), 'took up Darwinian anxieties as the basis for terror', mixing among others, Joris Karl Huysmans, Walter Pater, *La Queste del Sante Graal* and Sherlock Holmes.[41] In *The Great God Pan* (1894), to take one example, a doctor operates on a young girl to open her 'inner eye' to the existence of Pan. The resulting visionary power eventually drives her mad, and when the hell-child born after her coupling with the Great God dies, it passes through all the stages of biological species reversion, ending up as primal slime. Parallels with 'The Lemon' and other works by Thomas might be drawn, but the important link lies in the resemblances between Machen's biological and physical emphases and Thomas's concern with cycles of inter-involved growth, biological recapitulations and pre-human states of consciousness. It is this kind of influence, of course, which can be used to counter the 'glandular' charge so often levelled against Thomas's work.[42]

This aspect of the work also needs to be seen in the light of a powerful Modernist influence other than Eliot: that of D. H. Lawrence. There are many obvious similarities between Lawrence and Thomas. They were outsider figures in terms of provincial location and social class, and shared a Nonconformist background. Both writers also emphasize redemption through the flesh, rather than the disembodied intellect, in their work. The relationship of Thomas and Lawrence to the dominant metropolitan styles of the day was also similar. Tony Pinkney has argued that Lawrence attacked the classicizing Modernism of Katherine Mansfield, Ezra Pound, James Joyce, T. S. Eliot and Wyndham Lewis in order to forge an alternative Expressionist, northern Gothic variety.[43] Lawrence's fiction generally rejects the Hellenism running through English culture, from Arnold to Hulme and Eliot, in which "'criticism", "consciousness" and "irony" are cardinal virtues', in favour of the creaturely virtues of a more 'native' tradition, deriving from William Morris and John Ruskin.[44] It is this form of Modernism that, in the Lincoln Cathedral pages of *The Rainbow*, is shown as incorporating classicism's 'virtues' within its host of small details rather than expelling them. As Pinkney remarks of the Gothic,

> [it] deconstructs the rigid model of inside/outside . . . . Its outside is its inside; even the sly stone faces that denounce its incompletion are, after all, part of it. The Gothic contains its own 'negation', which thereafter ceases to be its negative pure and simple, and is rather granted a local validity within a more generous system which exceeds it.[45]

In terms of Welsh influence, essential to an appreciation of Thomas's Welsh Modernist Gothic context is the work of Caradoc Evans. (Thomas's Jarvis Valley can be read as a version of Evans's Manteg.) Evans was the author of the pioneering short-story collection *My People* (1915), described as the Welsh equivalent of James Joyce's *Dubliners*.[46] The stories of this collection combine anecdotal structure with savage, grotesque realism in an attack on rural Welsh Nonconformity, hypocrisy, greed and cruelty, and made Evans 'the most reviled man in his country'.[47] There is no doubt that Thomas, who visited Evans in 1936, saw him as a literary hero (*CLDT*, 172). But Evans is also a literary forerunner in the sense that his tales reverberate with the discourses of Nonconformity; their language, according to John Harris is 'simple, often majestic, and suggestive also of parable and myth',[48] while mocking those who use it for blatantly repressive ends. As in Thomas's poetry, religion's musical and rhetorical resources, part of its radical tradition, were exploited, even as the social forms it had capitulated to were critiqued.

Yet, as well as belonging to a later generation, very different forces intersect in Thomas's and Evans's work. Thomas's upbringing was freethinking, his surroundings suburban and his literary and political contexts more radical and cosmopolitan. It would be wrong, though, to see this as a simple split along urban–rural lines. Swansea lay at the westernmost point of English-speaking south Wales, its frontier, liminal situation complicated by the fact that it also represented the class divide which Thomas's parents had crossed in order to achieve middle-class respectability. Even in the 1920s, the Welsh-speaking farming communities of Carmarthenshire lay within easy reach of Thomas's home; Swansea was a mainly, but not totally, English-speaking town, hemmed around to the north and west by its Welsh-speaking industrial hinterland. Whilst the effects of the First World War and the economic crisis which gripped Wales in the 1920s post-dated *My People*, their effects can more readily be seen in Thomas's treatment of Welsh identity as ambiguity and repression.

If Wales was more closely tied to England than any other of the UK's component parts, its economy, lopsided to serve imperial rather than domestic needs, produced what Gwyn A. Williams has called an 'offshore working class', with its middle-class appendages.[49] It was thus especially vulnerable to the decline of British power, and, as a result, recession bit more deeply and earlier in Wales than anywhere else in Britain. The Depression pushed the already high Welsh unemployment level up to 32 per cent, a figure around which it lingered until the end of the 1930s. The demographic effects were devastating; over half a million people left Wales in the 1930s, most of them from the south. Though it was one of the more advanced areas of the south Walian economy, 'even Swansea with its poets and musicians . . . fell into . . . neglect and depression, a collapse of social capital and a dismal legacy in bad housing, ill-health, poor environment'.[50] Thomas's own (dis)location ensured both relative personal comfort and an inescapable awareness of suffering; his political response was a socialism as intense but more diffuse and durable than those of the more overtly Left poets of the 1930s. The general disaster of the times sharpened the differences between a generation of radicalized English-language Welsh writers and Welsh-language writers, whose nationalism and rural values were occasionally reinforced by isolated flirtations with fascism.[51] As Tony Conran claims, 1930s Anglo-Welsh writers had nowhere to go but London; 'They either stayed in Wales and festered in isolation, or they offered themselves as international or colonial recruits to the London intelligentsia. Nationalism was hardly an option for most of them.'[52]

This is an important point, given recent attempts to interpret Modernism in nationalist terms. Robert Crawford's *Devolving English Literature*, for example, argues that Modernism should be read as a provincial revolution against a complacent anglocentric literary establishment, and this can clearly be applied in some measure to Dylan Thomas. Crawford is certainly on firm ground when he opposes what he calls 'cursory' accounts of Modernism, which stress its 'cosmopolitanism and internationalism to present it as a facet of "high" metropolitan culture'.[53] Yet, the resultant claim that the provincial/demotic on the one hand and cosmopolitanism on the other 'are not opposites; they complement one another' is too neat a reversal, a too-easy overcoming of very real and material differences of class, gender and so on within the nation, and within Modernism as a literary formation.[54] In this way, Crawford overlooks the role of bourgeois nationalist culture in submerging the kinds of internal national differences which produce hybrid, mixed, boundary writings: for his argument to work, the desire to integrate within the London literary and social mainstream on the part of writers like Thomas and MacNeice also has to be seen in purely personal terms as an error of judgement. Again, recent work on Irish writing provides something of a corrective. A similar critique of Crawford is made by Peter McDonald, who notes the 'useful warning' sounded in his book, but also the contradictions involved in desiring that a new identity-discourse of nationalism would subvert the old one (of Englishness concealed by 'Britishness'): 'A complacent Englishness is no more subverted by (say) a complacent Scottishness than it is by the strident assertion of Irish identity; it is much more likely, in fact, to be reinforced by such pre-programmed systems of declaration.'[55] To view Modernism chiefly as an outgrowth of a wholly positive nationalist self-assertion, then, is to depoliticize both nationalism and Modernism; Crawford's celebration of national difference erases internal difference and ignores nationalism's reactionary potential. Crawford ultimately settles for the kind of cultural identity politics outlined earlier, according to which Thomas can be interpreted only as either 'genuinely' Welsh or an inauthentic showman.

We have seen how claims for identifiably Welsh elements in Thomas's early poetry can be made, but are normally limited to cursory allusion-hunting or reference searches. Further, even those rare but imaginative and ingenious attempts to detect more subtly the influence of *cynghanedd* or Welsh speech rhythms (presumed to result from métèque status) are thwarted by the poetry's lack of obvious markers of nationality.[56] Although, perhaps, a more oblique influence may be detected in his ability to take an outsider's advantage of the English language, it can scarcely be distinguished from the kinds of linguistic subversion that mark many poets, regardless of origin, and particularly those who write, as Thomas did, in a transitional historical period.

As I have argued, though, what is more significant in Thomas's work is its concern with ambiguous and fragmented identities, which also manifested itself in his perception of fixed identities as constraining. His own ambivalence towards nationality was expressed not so much in outright denials as in tongue-in-cheek self-styling as the 'Rimbaud of Cwmdonkin Drive', a *voyant* who felt lost without 'the aspidistra, the provincial drive, the morning cafe [and] the evening pub' of suburbia (*CLDT*, 487, 222). Tony Conran deems Thomas's national identity 'largely a negative thing – he is not English', but in the Machereyan sense, the 'negative thing' is also an absence that speaks. Most often in Thomas's case it speaks of an enabling isolation, a calculated philistinism and defensive humour that allowed for a transgressive miscegenation of modes and genres in his work that can be said to be characteristic of a truly (in)authentic Welsh Modernism.[57]

Conclusion

'The judge-blown bedlam':
after the 1930s

As soon as I heard on the wireless of the outbreak of war, Galway became unreal. And Yeats and his poetry became unreal also.

This was not merely because Galway and Yeats belong in a sense to the past order of things. The unreality which overtook them was also overtaking in my mind modern London, modernist art, and Left Wing politics.

Louis MacNeice[1]

Once it was the colour of saying
Soaked my table the uglier side of a hill
With a capsized field where a school sat still
And a black and white patch of girls grew playing;
The gentle seaslides of saying I must undo
That all the charmingly drowned arise to cockcrow and kill.
When I whistled with mitching boys through a reservoir park
Where at night we stoned the cold and cuckoo
Lovers in the dirt of their leafy beds,
The shade of their trees was a word of many shades
And a lamp of lightning for the poor in the dark;
Now my saying shall be my undoing,
And every stone I wind off like a reel.

(CPDT, 74)

The Second World War changed the work of both MacNeice and Thomas. In part, this was an outcome of the new realities of existence during a time of war. As Robert Hewison remarks in *Under Siege: Literary Life in London 1939–1945*, caught in the process of total war, the individual was interpellated as never before; mass mobilization, conscription, increased bureaucratization and the incorporation of artists and writers (including both MacNeice and Thomas) into an expanding propaganda machine, all contributed to the subduing of the self-determining subject.[2] In MacNeice's work these changed circumstances would lead to a postmodern parabolic writing, closely attuned to the historical anxieties of the war and post-war periods; in Thomas's, to a gradual easing of the obscurity and bodily anxieties of his poetry of the 1930s into a more exuberant, exorbitant even, referential aesthetic. In the same way that, as I have argued, there was no clean and absolute break between the poetry of the 1920s and that of the 1930s, the changes in MacNeice's and Thomas's work between the 1930s and 1940s were gradual, rather than immediate. Further, it is important to note that in both cases the changes in direction had begun before the declaration of war on 3 September 1939.

In any case, the crucial turning-point was 1938, not 1939. By that time the aggressive dictatorships of the Anti-Comintern Pact had effectively undermined any remaining vestiges of the authority of the League of Nations. Japan had successfully attacked Manchuria, Italy had conquered Abyssinia, Germany had reoccupied the Rhineland and General Franco's position of authority in the Spanish Civil War had become absolute, unchallenged by France and Britain. This was, of course, precisely the source material for *Autumn Journal*, though 1938 also saw the publication of *Modern Poetry: A Personal Essay*, whose concluding sentence muses upon the coming 'crisis' and its potential effects on creative and critical activity.[3] If the historical realities of the late 1930s explicitly inform the work of MacNeice, they are implicit in Thomas's. There, 1938 was not only the year of the monstrous threat of 'How shall my animal', a poem in which, as I have argued, aggressive masculinity is unwritten, but also of 'Once it was the colour of saying' and 'On no work of words'. Both poems reflect on the same issue of the nature of poetic representation, with the former writing against 'the colour of saying' to be found in *18 Poems* (1934) and *Twenty-five Poems* (1936), and the latter criticizing the unworldliness of the poet's 'lovely gift of the gab' (*CPDT*, 74, 78). All three of these poems are to be found in Thomas's transitional collection, *The Map of Love*, which was published nine days before Britain declared war on Germany.

As James A. Davies notes, the poems of Dylan Thomas's wartime volume, *Deaths and Entrances* (1946), can be divided into two groups: those written between 1939 and 1941, and those written between 1944 and 1945.[4] Whereas, in Thomas's pre-war collections, the majority of the poems are versions of early notebook drafts, only three of the poems of *Deaths and Entrances*, all of which were written between 1939 and 1941, can be traced back to the notebooks. (These are 'The hunchback in the park', 'On the Marriage of a Virgin', and 'Holy Spring'.) As a result, there are clear differences between the poetry of *Deaths and Entrances* and that of the earlier collections. Most markedly, the poems are no longer concerned with the internal and external processes of the body, the identities no longer in flux prior to birth. Instead, there are repeated attempts to register the traumatic eventhood of the war by reconciling the public and the private. Hence, 'A Refusal to Mourn the Death, by Fire, of a Child in London', or the anxiety of representation in 'Among those Killed in the Dawn Raid was a Man Aged a Hundred' (*CPDT*, 85, 112). However, there are also similarities with the earlier work. Whilst the obscurity of the early poetry gives way in *Deaths and Entrances* to a more referential language, that language is still Modernist in its density and materiality. As with *18 Poems*, *Twenty-five Poems* and *The Map of Love*, this volume contains several poems about the processes of creativity and writing, and Thomas's interest in childhood states persists.

In an analogous fashion, there are similarities and differences between Louis MacNeice's pre-war poetry and his wartime collections. Although the war is a notable presence in the poetry he wrote between 1941 and 1944, especially in the excesses of poems such as 'Brother Fire' and 'The Trolls', much of his war poetry is thematically continuous with that of the 1930s. The sense of fragmented or disoriented consciousnesses situated perilously between spaces, places, states or subject positions, for example, is as prevalent in the poems of *Plant and Phantom* (1941) and *Springboard* (1944) as it is in *Poems*, *The Earth Compels* (1938) and *Autumn Journal*. In fact, in its concerns with the insecurity of self (for example in 'Plant and Phantom'), and its historiographic interventions (for example in 'Entered in the Minutes'), *Plant and Phantom* might well be read as a continuation of *Autumn Journal*, its 'sixth act', as Edna Longley puts it (*CPLM*, 159–60, 186–7).[5]

However, as MacNeice commented in a letter to E. R. Dodds of February, 1940 (albeit in the different context of his renewed relationship with Eleanor Clark in America), 'I am going to write (at least I hope) new kinds of poetry', and there are significant differences to be found in his poetry of the war.[6] In 'To Hedli', the dedicatory poem to *Springboard*, MacNeice gives an indication of the aesthetic modifications and variations that he attempts in this volume:

> Because the velvet image,
> Because the lilting measure,
> No more convey my meaning

> I am compelled to use
> Such words as disabuse
> My mind of casual pleasure
> And turn it towards a centre –
> A zone which others too
> And you
> May choose to enter.

(CPLM, 191)

The poem articulates a delicate simultaneous sense of an unemotional awareness of the weight of external events upon the individual and a cautious suggestion of a utopian space. The employment of the word 'compelled' is a creative benchmark for the experiences of a social formation constructed in the state of total war. In this, it can be contrasted with his use of the word to signify (at least in part) the surface attraction of the things of the world in the title of his collection *The Earth Compels*. In such circumstances it is understandable that MacNeice, like Thomas, regarded 'the velvet image' and 'the lilting measure' as inadequate responses to the nature of war. However, in MacNeice's case, these poetic constructions are discarded not simply because of their inadequacy, but also because they entertain the prospect of self-satisfied expression. As he writes in *The Poetry of W. B. Yeats* (1941):

> If the war made nonsense of Yeats's poetry and of all works that are called 'escapist', it also made nonsense of the poetry that professes to be 'realist'. My friends had been writing for years about guns and frontiers and factories, about the 'facts' of psychology, politics, science, economics, but the fact of war made their writing seem as remote as the pleasure dome in Xanadu. For war spares neither the poetry of Xanadu nor the poetry of pylons.[7]

Accordingly, the poet will 'turn' his mind instead, as he states in 'The Trolls', to spelling 'out Death correctly' (*CPLM*, 197).

Reflecting back on *Plant and Phantom* and *Springboard* in 'Experiences with images', MacNeice offers examples of poems from both collections to demonstrate a new 'structural type of image' in his work.[8] What MacNeice is referring to here is his use of parable, which comes to dominate his poetry after the war. A few months before his untimely death in September 1963, he delivered, as part of the Clark Lectures in Cambridge, seven discussions, under the title 'Varieties of Parable', which were published posthumously in 1965 as *Varieties of Parable*. As well as offering alert readings of a number of writers, from Edmund Spenser to Samuel Beckett, who have engaged with different forms of the parabolic, *Varieties of Parable* is, arguably, an indispensable companion to MacNeice's post-war writing. Although contemporary reviews of MacNeice's late poetry, specifically reviews of the two final volumes – *Solstices* (1961) and *The Burning Perch* (1963) – do not mention the word parable, they do acknowledge the formal and thematic innovations of these collections, which distinguish them from the supposed looseness and indulgence of *Ten Burnt Offerings* (1952) and *Autumn Sequel* (1954), or the greater attention to public events that is readily discernible in the work of the 1930s and 1940s.[9] The anonymous reviewers of *Solstices* and *Ten Burnt Offerings* in the *Times Literary Supplement* are conscious of MacNeice's development of a poetry that is somehow more precise than his previous work, and that rarely 'deals directly with politics of the public world'; they recognize the finely tuned use of symbolism and the growing sense of solemnity.[10] The formal structures that MacNeice mobilizes to provide his work with a series of frames are not, though, mentioned. It is only in *Varieties of Parable* that MacNeice himself draws together the strands of allegory, fantasy, fable, myth and his own 'double-level writing', under the uneasy expression of 'parable'.[11] Indeed, as well as representing a postmodern starting point for contemporary Irish poets (Paul Muldoon, Ciaran Carson and Tom Paulin), there is a long tradition of writing allegory and parable in Irish literature. According to W. J. McCormack, this arises out of a gap between what is desired by the modern nation-state that is autonomous and self-sufficient and has an established cultural tradition, and the reality of dependency and peripheralization. Allegory serves to fill a lack generated by Ireland's ambivalent metropolitan–colonial status because it asks to be read on many different levels: political, ethical, fantastic, symbolic. While its origins lie in the expression of a conservative anguish at being displaced from history, suffered by the Ascendancy caste, it also has a potential for radical suspicion and scepticism; unbelonging has its subversive charge in dealing with essentialism and traditionalism. In MacNeice's work, including *The Dark Tower* (1947), parabolic strategies are a version of such historically conditioned allegorical usages.[12]

The later poems are nightmarish, and in them the poet is haunted by his own ghostly status. Indeed, if the world had seemed an unreal place during the 1940s, arguably it was more so after the war. The pursuit of an instrumental rationality had resulted in the emergence of a mythic barbarism, which produced the Holocaust. Further, the conclusion to the Second World War with the dropping of the A-bomb had also altered future human relations, in an unprecedented manner. MacNeice discusses this terrifying atomic innovation in *Varieties of Parable*:

in fact the one really peculiar reality in our world is the Bomb; and as Arthur Koestler has pointed out, however much we have realized the implications of that with our heads, we have not yet grown into that realization: the possibility of death for the whole human race is not something we live with like the certainty of our individual deaths.[13]

Further, it is significant that the re-emergence of MacNeice's poetic imagination in the 1950s coincides with the growth of the Cold War balance of terror between the USA and the Soviet Union, as the threats of the later poems are terrible, but unspecified. In 'The Taxis', for example, the narrator is a sinister ghostly presence, unaware of his other selves sitting beside and opposite him, whilst in 'Charon' the destination of the bus ferrying its passengers through London is revealed as Hades (*CPLM*, 522, 530).

Thomas's post-war work also engages in an oblique and parabolic way with the historical realities of the period. In a broadcast of 25 September 1950, Thomas referred to a 'long poem in preparation' which was to be called 'In Country Heaven', to be composed according to a 'grand and simple plan':

> The poem is to be called 'In Country Heaven'. The godhead, the author, the milky-way farmer, the first cause, architect, lamplighter, quintessence, the beginning Word . . . – He, on top of a hill in Heaven, weeps whenever, outside that state of being called his country, one of his worlds drops dead, vanishes screaming, shrivels, explodes, murders itself. . . . . The Earth has killed itself. It is black, petrified, wizened, poisoned, burst; insanity has blown it rotten; and no creatures at all, joyful, despairing, cruel, kind, dumb, afire, loving, dull, shortly and brutishly hunt their days down like enemies on that corrupted face.[14]

In many ways, several of Thomas's poems composed after 9 August 1945 are conditioned by the threat of nuclear extinction. The childhood pastoral recapitulations of 'Fern Hill', 'Poem on his Birthday' and 'Lament' all idealize a pre-nuclear past, and, as John Goodby notes, several of their images demand to be read in the context of the dropping of the two atomic bombs on Hiroshima and Nagasaki, and the continuing American and Russian A- and H-bomb tests in the late 1940s and early 1950s.[15]

If, as I have argued, MacNeice's and Thomas's work of the 1930s can be regarded as Modernist, their post-war writing may usefully (though not unproblematically) be considered postmodern. Over the course of MacNeice's career there is a shift from attempts to locate a space in which the autonomous self may be reconstructed, towards a recognition of the limits of subject positioning, predicated on the lack of any monadic sense of identity or coherent selfhood. This is revealed in the consistent plight of the subjects of MacNeice's later poems, which are generally involved in thwarted attempts to acquire agency. The journey is from a Modernist search for autonomy towards a postmodernist recognition of its impossibility. Through their status as 'events', several of Thomas's early poems resist a similarly historicized postmodernism. Thus, while MacNeice's parabolic darkness is one face of the postmodern sublime, the other, its euphoric aspect, is figured in the linguistic surplus and hyperbolic praise that can be glimpsed in Thomas's later poems. (But just as MacNeice's grim parables have a counter-impulse of resilience, so Thomas's baroque superabundance skates over the void of 'a yawning wound'.) Both play with elements of postmodernism, but the postmodern sensibility (recognized as such) had not at this stage fully emerged. That their later work has yet to be read in this way is another indication of the lack of engagement with recent developments in criticism by those writing about MacNeice and Thomas. To trace the full implications of such a postmodern reading would require, however, another book.

This book has attempted to argue against anti-Modernist and anti-theoretical accounts of the 1930s poetry of MacNeice and Thomas by following recent work that has problematized the notion of Modernism as a monolithic phenomenon. As such, it argues for a new critical awareness of the diversity of the writing of the 1930s. But in so doing, its aim is neither to expel Auden from critical accounts of the literature of the period in order to replace him with a hybrid Dylan MacNeice or Louis Thomas, nor to argue against the influence and status of Auden as a crucial poet of the mid century. Rather, this book contends that the liminal, hybrid and transgressive qualities which Welsh and Irish origins afforded Thomas and MacNeice resulted in poetries that, read together, provide a Derridean *supplement*, which completes and undermines the standard, 'audenary' histories of 1930s literature. The fudging of issues that has led directly to continued misrepresentations of both poets – of Thomas as solely a regional late Romantic and MacNeice as merely an acolyte of Auden – is, I would argue, no longer tenable.

Notes

Introduction: 'Night-bound doubles'

1 Adrian Caesar, *Dividing Lines: Poetry, Class and Ideology in the 1930s* (Manchester: Manchester University Press, 1991), p. 6.
2 *CPLM*, p. 411.
3 Steven Matthews and Keith Williams (eds), *Rewriting the Thirties: Modernism and After* (London: Longman, 1997), p. 1.
4 Samuel Hynes, *The Auden Generation: Literature and Politics in England in the 1930s* (London: Bodley Head, 1976).
5 Caesar, *Dividing Lines*, p. 2.
6 A. T. Tolley, *The Poetry of the Thirties* (London: Victor Gollancz, 1975).
7 Bernard Bergonzi, *Reading the Thirties: Texts and Contexts* (London: Macmillan, 1978), p. 1; Valentine Cunningham, *British Writers of the Thirties* (Oxford: Oxford University Press, 1988), p. 17.
8 Caesar, *Dividing Lines*, p. 36; Bergonzi, *Reading the Thirties*, pp. 8–9; Hynes, *The Auden Generation*, pp. 10–11.
9 Peter McDonald, *Louis MacNeice: The Poet in his Contexts* (Oxford: Clarendon Press, 1991), p. 1.
10 Cunningham, *British Writers of the Thirties*, pp. 17, 20.
11 Stephen Spender, *World Within World* (London: Hamish Hamilton and the Book Society, 1951), p. 119.
12 Malcom Bradbury and James McFarlane (eds), *Modernism: A Guide to European Literature 1890–1930* (London: Penguin, 1991), pp. 51–2.
13 Alan Wilde, *Horizons of Assent: Modernism, Postmodernism and the Ironic Imagination* (Baltimore, MD: Johns Hopkins University Press, 1987), p. 41.
14 See, for example, Peter Nicholls, *Modernisms: A Literary Guide* (Basingstoke: Macmillan, 1995), or Marjorie Perloff, *Radical Artifice: Writing in the Age of Media* (Chicago: University of Chicago Press, 1991).
15 See, for example, Terry Eagleton, *Criticism and Ideology: A Study in Marxist Literary Theory* (London: Verso, 1976); Robert Crawford: *Devolving English Literature* (Oxford: Clarendon Press, 1992), and Cairns Craig, *Out of History: Narrative Paradigms in Scottish and British Culture* (Edinburgh: Polygon, 1996).

NOTES

16 Longley's insistence upon the notion of Modernism as a wrong turning in the progression of British poetic achievement and her New Critical/Leavisite insistence on close reading, with a consequent denial of the importance of context, are well known. Both can be seen at the beginning of *Poetry in the Wars*, wherein she takes Stan Smith to task for what she refers to as 'simple cause and effect' Marxist criticism. That one of the ways she does so is by throwing MacNeice's comments at Smith is interesting, as is her skirting around the issue of MacNeice's politics (or lack of it) in the same book: 'the new situation [of the end of the 1930s], blurring issues of left and right, clarifying those of right and wrong, was simply more susceptible to his political and aesthetic individualism'. Edna Longley, *Poetry in the Wars* (Newcastle upon Tyne: Bloodaxe, 1988), pp. 9, 83. Several of Thomas's critics do acknowledge briefly the Modernism of some of his work (see chapter 6 of this book).

17 Edward Said, 'Yeats and decolonization', in Barbara Kruger and Phil Mariani (eds), *Making History*, Discussions in Contemporary Culture, 4 (Seattle: Bay Press, 1989), p. 6. Jameson is cited in Liam Kennedy, 'Modern Ireland: post-colonial society or post-colonial pretensions?', *Irish Review*, 13 (Winter 1992/3), 107.

18 Tony Conran, *Frontiers in Anglo-Welsh Poetry* (Cardiff: University of Wales Press, 1997), p. 1.

19 Said, 'Yeats and decolonization', p. 14; ibid., pp. 15, 13.

20 Kennedy, 'Modern Ireland', pp. 13, 114. And even in 1991 the World Bank, using yardsticks such as infant mortality rates, life expectancy, reliance upon agriculture, literacy, diet, etc., stated specifically that Ireland was not a member of the Third World, *The World Development Report, 1991.*

21 Ibid., p. 110.

22 Luke Gibbons, *Transformations in Irish Culture* (Cork: Cork University Press in association with Field Day, 1996), pp. 1, 9, 11.

23 Claims for Ireland's current economic status as First World abound, due to the perceived success of the 'Celtic Tiger'. Accordingly, Ireland was seen as 'the fastest growing economy in the European Union throughout the 1990s . . . [and it had] also made huge strides in improving growth and competitiveness'. *Global Competitiveness Report 1997* (Geneva: World Economic Forum), p. 41. The national economy, it was then claimed, was growing at a rate of more than 7 per cent, over double that of western Europe, as was reported in *The Economist* in 1997, 'Miracles do happen you know: look at the Irish economy'; *The Economist*, 17 May 1997, 12. Recently, though, Ireland is showing signs of boom-time stress, as house prices have risen 180 per cent in Dublin since 1992, credit levels are rising rapidly and workforce wage restraints are in place. For a wide-ranging institutional critique of the Celtic Tiger, see *The Workers' Solidarity Movement Pages* @ «www. Flag.blackened.net/revolt/ws98/ws53_tiger.html»

24 Declan Kiberd, *Inventing Ireland: The Literature of the Modern Nation* (London: Vintage, 1996), p. 5.

126

1 'Poised on the edge of absence': Louis MacNeice, Modernism and the 1930s

1 Alan Wilde, *Horizons of Assent: Modernism, Postmodernism and the Ironic Imagination* (Baltimore, MD: Johns Hopkins University Press, 1987), p. 4.
2 *CPLM*, 5.
3 John Hilton, 'Louis MacNeice at Marlborough and Oxford', in *TSAF*, Appendix B, p. 248; Louis MacNeice, *Modern Poetry: A Personal Essay* (Oxford: Oxford University Press, 1938), pp. 53–4.
4 Ibid., p. 55.
5 Louis MacNeice, *Blind Fireworks* (London: Victor Gollancz, 1929), 'Foreword'.
6 Edna Longley, *Louis MacNeice: A Study* (London: Faber & Faber, 1988), pp. 44, 103; Robyn Marsack, *The Cave of Making: The Poetry of Louis MacNeice* (Oxford: Clarendon Press, 1982), pp. 4, 7; Peter McDonald, 'The falling castle: MacNeice's poetry (1936–39)', in Jacqueline Genet and Wynne Hellegouarch (eds), *Studies on Louis MacNeice* (Caen: Centre de Publications de l'Université de Caen, 1988), p. 30.
7 Louis MacNeice, *The Poetry of W. B. Yeats* (London: Faber & Faber, 1941), p. 81; MacNeice, *Modern Poetry*, pp. 12, 13–15, 154–77.
8 Ibid., pp. 27, 164.
9 Ibid., pp. 12, 14.
10 Ibid., p. 163.
11 MacNeice, *The Poetry of W. B. Yeats*, pp. 156–7.
12 McDonald, 'The falling castle', p. 27.
13 MacNeice, *Modern Poetry*, p. 52.
14 Jon Stallworthy, *Louis MacNeice* (London: Faber & Faber, 1996), pp. 95–6.
15 MacNeice, *Modern Poetry*, pp. 15, 52.
16 Edna Longley, 'Louis MacNeice: aspects of his aesthetic theory and practice', in Glenet and Hellegonarch (eds), *Studies on Louis MacNeice*, p. 54. However, it could well be said that her phrase 'human wholeness' has itself an element of 'symbol or pastiche' about it.
17 Georg Lukács's critique of Modernism began, of course, in the 1930s, and is most thoroughly articulated in 'The ideology of Modernism', *The Meaning of Contemporary Realism*, trans. John and Necke Mander (London: Merlin Press, 1963 [1937]).
18 M. H. Abrams, *A Glossary of Literary Terms* (Fort Worth: Holt Rinehart and Winston, 1988), p. 127; J. A. Cuddon, *The Penguin Dictionary of Literary Terms and Literary Theory* (Harmondsworth: Penguin, 1991), p. 267.
19 Louis A. Montrose, '"Eliza, Queen of shepheardes", and the pastoral of power', *English Literary Renaissance*, 10 (1980), 153.
20 Annabel Patterson, *Pastoral and Ideology: Virgil to Valéry* (Oxford: Clarendon Press, 1988), p. 3.
21 Stephen Spender, *World Within World* (London: Hamish Hamilton and the Book Society, 1951), pp. 249–50. It is equally possible to read his claim the opposite

way to the one posited here, as suggesting that there *is* a politics in a pastoral stance: that a conscious refusal to write political poetry is itself a political act.

22 William Empson, *Some Versions of Pastoral* (London: Chatto & Windus, 1935), p. 22. Christopher Norris, *William Empson and the Philosophy of Literary Criticism* (London: Athlone Press, 1978), p. 44; Norris, *The Truth about Postmodernism* (Oxford: Blackwell, 1993), p. 122. See also Paul Alpers, *What is Pastoral?* (Chicago: University of Chicago Press, 1996), pp. 37–43; Christopher Norris, *The Truth about Postmodernism*, pp. 120–33.

23 It is interesting to note that Edna Longley has written that 'An Eclogue for Christmas' 'derives and deviates from' *The Waste Land*. Edna Longley, 'Traditionalism and modernism in Irish poetry since 1930: the role of Louis MacNeice', in Geert Lernout (ed.), *The Crows Behind the Plough: History and Violence in Anglo-Irish Poetry and Drama* (Amsterdam: Rodopi, 1991), p. 163. For Robyn Marsack, it is 'The Love Song of J. Alfred Prufrock', that lies behind the poem: 'Perhaps this passage is the residue of MacNeice's reading of 'Prufrock', the speaker standing aside to assess what society has made of its victim. While Prufrock considers spiritual consequences, A sees the result in aesthetic terms and in autobiographical ones, if we identify 'A' with MacNeice', which she does. Marsack, *The Cave of Making*, p. 26.

24 See for example, 'Elephant Trunk', quoted as epigraph to the chapter. Other examples include 'The Sunlight on the Garden', 'The Brandy Glass', 'An Eclogue for Christmas' and 'Cuckoo'.

25 T. S. Eliot, 'Fragment of an Agon', in *The Complete Poems and Plays* (London: Faber & Faber, 1969), p. 124.

26 Anthony Burgess, *A Mouthful of Air: Language and Languages, Especially English* (London: Vintage, 1993), pp. 309–10.

27 In the context of MacNeice's interest in surface images and sensory impressions it is interesting to consider his use of 'mauve' in the eighth line of the passage quoted. Mauve is a synthetic dye, rather than a 'natural' colour, discovered by mistake, following an experimental attempt to produce quinine, in 1856 by William Perkin. Perkin's factory was in the first city of the industrial revolution, Manchester (Birmingham is the second), and during its original period of manufacture, the factory regularly contaminated the local environment, and particularly the water supply, with the dye. This may be related, in line with the reading of the poem that ensues, to 'Birmingham's production of 'the sky, plum after sunset, merging to duck's egg, barred with mauve' (*CPLM*, 18). See Simon Garfield, *Mauve* (London: Faber & Faber, 2001).

28 Cuddon, *The Penguin Dictionary of Literary Terms and Literary Theory*, p. 360. See Marjorie Perloff, *The Futurist Moment: Avant-Garde, Avant Guerre, and the Language of Rupture* (Chicago: University of Chicago Press, 1986); John J. Whites, *Literary Futurism: Aspects of the First Avant-Garde* (Oxford: Clarendon Press, 1991); Leon Trotsky, *Literature and Revolution* (Ann Arbor: University of Michigan Press, 1960).

29 See René Wellek, *A History of Modern Criticism: 1750–1950*, volume 7, *German, Russian, and Eastern European Criticism, 1900–1950* (New Haven: Yale Univer-

sity Press, 1991), pp. xvii, 458; Victor Shklovsky, 'Art as technique', in Rick Rylance (ed.), *Debating Texts: Readings in 20th Century Literary Theory and Method* (Toronto: University of Toronto Press, 1987), pp. 48–9.

30 *Selected Literary Criticism of Louis MacNeice*, ed. Alan Heuser (Oxford: Clarendon Press, 1987), pp. 160–1.

31 MacNeice, *Modern Poetry*, p. 74. This might serve as a useful reminder of the dangers of a careless and crude association of poet and critic, for, as I have argued, 'Birmingham' can also be read as demonstrating the appeal of sensory impressions and surfaces ('*décor*') to MacNeice.

32 Geoffrey Grigson, *Poetry of the Present: An Anthology of the Thirties and After* (London: Phoenix House, 1949), p. 77.

33 W. H. Auden, 'Consider this and in our time', in *The English Auden: Poems, Essays and Dramatic Writings 1927–1937*, ed. Edward Mendelson (London: Faber & Faber, 1977), p. 46.

34 See Bernard Bergonzi, *The Myth of Modernism and Twentieth Century Literature* (New York: St Martin's Press, 1986), p. 120; *Reading the Thirties: Texts and Contexts* (London: Macmillan, 1978), pp. 52–4. Bergonzi points out that the list is a characteristic feature of 1930s poetry, for which he cites Auden's 'Spain' as the prime example. For an alternative view, see Janet Montefiore, *Men and Women Writers of the 1930s: The Dangerous Flood of History* (London: Routledge, 1996), p. 15.

35 W. H. Auden, 'Spain 1937', in Robin Skelton (ed.), *Poetry of the Thirties* (Harmondsworth: Penguin, 1964), pp. 133–4.

36 W. H. Auden, *Collected Poems*, ed. Edward Mendelson (London: Faber & Faber, 1976), p. 201.

37 In *The Strings are False*, MacNeice provides an account of the association of flux and form in his work of the 1920s: 'Style remained more important than subject. The magic words – Relativity and the Unconscious – were always on our lips and we were pathetically eager to be realist (which meant the mimesis of flux), but we always fell back upon Form. This paradox came out in our admiration for contemporary novelists – Joyce, D. H. Lawrence, Virginia Woolf – who give you the flux but serve it on golden platters. We considered them good because they were the acolytes of Flux, but it was the *gold* and the ritual that fetched us. For they each had something positive to offer: Lawrence had his crusading enthusiasm, his wonderful pictorial sense; Joyce had the solid ground against which he kicked; Woolf had at least a precision of picture and cadence. The flux is the reality, so has to be recognised, but you can make this recognition with style. What you do does not matter, but how you do it; Picasso can make a picture out of any thing' (*TSAF*, 118, 119).

38 Ezra Pound, *The Cantos* (London: Faber & Faber, 1998), pp. 6–10.

39 Hugh Kenner, *The Poetry of Ezra Pound* (London: Faber & Faber, 1951), p. 318.

40 The passage is from a letter to his father of 11 April 1927 describing a number of Cantos, *The Letters of Ezra Pound: 1907–1941*, ed. D. D. Paige (London: Faber & Faber, 1951), p. 285.

41 Edna Longley, 'Traditionalism and Modernism in Irish poetry since 1930',
    p. 154.
42 Jon Stallworthy states that the '"camp" phrase, "my dear" suggests that Wystan
    is the communist addressed'. Stallworthy, *Louis MacNeice*, p. 154. The poem
    may, alternatively, be addressed to Anthony Blunt – an aesthete Marxist, if there
    ever was one. Stallworthy, however, states that this is unlikely, as it is improbable
    that Blunt discussed communism with MacNeice before 1934.
43 In France, following the election of the Popular Front, the industrial action
    mounted by the majority of workers in the country did initially realize substantial
    victories (including increased pay for workers and financial allowances for the
    unemployed). However, although the Popular Front was the official governmental
    organization through which reform was undertaken, it ultimately stalled the
    extension of reform (a deal had been arranged between its leadership and the
    bourgeoisie to disband the revolutionary movement). Indeed, when further
    strikes reached revolutionary potential, the PCF (French Communist Party) and
    PSF (French Socialist Party) worked to restrain the workers, so that the PCF's
    alliance with the bourgeoisie could be maintained. The result was, it has been
    argued, twofold: two years later, a full-scale attack on the gains made by a
    resurgent bourgeois reaction, and, after the start of the Second World War, the
    imposition of the pro-Hitler Vichy dictatorship by the French ruling class, under
    the banner 'Better Hitler than the Popular Front' (see also n. 41). In Spain, a
    fascist revolt took place within six months of the election of the Second Popular
    Front government, signalling the beginning of a bloody civil war between (in
    crude terms) the working classes on the one side, and the Spanish bourgeoisie,
    who supported Franco's fascist forces, on the other. Though made up of the
    Socialist Party, the Communist Party and the left-wing POUM (Party of Marxist
    Unification), the leadership of the Popular Front in Spain was predominantly
    Stalinist and suppressed any manifestation of the working-class struggle against
    capitalism. One example of this was the suppression of the Barcelona workers'
    uprising in May 1937 and the murder of leftist leaders (Andres Nin, leader of
    the POUM, for instance). That this suppression of workers' revolution in favour
    of 'democratic' capitalism took place in a country where the vast majority (if
    not all) of the capitalist class supported fascism and the break-up of workers'
    organizations is significant, as it has been argued that the Popular Front was
    responsible for the installation of Franco and the subsequent forty years of fascist
    dictatorship in Spain. In this way, the policy of Popular Frontism was as disastrous
    in Spain for the working class as it was in France. See Helen Graham and Paul
    Preston (eds), *The Popular Front in Europe* (London: Macmillan, 1987); Anthony
    Beevor, *The Spanish Civil War* (London: Cassell, 1999), pp. 39–51; Michael
    Alpert, *A New History of the Spanish Civil War* (London: Macmillan, 1994),
    pp. 13–50.
44 See, for example, Frank Borkenau, *World Communism* (Ann Arbor: University
    of Michigan Press, 1962), pp. 337–47, or Arthur Koestler, *The God that Failed:
    Six Studies in Communism*, ed. Richard Crossman (London: Hamish Hamilton,
    1950), pp. 43–63. The thrust of their arguments is that, had it not been for the

conflict and division between the Communist Party (KPD) and the German Socialist Party (SDP), the rise of Hitler could have been halted. See also George Orwell, *Homage to Catalonia* (Harmondsworth: Penguin, 1974), pp. 51–70.

[45] Ihab Hassan, 'The culture of postmodernism', *Theory, Culture and Society*, 2 (1985), 123–4.

2 'Our modern formula/of death to sense and dissolution': Dylan Thomas, Modernism and Surrealism in the 1930s

[1] T. S. Eliot, *Selected Essays* (London: Faber & Faber, 1951), p. 27. Terry Eagleton has glossed Eliot's 'Whiggism' in an English context as 'protestantism, liberalism, Romanticism, humanism'. Terry Eagleton, *Criticism and Ideology: A Study in Marxist Literary Theory* (London: Verso, 1976), p. 146. Welsh Dissent, socialism and 'Celtic' emotionalism might be taken to represent extreme versions of these categories.

[2] T. S. Eliot, *The Complete Poems and Plays* (London: Faber & Faber, 1969), p. 122. See also John Bayley, 'Dylan Thomas', in C. B. Cox (ed.), *Dylan Thomas: A Collection of Critical Essays* (Englewood Cliffs, NJ: Prentice Hall, 1966), p. 165.

[3] Dylan Thomas, 'Poetic manifesto', in *Early Prose Writings*, ed. Walford Davies (London: Dent, 1971), p. 158.

[4] J. Hillis Miller, *Poets of Reality: Six Twentieth-Century Writers* (Cambridge, MA: Harvard University Press, 1966), p. 195.

[5] Walford Davies, *Dylan Thomas: An Open Guide* (Milton Keynes: Open University Press, 1986), p. 105.

[6] See also Terry Eagleton's comment that 'The phenomenal text, to use one of Eliot's own metaphors, is merely the meat with which the burglar distracts the guard-dog while he proceeds with his stealthy business.' Eagleton, *Criticism and Ideology*, p. 150.

[7] Neil Corcoran, *English Poetry since 1940* (London: Longman, 1993), pp. 44–5.

[8] Davies, *Dylan Thomas: An Open Guide*, p. 118.

[9] M. H. Abrams, *A Glossary of Literary Terms* (Fort Worth: Holt Rinehart and Winston, 1988), p. 65.

[10] Davies, *Dylan Thomas: An Open Guide*, p. 114.

[11] See Stewart Crehan, 'The lips of time', in Alan Bold (ed.), *Dylan Thomas: Craft or Sullen Art* (London: Vision Press, 1990), p. 38.

[12] For an explanation and full discussion of Saussure's linguistic theories see Jonathon Culler, *Saussure* (London: Fontana, 1976), p. 23ff.

[13] See Julia Kristeva, *Powers of Horror: An Essay on Abjection* (New York: Columbia University Press, 1982).

[14] Elizabeth A. Grosz, *Sexual Subversions: Three French Feminists* (Winchester, MA: Unwin Hyman, 1989), p. 43.

[15] See Crehan, 'The lips of time', p. 38. Interpellation is the term coined by Louis Althusser to refer to the process by which the ideologies which permeate society

'call up' or 'recruit' human subjects. See Louis Althusser, 'Ideology and ideological state apparatuses', in *Lenin and Philosophy and Other Essays*, trans. B. Brewster (London: NLB, 1971).

16 For example, Bernard Bergonzi reads Thomas as a 'visceral rather than social poet'. Bernard Bergonzi, *Reading the Thirties: Texts and Contexts* (London: Macmillan, 1978), p. 125.

17 Maud Ellmann, 'Eliots's abjection', in John Fletcher and Andrew Benjamin (eds), *Abjection, Melancolia and Love: The Work of Julia Kristeva* (London: Routledge, 1990), p. 187.

18 Ibid., p. 179.

19 Ibid., p. 181.

20 Ibid., pp. 192–3. Eliot refers to Milton's work in the following terms: 'In Milton, there is always the maximal, never the minimal, alteration of ordinary language. Every distortion of construction, the foreign idiom, the use of a word in a foreign way or with the meaning of the foreign word from which it is derived rather than the accepted meaning in English, every idiosyncrasy is a particular act of violence which Milton has been the first to commit . . . Of all modern writers of verse, the nearest analogy seems to me to be Mallarmé, a smaller poet, though still a great one.' T. S. Eliot, 'Milton II', in *On Poetry and Poets* (London: Faber & Faber, 1969), p. 156.

21 Eliot, 'Tradition and the individual talent', in *Selected Essays* pp. 13–22. As Judith Butler points out, the body is discursively constructed, and its very materiality is a product of power. See Judith Butler, *Bodies That Matter: On the Discursive Limits of 'Sex'* (New York and London: Routledge, 1993). As such, the body is a site for continuing conflict over its meanings and significance within the body politic, the consequences of which have important repercussions for an investigation of the subject and subjectivity. What might be termed the historical deconstruction of Michel Foucault, which attends to historical discontinuities to the same degree that it does to historical connections, lies behind much of this critical work. See H. L. Dreyfus and P. Rabinow, *Michel Foucault: Beyond Structuralism and Hermeneutics* (New York and London: Harvester Wheatsheaf, 1982), p. 104–25.

22 Kristeva, *Powers of Horror*, p. 4. See also Ellmann, 'Eliot's abjection', p. 181: 'In the semantic landscape of the text, sinking banks imply dissolving definitions. In fact, the horror of *The Waste Land* lies in its osmoses, exhalations, and porosities, for this miasma is the symptom of disintegrating boundaries.'

23 Sigmund Freud, *Three Essays on the Theory of Sexuality*, *The Standard Edition of the Complete Psychological Works*, VII (London: Hogarth Press and the Institute of Psychoanalysis, 1953), trans. from *Gesammelte Werke* (vols I–XVIII) (London and Frankfurt: 1940–68), pp. 123–246.

24 Kristeva, *Powers of Horror*, p. 16.

25 Toril Moi explains the Law of the Father in the following terms: 'The Oedipal crisis represents the entry into the symbolic order. This entry is also likened [by Lacan] to the acquisition of language. In the Oedipal crisis the father splits up the dyadic unity between the mother and child and forbids the child further

access to the mother and the mother's body. The phallus, representing the Law of the Father (or the threat of castration), thus comes to signify separation and loss to the child. . . . To enter into the symbolic Order means to accept the phallus as the representation of the Law of the Father. All human culture and all life in society is dominated by the Symbolic Order.' Toril Moi, *Sexual/Textual Politics: Feminist Literary Theory* (London: Routledge, 1991), pp. 99–100.

[26] Freud, *Three Essays on the Theory of Sexuality* pp. 191, 167.

[27] Jacques Derrida, *Of Grammatology*, trans. Gayatri Chakravorty Spivak (Baltimore, MD: Johns Hopkins University Press, 1976), pp. 154–5.

[28] Herbert Read, 'The map of love', *Seven*, 6 (1939), 20.

[29] Louis MacNeice, *Modern Poetry: A Personal Essay* (London: Faber & Faber, 1938), pp. 59–60.

[30] Paul C. Ray, *The Surrealist Movement in England* (Ithaca: Cornell University Press, 1971), pp. 277, 278.

[31] For a detailed account of the exhibition see Ray, *The Surrealist Movement in England*, pp. 134–66.

[32] Alan Young, *dada and after: extremist modernism and english literature* (Manchester: Manchester University Press, 1981), p. 222.

[33] Henry I. Schvey, 'Dylan Thomas and surrealism', *Dutch Quarterly Review*, 5 (1975), 97–8.

[34] See, for example, Paul Ferris, *Dylan Thomas* (Harmondsworth: Penguin, 1978), p. 62; Davies, *Dylan Thomas: An Open Guide*, pp. 109–10.

[35] Constantine Fitzgibbon, *The Life of Dylan Thomas* (London: Dent, 1965), p. 196.

[36] Thomas, *Early Prose Writings*, p. 150.

[37] Davies, *Dylan Thomas: An Open Guide*, pp. 109, 110.

[38] André Breton, 'Premier manifeste', in *Manifestes du surréalisme* (Paris: Jean-Jacques Pauvert, 1962), p. 40; Theodor Adorno, 'Looking back on surrealism', in *Notes to Literature*, vol. 1, ed. Rolf Tiedemann, trans. Shierry Weber Nicholsen (New York: Columbia University Press, 1991), pp. 90–2.

[39] Davies, *Dylan Thomas: An Open Guide*, p. 110.

[40] Adorno, 'Looking back on surrealism', p. 90.

[41] See also Elizabeth Wright, 'The uncanny and surrealism', in Peter Collier and Judy Davies (eds), *Modernism and the European Unconscious* (Cambridge: Polity Press, 1990), p. 268.

[42] Thomas, *Early Prose Writings*, p. 150.

[43] See, for example, any of David Holbrook's studies of Thomas: *Llareggub Revisited: Dylan Thomas and the State of Modern Poetry* (London: Bowes & Bowes, 1962); *Dylan Thomas: The Code of Night* (London: Athlone Press, 1972).

[44] Wright, 'The uncanny and surrealism', p. 265.

[45] Alex Callinicos, *Against Postmodernism: A Marxist Critique* (Cambridge: Polity Press, 1989), p. 23.

[46] Wright, 'The uncanny and surrealism', p. 268.

[47] Picasso also produced the cover of 1933's *Minotaure*.

[48] This distinction between the regressive and the subversive is suggested by Wright, 'The uncanny and surrealism', p. 268.

49 Ferris, *Dylan Thomas*, p. 30.
50 See John Harvey, *The Art of Piety: The Visual Culture of Welsh Nonconformity* (Cardiff: University of Wales Press, 1995); John Davies, *A History of Wales* (London: Penguin, 1994), p. 289.
51 Familiarity with the work of Caradoc Evans is useful to an understanding of Thomas's use of Welsh Nonconformity. This is discussed in chapter 6.
52 M. Wynn Thomas comments that 'Thomas's approach to "making art objective to itself", that distinctively Modernist strategy, is via his experience of Welsh Nonconformity's mistrustful highlighting of the artfulness of art.' M. Wynn Thomas, *Corresponding Cultures: The Two Literatures of Wales* (Cardiff: University of Wales Press, 1999), p. 80.
53 This is also a more rewarding explanation of Thomas's participation in the 1936 Surrealist Exhibition.
54 Terry Eagleton, *The Ideology of the Aesthetic* (Oxford: Blackwell, 1990), pp. 321, 322.
55 Ibid., p. 322.

3 *'The woven figure': Louis MacNeice's Ireland*

1   Edward Said, 'Yeats and decolonization', in Barbara Kruger and Phil Mariani (eds), *Making History, Discussions in Contemporary Culture, 4* (Seattle: Bay Press, 1989), p. 3.
2   'Prologue', in Terence Brown and Alec Reid (eds), *Time Was Away: The World of Louis MacNeice* (Dublin: Dolmen Press, 1974), pp. 1–4. Also quoted in Peter McDonald, *Mistaken Identities: Poetry and Northern Ireland* (Oxford: Clarendon Press, 1997), p. 38.
3   All possible efforts have been made to track down and reference the programme, which was aired on BBC Radio 4 in 1995.
4   *The Selected Poetry of W. B. Yeats*, ed. A. Norman Jeffares (London: Macmillan, 1974), p. 208.
5   Declan Kiberd, *Inventing Ireland: The Literature of the Modern Nation* (London: Vintage, 1996), p 5.
6   Colin Graham, 'Post-colonial Theory and Kiberd's "Ireland"', *Irish Review*, 19 (Spring/Summer 1996), 62.
7   Colin Graham, 'Liminal spaces: post-colonial theories and Irish culture', *Irish Review*, 16 (Autumn/Winter, 1994), 29–43.
8   Homi K. Bhabha, 'Cultural diversity and cultural differences', in Bill Ashcroft, Gareth Griffiths and Helen Tiffin (eds), *The Post-Colonial Studies Reader* (London: Routledge, 1995), p. 207.
9   Ella Shohat and Robert Stam, *Unthinking Eurocentrism: Multiculturalism and the Media* (New York: Routledge, 1994), p. 42.
10 W. J. McCormack, *Ascendancy and Tradition in Anglo-Irish Literary History from 1789 to 1939* (Oxford: Clarendon Press, 1985), p. 7.

[11] *The Selected Prose of Louis MacNeice*, ed. Alan Heuser (Oxford: Clarendon Press, 1990), p. 23.

[12] Paul Muldoon (ed.), *The Faber Book of Contemporary Irish Poetry* (London: Faber & Faber, 1986), pp. 81–144. Most commentators note the influence of MacNeice on contemporary Northern Irish poetry. See, for example, Peter McDonald, *Louis MacNeice: The Poet in his Contexts* (Oxford: Clarendon Press, 1991), pp. 5, 7; Edna Longley, *Poetry in the Wars* (Newcastle upon Tyne: Bloodaxe, 1986), p. 211; Seamus Deane, *A Short History of Irish Literature* (London: Hutchinson, 1986), p. 230. This is not to deny that Edna and Michael Longley are attempting to construct their own version of 'the Irish tradition' in their polemics.

[13] F. R. Higgins and Louis MacNeice, 'Tendencies in modern poetry', *The Listener*, 27 July 1939, 186. Higgins's definition here is English, as he misrepresents Wordsworth's 'I have said that poetry is the spontaneous overflow of powerful feelings: it takes its origin from emotion *recollected in tranquillity*' (my italics). William Wordsworth, 'Preface to the Lyrical Ballads', in William Wordsworth and Samuel Taylor Coleridge, *Lyrical Ballads*, ed. R. L. Brett and A. R. Jones (Routledge: London and New York, 1991), p. 266. Higgins's language also recalls that which Yeats used in his 1930s writing, such as *On the Boiler* and 'The Statues', about race, land and the filthy tide of modernity: 'We Irish, born into that ancient sect/But thrown upon the filthy modern tide'. W. B. Yeats, *Selected Poems*, ed. A. Norman Jeffares (London: Pan, 1974), p. 196.

[14] John Hewitt, 'The bitter gourd: some problems of the Ulster writer', in Tom Clyde (ed.), *Ancestral Voices: The Selected Prose of John Hewitt* (Belfast: Blackstaff Press, 1987).

[15] Ibid., pp. 92–4.

[16] For more on Hewitt's attempt at a regional nationalism, see McDonald, *Mistaken Identities*, pp. 20–24.

[17] Quoted by Edna Longley, *The Living Stream: Literature and Revisionism in Ireland* (Newcastle upon Tyne: Bloodaxe), p. 65.

[18] Kiberd, *Inventing Ireland*, p. 474.

[19] Derrida's *différance* derives, of course, from a conflation of two definitions of the French *différer*, meaning 'to defer, postpone, delay' and also 'to differ, be different from'. It connotes that meaning is continuously and endlessly deferred, since a word's meaning is an effect of its relationships within a system of signifiers, none of which has any inherent meaning.

[20] Michel Foucault, 'What is enlightenment?', in Patricia Waugh (ed.), *Postmodernism: A Reader* (London: Edward Arnold, 1992), pp. 101–2.

[21] The term *flâneur* is from Charles Baudelaire, *The Painter of Modern Life and Other Essays*, trans. Jonathon Mayne (London: Phaidon, 1964), p. 13. The term is often used in discussions of the postmodern.

[22] Michael Longley, Introduction to *Louis MacNeice: Selected Poems*, ed. Michael Longley (London: Faber & Faber, 1988), p. xxii.

[23] Louis MacNeice, *Zoo* (London: Michael Joseph, 1938), p. 78.

[24] Ibid., p. 78.

[25] Terence Brown, 'Louis MacNeice's Ireland', in Terence Brown and Nicholas Grene (eds), *Tradition and Influence in Anglo-Irish Poetry* (Totowa, NJ: Barnes & Noble, 1989), p. 84.

[26] W. J. McCormack, *The Battle of the Books: Two Decades of Irish Cultural Debate* (Mullingar: Lilliput Press, 1986), p. 66.

[27] McCormack, *Ascendancy and Tradition*, p. 333.

[28] Peter McDonald, *Mistaken Identities*, pp. 227–8.

[29] See Richard Kearney 'Myth and motherland', in Field Day Theatre Company (ed.), *Ireland's Field Day* (London: Hutchinson, 1985), pp. 61–80. Seamus Heaney, for example, famously celebrates female essentialism in 'Bog Queen', *North* (London: Faber & Faber, 1975), p. 47.

[30] Seamus Heaney, *The Redress of Poetry: Oxford Lectures* (London: Faber & Faber, 1995), p. 199.

[31] A Machereyan criticism 'sets out to deliver the text from its own silences, by coaxing it into giving up its true, latent or hidden meaning'. Quoted from Tony Bennett, *Formalism and Marxism* (London: Methuen 1979), p. 107. For Macherey, the gaps, omissions and lapses of a text, its 'unsaid', are as important as that which is 'said'; they reveal its 'real' meaning, rather than its 'intended' one. See Pierre Macherey, *A Theory of Literary Production*, trans. G. Wall (London: Routledge 1978).

[32] Jacques Derrida, *Glas*, trans. John P. Leavey, Jr. and Richard Rand (Lincoln: University of Nebraska Press, 1986), p. 136.

[33] Marina Warner, *Alone of All her Sex: The Myth and Cult of the Virgin Mary* (London: Picador, 1985), p. 77. The position of priesthood might also be considered an idealized female role, as it is asexual. See also Tom Inglis, *Moral Monopoly: The Catholic Church in Modern Irish Society* (Dublin: Gill and Macmillan, 1987). Clair Wills writes of representations of Mother Ireland in the following terms: 'I should make it clear that it is certainly not the case that the symbolic power given to women, for example in the representations of Mother Ireland and the authority invested in the figure of the Virgin Mary, has resulted in any greater role for women in society. Quite the reverse, the requirements of purity within the family and nation have forced women into the most restricted modes of behaviour in order to conform to the Catholic and nationalist ideology of femininity.' Clair Wills, *Improprieties: Politics and Sexuality in Northern Irish Poetry* (Oxford: Clarendon Press, 1993), p. 66.

[34] Louis MacNeice, *Modern Poetry: A Personal Essay* (London: Faber, 1938), pp. 88–9.

[35] MacNeice, *Zoo*, p. 79.

[36] For a full account of the terror of her regime see Jon Stallworthy, *Louis MacNeice* (London: Faber & Faber, 1996), pp. 28–30.

[37] Terence Brown, *Louis MacNeice: Sceptical Vision* (Dublin: Gill & Macmillan, 1975), p. 10.

[38] Tom Paulin, *Ireland and the English Crisis* (Newcastle upon Tyne: Bloodaxe, 1984), pp. 75–80.

[39] Homi K. Bhabha, *The Location of Culture* (London: Routledge, 1994), p. 113. A fuller discussion of Bhabhan hybridity can be found in chapter 6.

4 'Here Lie the Beasts': Dylan Thomas's Monsters, Monstrous Dylan Thomas

1 David E. Musselwhite, *Partings Welded Together: Politics and Desire in the Nineteenth-Century English Novel* (London: Methuen, 1987), pp. 58–9.

2 *Sunday Referee*, 3 September 1933.

3 Also of interest in this regard is Thomas's January 1933 essay, first published in the *South Wales Evening Post*, 'Genius and madness akin in the world of art', in which he discusses the idea that the poet walks a line where it is 'difficult to differentiate, with any sureness, between insanity and eccentricity' and asserts that 'the borderline of insanity is more difficult to trace than the majority of people, comparatively safe within the barriers of their own common-sensibility, can realise.' Dylan Thomas, *Early Prose Writings*, ed. Walford Davies (London: Dent, 1971), p. 122.

4 Fred Botting, *Gothic* (London: Routledge, 1996), p. 3.

5 Stewart Crehan, 'The lips of time', in John Goodby and Chris Wigginton (eds), *Dylan Thomas: New Casebook* (Basingstoke: Palgrave, 2001), p. 56.

6 Botting, *Gothic*, p. 3.

7 Dylan Thomas, *The Poems*, ed. Daniel Jones (London: Dent, 1971), p. 81; Paul's First Epistle to the Romans, VI, The Bible, Authorized Version (Oxford: Oxford University Press, n. d.), p. 912; Mary Shelley, *Frankenstein or The Modern Prometheus* (Oxford: Oxford University Press, 1993), p. 202.

8 Elza Adamowicz, 'Monsters in surrealism: hunting the human-headed bombyx', in Peter Collier and Judy Davies (eds), *Modernism and The European Unconscious* (Cambridge: Polity Press, 1990), p. 299.

9 Ibid., pp. 286, 287.

10 Thomas was familiar with Ernst's work prior to staying with him in America in 1952.

11 Aristotle, *Generation of Animals*, trans. A. L. Peck (Cambridge, MA: Harvard University Press, 1943), section IV, iv, pp. 417, 425.

12 *The Oxford English Dictionary*, 2nd edn (Oxford: Clarendon Press, 1989), pp. 1036–7.

13 Katherine Park and Lorraine J. Daston, 'Unnatural conceptions: the study of monsters in sixteenth and seventeenth-century France and England', *Past and Present*, 92 (1981), 23.

14 *Oxford English Dictionary*, pp. 1036–7.

15 Michel Foucault, *Madness and Civilisation: A History of Insanity in the Age of Reason*, trans. Richard Howard (London: Tavistock, 1967), p. 70.

16 Michel Foucault, *Discipline and Punish* (New York: Random House, 1977), pp. 100–1. It is worth noting that Kristeva does link criminality with abjection: 'The traitor, the liar, the criminal with a good conscience, the shameless rapist, the killer who claims he is a saviour . . . Any crime, because it draws attention to the fragility of the law, is abject, but premeditated crime, cunning murder, hypocritical revenge are even more so because they heighten the display of such

fragility. He who denies morality is not abject; there can be grandeur in amorality and even in crime that flaunts its disrespect for the law – rebellious, liberating, and suicidal crime. Abjection, on the other hand, is immoral, sinister, scheming, and shady: a terror that dissembles, a hatred that smiles, a passion that uses the body for barter instead of inflaming it, a debtor . . . a friend who stabs you . . .' Julia Kristeva, *Powers of Horror: An Essay on Abjection* (New York: Columbia University Press, 1982), p. 4. 'Corruption is its most common, most obvious appearance. That is the socialised appearance of the abject . . . An unshakeable adherence to Prohibition and Law is necessary if that perverse interspace of abjection is to be hemmed in and thrust aside. Religion, Morality, Law. Obviously always arbitrary, more or less; unfailingly oppressive, rather more than less; laboratory prevailing, more and more so.' Ibid., p. 16

[17] James A. Davies, *A Reference Companion to Dylan Thomas* (Westport, CT: Greenwood Press, 1998), p. 263.

[18] W. H. Mellors, 'The bard and the prep school', *Scrutiny*, 9 (1940), 77; Robin Mayhead, Review of *Collected Poems 1934–1952*, *Scrutiny*, 19 (1952–3), 146. Robert Graves is quoted by Crehan, in 'The lips of time', p. 92.

[19] See Marjorie Levinson, *Keats's Life of Allegory* (Oxford: Blackwell, 1988).

[20] Michael Roberts, 'The brassy orator', *London Mercury*, 9 October 1939, 780, 782; Cyril Connolly, 'Comment', *Horizon*, June 1940, 391; Geoffrey Grigson, 'A letter from England', *Poetry*, November 1936, 102–3; Geoffrey Grigson, 'How much me your verbal acrobatics amaze', in *The Harp of Aeolus and Other Essays* (London: Routledge, 1948), pp. 151–60. See also Davies, *A Reference Companion to Dylan Thomas*, pp. 262–91.

[21] Hugh Gordon Porteus, 'Map of Llareggub', *New English Weekly*, 7 September 1939, 269–70.

[22] Michel Foucault, *The Order of Things: An Archaeology of the Human Sciences* (London: Tavistock, 1970), pp. xv, xvi.

[23] Jacques Derrida, *Of Grammatology*, trans. Gayatri Chakravorty Spivak (Baltimore, MD: Johns Hopkins University Press, 1976), p. 5.

[24] Jacques Derrida, 'Traumatism to promise', in *Points: Interviews 1974–1994*, ed. Elizabeth Weber (Stanford: Stanford University Press, 1995), p. 387.

[25] Jean-François Lyotard, *The Postmodern Condition: A Report on Knowledge*, Theory and History of Literature, vol. 10 (Minneapolis: University of Minnesota Press, 1984), p. xxiv.

[26] Jean-François Lyotard, 'Answering the question: what is postmodernism', in Patricia Waugh (ed.), *Postmodernism: A Reader* (London: Edward Arnold, 1992), p. 125.

[27] Ibid., p. 124.

[28] André Breton, *Manifestos of Surrealism*, trans. Richard Seaver and Helen R. Lane (Ann Arbor: University of Michigan Press, 1972), p. 241; Walter Benjamin, *One Way Street and Other Writings*, trans. Edmund Jephcott and Kingsley Shorter (London: NLB, 1979), p. 236.

[29] André Breton, 'Premier manifeste', in *Manifestes du surrealisme* (Paris: Jean-Jacques Pauvert, 1962), p. 11. Peter Bürger, *Theory of the Avant-Garde*, trans. Michel Shaw (Minneapolis: University of Chicago Press, 1984), pp. 12–13.

5 *'But one – meaning I':* Autumn Journal*'s histories and voices*

[1] Letter to Eleanor Clark, 21 May 1940. This was written forty-two days after Hitler had invaded Denmark and Norway, eleven days after the invasion of Belgium and Holland and two days after the beginning of the British retreat towards Dunkirk. Quoted in full by Jon Stallworthy in *Louis MacNeice* (London: Faber & Faber, 1996), pp. 273–7.

[2] Samuel Hynes, *The Auden Generation: Literature and Politics in England in the 1930s* (London: Bodley Head, 1976), p. 37.

[3] Ibid., p. 367.

[4] Edna Longley, *Poetry in the Wars* (Newcastle upon Tyne: Bloodaxe, 1996), p. 79. A similar list of the contents of the poem is provided by the author himself in a letter to T. S. Eliot: 'It contains rappotage [*sic*], metaphysics, ethics, lyrical emotion, autobiography, nightmare.' Quoted by Robyn Marsack, *The Cave of Making: The Poetry of Louis MacNeice* (Oxford: Clarendon Press, 1982), p. 43.

[5] Julian Symons, quoted in Edna Longley, *Louis MacNeice: A Study* (London: Faber & Faber, 1988), p. 61; Hynes, *The Auden Generation*, p. 295.

[6] D. E. S. Maxwell, *Poets of the Thirties* (London: Macmillan, 1969), p. 61.

[7] The term *performative* was introduced by J. L. Austin, to refer to language which is different from what he refers to as 'constantive' language. The former, according to Austin, is language whose primary function is to do something, the latter, language whose primary use is to say something. See *How to Do Things with Words* (Cambridge, MA: Harvard University Press, 1962), pp. 13–14. See also J. L. Austin, 'Performative–constantive', in John R. Searle (ed.), *The Philosophy of Language* (Oxford: Oxford University Press, 1971), pp. 13–22. Performatives are, though, intelligible only within a certain social context. See 'Performative acts and gender constitution: an essay in phenomenology and feminist theory', in Sue-Ellen Case (ed.), *Performing Feminism: Feminist Critical Theory and Theatre* (Baltimore, MD: Johns Hopkins University Press, 1990), pp. 270–82. See also Judith Butler's *Excitable Speech: A Politics of the Performative* (London: Routledge, 1997). I use the term to imply that, as a semiotic gesture, *Autumn Journal* is a doing as well as a being, or, more accurately, that the poem is a process that performs what it describes. See also Antony Shuttleworth's welcome corrective and 'postmodern' reading of MacNeice, *'The Poetics of Impurity': Louis MacNeice, Writing and the Thirties*, Ph.D., University of Warwick.

[8] As MacNeice commented after the start of the Second World War: 'If the war made nonsense of Yeats's poetry and all works that are to be called "escapist", it also made nonsense of poetry that professes to be "realist". My friends had been writing for years about guns and frontiers and factories, about the "facts" of psychology, politics, science, economics, but the fact of war made their writing seem as remote as the pleasure dome in Xanadu. For war spares neither the poetry of Xanadu nor the poetry of pylons.' *The Poetry of W. B. Yeats* (London: Faber & Faber, 1967), pp. 17–18.

[9] Christopher Isherwood, *Goodbye to Berlin* (London: Minerva, 1989), p. 9.

[10]   M. H. Abrams defines the 'palinode' as 'A poem or poetic passage in which the
       poet disavows or retracts an earlier poem or type of subject matter'. M. H. Abrams,
       A Glossary of Literary Terms (Fort Worth: Holt Rinehart and Winston, 1988),
       p. 139.
[11]   See, for example, Bernard Bergonzi, *Reading the Thirties: Texts and Contexts*
       (London: Macmillan, 1978), p. 145. On the increasing space and time for leisure
       and personal development in the 1930s, see Noreen Branson and Margot
       Heinemann, *Britain in the Nineteen Thirties* (London: Weidenfeld & Nicolson,
       1971), pp. 216–57.
[12]   Edna Longley, *Louis MacNeice: A Study* (London: Faber & Faber, 1988), p. 74.
[13]   Lynne Pearce, *Reading Dialogics* (London: Edward Arnold, 1994), p. 152.
[14]   Lynne Pearce writes that 'we are interested not in the construction of a universal
       model of the subject but of many subjects; in the differences between
       subjectivities, and in the difference within a single subjectivity'. Ibid., p. 152.
[15]   Longley, *Poetry in the Wars*, p. 81.
[16]   'Spider, spider, twisting tight' echoes 'Tyger Tyger, burning bright', William
       Blake, *The Complete Poems*, ed. Alicia Ostriker (Harmondsworth: Penguin, 1977),
       p. 125. '*Noli me tangere*' ('touch me not') is from both 'Who so list to hount I
       knowe where is an hynde', *The Penguin Book of Renaissance Verse 1509–1659*,
       ed. H. R. Woudhuysen (Harmondsworth: Penguin, 1993), p. 182, and the Gospel
       according to St John, XX, The Bible, Authorized Version (Oxford: Oxford
       University Press, n.d.), p. 875.
[17]   Plato, *Gorgias*, trans. W. Hamilton (Harmondsworth: Penguin, 1960), pp. 94–7.
[18]   The nirvana principle is a term used in Freudian psychoanalytic theory to refer
       to the attraction of the psyche to a state of non-existence. This would counter
       the effects of the pleasure principle. Sigmund Freud, 'Beyond the pleasure
       principle', in *On Metapsychology: The Theory of Psychoanalysis*, Pelican Freud
       Library XI, ed. and trans. Angela Richards (Harmondsworth: Penguin, 1984),
       p. 329.
[19]   E. M. Forster, *A Passage to India*, ed. Oliver Stallybrass (Harmondsworth:
       Penguin, 1979), p. 50.
[20]   *Oxford English Dictionary*, 2nd edn (Oxford: Clarendon Press, 1989), p. 851.
[21]   See Homer, *The Iliad of Homer*, trans. Richard Lattimore (Chicago: University
       of Chicago Press, 1971), Book VI, lines 152–5, p. 157; Homer, *The Odyssey*,
       trans. E. V. Rieu (Harmondsworth: Penguin, 1991), Book XI, lines 592–600,
       pp. 176–7. See also Ovid, *Metamorphoses*, trans. Mary M. Innes (Harmondsworth:
       Penguin, 1985), Book IV, lines 465–75, Book XIII, lines 27–32, pp. 166, 285,
       286.
[22]   Albert Camus, *The Myth of Sisyphus*, trans. Justin O'Brian (Harmondsworth:
       Penguin, 1986), pp. 108–9.
[23]   Ibid., pp. 109, 111.
[24]   See 'The Gift of Autumn', BBC Radio 3, October 1990, devised by Anne Mann,
       produced by Piers Plowright.
[25]   Stallworthy, *Louis MacNeice*, pp. 23–34.

26 George Orwell, 'Looking back on the Spanish Civil War', *Collected Essays, Journalism and Letters*, 2 (Harmondsworth: Penguin, 1954), p. 294. Further, Edna Longley has written that 'In its attitudes to totalitarianism, and to the propagandist abuse of language and thought, *Autumn Journal* anticipates Orwell's *Animal Farm* and *Nineteen Eighty-Four*'. Longley, *Louis MacNeice*, pp. 68–9.

27 Ibid., p. 65.

28 Edna Longley, *The Living Stream: Literature and Revisionism in Ireland* (Newcastle upon Tyne: Bloodaxe, 1994), p. 262.

29 Longley, *Poetry in the Wars*, p. 81.

30 Maurice Merleau-Ponty, *Phenomenology of Perception*, trans. Colin Smith, (London: Routledge, 1962), p. 377.

31 Ibid., p. xxi. Phenomenology was a cognate philosophical movement of the time of the writing of the poem. Merleau-Ponty summarizes his own (circumspect) phenomenology in the following terms: 'Inside and outside are inseparable. The world is wholly inside and I am wholly outside myself . . . In one of his celebrated *pensées*, Pascal shows that in one way I understand the world, and in another it understands me. We must add that it is in the same *way*: I understand the world because there are for me things near and far, foregrounds and horizons, and because in this way it forms a picture and acquires significance before me, and this finally is because I am situated in it and it understands me.' Ibid., p. 407–8.

32 Ibid., p. xvi-xvii. For Merleau-Ponty, truth may be found only in the 'chiasm', the intertwined and complex relationships between self and world. Maurice Merleau-Ponty, *The Visible and the Invisible*, ed. Claude Lefort, trans. Alphonso Lingis (Illinois: Northwestern University Press, 1968), pp. 131–2.

6 'Crying with hungry voices in our nest': Wales and Dylan Thomas

1 Address to the Scottish Society of Writers in Edinburgh. From *Adam: International Review, A Literary Monthly in English and French: Dylan Thomas Memorial Number*, ed. Miron Grindea, 238 (1953), 68.

2 Dylan Thomas, *The Poems*, ed. Daniel Jones (London: Dent, 1971), p. 74.

3 James A. Davies argues that 'The Welsh element of Thomas's critical history . . . involves prejudice, stereotyping, and tense discussion of his relationship with Wales and its literature'. James A. Davies, *A Reference Companion to Dylan Thomas* (Westport, CT: Greenwood Press, 1998), p. 263.

4 Ibid., p. 266.

5 T. Gwynn Jones, 'The modern trend in Welsh poetry', *Western Mail*, 19 July 1939, 11. Gwynn Jones's comment should be qualified, however, by noting that Thomas was not named, and that, as James A. Davies points out, Gwynn Jones's article was written in response to 'the deplorable standard of poems in Welsh submitted for various eisteddfod competitions'. Davies, *A Reference Companion to Dylan Thomas*, p. 266.

6 Bobi Jones, 'Imitations in death', *Welsh Anvil*, 7 (1955), 85–6.

7   *Tin Gods*, Fulmar Television for HTV Wales, November 2001. In fact, the documentary was a tissue of unsubstantiated rumours, gossip, anecdote and incomplete research, with the presenter, journalist Patrick Hannan, despite appearances, interviewing none of the contributors and imposing a narrow view of Thomas onto the final programme.

8   Saunders Lewis, *Is there an Anglo-Welsh Literature?* (Cardiff: Guild of Graduates of the University of Wales, 1939), p. 5. See also M. Wynn Thomas '"He belongs to the English": Welsh Dylan and Welsh-language culture', *Swansea Review*, 20 (2000), 122–134.

9   Lewis, *Is there an Anglo-Welsh Literature?*, p. 9.

10 *Dock Leaves*, 5, 'A Dylan Thomas number', ed. Raymond Garlick, 13 (Spring 1954), p. 9.

11 Walford Davies, for example, writes that Thomas is 'essentially a Modernist poet: he forces us to draw our meanings from the logic of the poem itself, in concrete terms, and not from an appeal to general experience outside'. Walford Davies, *Dylan Thomas: An Open Guide* (Milton Keynes: Open University Press, 1986), p. 57. Tony Conran contends that 'Dylan Thomas is a modernist in the symbolist tradition . . . he looks to an international horizon that began (more or less) in France in the third quarter of the nineteenth century'. Tony Conran, *Frontiers in Anglo-Welsh Poetry* (Cardiff: University of Wales Press, 1997), p. 114.

12 'A Letter to my Aunt discussing the Correct Approach to Modern Poetry', Thomas, *The Poems*, p. 83.

13 See, for example, Jane Aaron, Teresa Rees, Sandra Betts and Moira Vincentelli (eds), *Our Sisters' Land*, (Cardiff: University of Wales Press, 1994); Linden Peach, *Ancestral Lines* (Bridgend: Seren, 1993). See also, as an example, Meic Stephens (ed.), *Rhys Davies: Decoding the Hare* (Cardiff: University of Wales Press, 2001).

14 *Welsh Writing in English: A Yearbook of Critical Essays*, ed. Tony Brown, began in 1995 and is currently in its twelfth volume.

15 M. Wynn Thomas, *Corresponding Cultures: The Two Literatures of Wales* (Cardiff: University of Wales Press, 1999), pp. 49, 77.

16 Homi K. Bhabha, *The Location of Culture* (London: Routledge, 1994), pp. 113, 116.

17 Ibid., p. 112.

18 Raymond Williams, *What I Came to Say*, ed. Neil Belton, Francis Mulhern and Jenny Taylor (London: Hutchinson Radius, 1989), p. 57.

19 Conran, *Frontiers in Anglo-Welsh Poetry*, p. 1. *Welsh Rural Communities*, eds. Elwyn Davies and Alwyn D. Rees (Cardiff: University of Wales Press, 1962).

20 Ibid., p. 2.

21 Ibid., p. 3.

22 M. Wynn Thomas, 'Keeping his pen clean: R. S. Thomas and Wales', in William V. Davis (ed.), *Miraculous Simplicity: Essays on R. S. Thomas* (Fayetteville: University of Arkansas Press, 1993), p. 68.

23 Tony Bianchi, 'R. S. Thomas and his readers', in Davis (ed.), *Miraculous Simplicity*, p. 88.

24 R. S. Thomas, *Collected Poems* (London: Dent, 1983), p. 36.

25 Ibid., p. 262.

26 Again, here is a heavily gendered image, this time of the mother, with its connotations of 'mother tongue' and 'motherland'.

27 'Confessions of an Anglo-Welshman', *Wales*, 2 (1943), 49.

28 Brinley Thomas, 'Wales and the Atlantic economy', in Brinley Thomas (ed.), *The Welsh Economy* (Cardiff: University of Wales Press, 1962), p. 26.

29 It should be noted, too, that both of Raymond Williams's constructions are also identity based, defining the self in terms of Welshness, either racially or culturally.

30 Bianchi, 'R. S. Thomas and his readers', p. 80.

31 Niall Griffiths, lecture at Trinity College, Carmarthen, 20 February 2002. Griffiths also argues, interestingly, that R. S. Thomas's writing might also be read as hybrid and threatening to an English audience.

32 Ralph Maud, *Entrances to Dylan Thomas's Poetry* (Pittsburgh: University of Pittsburgh Press, 1963), pp. 57, 80.

33 Ibid., p. 61.

34 Peter Barry offers a deconstructive reading of Thomas's 'A Refusal to Mourn the Death, by Fire, of a Child in London'. Peter Barry, *Beginning Theory: An Introduction to Literary and Cultural Theory* (Manchester: Manchester University Press, 1995).

35 Thomas, *The Poems*, p. 74.

36 In a letter of 1935 to Bert Trick, Thomas considers Wales and its relationship to his poetic subject-matter: 'My own eyes, I know, squint inwards: when, and if, I look at the exterior world I see nothing or me; I should like very much to say that I see *everything* through the inner eye, but all I see is darkness, naked and not very nice. What can be done about it?' (*CLDT*, 192). James A. Davies suggests an alternative reading of these poems, based on their references of war. 'Thomas reaches so readily', he writes, for the 'military image', and elsewhere argues that what have been referred to as Thomas's 'process' poems must be read as part of his obsession with the First World War. On the other hand, John Goodby foregrounds the dialectical relationship of Thomas's images: 'Likewise, favourite words - such as "drill" and "gear" – carry associations with machinery . . . The common claim that "organic" imagery dominates the early poems is a good example of critical expectation overriding evidence; what Thomas does do is yoke together organic and inorganic terms. . . . To note this is not to deny the concern with the mutuality of growth and decay, but to insist on the dialectical relationship between the two terms.' Davies, *A Reference Companion to Dylan Thomas*, p. 139; James A. Davies '"A mental militarist": Dylan Thomas and the Great War', in *Welsh Writing in English: A Yearbook of Critical Essays*, 2 (1996), pp. 62–81; Alex Davis and Lee M. Jenkins (eds), *Locations of Literary Modernism: Region and Nation in British and American Modernist Poetry* (Cambridge: Cambridge University Press, 2000), pp. 267–8.

37   Gareth Thomas, 'A freak user of words', in Alan Bold (ed.), *Dylan Thomas: Craft or Sullen Art* (London: Vision Press, 1990), p. 66.

38   Conran, *Frontiers in Anglo-Welsh Poetry*, p. 113.

39   Recently, interesting research on Wales and Gothic has begun to appear. See, for example, Kirsti Bohata, 'Apes and cannibals in Cambria: images of the racial and gendered other in Gothic writing in Wales', in *Welsh Writing in English: A Yearbook of Critical Essays*, 6 (2001); Harri Roberts, '"Tower of Babel": heteroglossia and the (de)construction of meaning in Glyn Jones's *The Valley, The City, The Village* and Niall Griffiths's *Grits*', in *Welsh Writing in English: A Yearbook of Critical Essays*, 7 (2002).

40   See, for example, Annis Pratt, *Dylan Thomas's Early Prose: A Study in Creative Mythology* (Pittsburgh: University of Pittsburgh Press, 1970).

41   David Punter, *The Literature of Terror: A History of Gothic Fictions* (London: Longman, 1980), p. 263.

42   See, for example, Geoffrey Grigson's comment that 'the self in Mr. Thomas's poems seems inhuman and glandular', and Neil Corcoran's statement that, 'In Thomas's own early work, of course, the 'melancholics' flood back: the body, in its most intimately glandular process, reasserts an obdurate primacy.' Geoffrey Grigson, 'How much me your verbal acrobatics amaze', in *The Harp of Aeolus and Other Essays* (London: Routledge, 1948), p. 152; Neil Corcoran, *English Poetry since 1940* (London: Longman, 1993), p. 40.

43   Tony Pinkney, *D. H. Lawrence* (Hemel Hempstead: Harvester Wheatsheaf, 1990). See, especially, chapter 2: 'Northernness and Modernism'.

44   Ibid., p. 73.

45   Ibid., p. 73.

46   See Chris Hopkins, '"James Joyce is an Irish Edition of Mr Caradoc Evans": two Celtic naturalists', *Irish Studies Review* (Autumn 1995), 23–6.

47   Caradoc Evans, *My People*, ed. John Harris (Bridgend: Seren, 1997), back cover.

48   Ibid., p. 10.

49   Gwyn A. Williams, *When Was Wales?* (Harmondsworth: Penguin, 1991), p. 253.

50   Ibid., p. 253.

51   Ibid., pp. 280–6.

52   Conran, *Frontiers in Anglo-Welsh Poetry*, p. 111.

53   Robert Crawford, *Devolving English Literature* (Oxford: Clarendon Press, 1992), p. 218.

54   Ibid., p. 219.

55   Peter McDonald, *Mistaken Identities: Poetry and Northern Ireland* (Oxford: Clarendon Press, 1997), pp. 193–4.

56   Davies, *Dylan Thomas: An Open Guide*. See also John Ackerman, 'The Welsh background', in C. B. Cox (ed.), *Dylan Thomas: A Collection of Critical Essays* (Englewood Cliffs, NJ: Prentice Hall, 1966).

57   Conran, *Frontiers in Anglo-Welsh Poetry*, p. 113. (Conran also remarks that 'Dylan's Welshness is a lack of Englishness as much as anything homespun from Wales'. Ibid., p. 52).

Conclusion: 'The judge-blown bedlam': after the 1930s

[1]   Louis MacNeice, *The Poetry of W. B. Yeats* (London: Faber & Faber, 1941), p. 17.

[2]   Robert Hewison, *Under Siege: Literary Life in London: 1939–1945* (Oxford: Oxford University Press).

[3]   Louis MacNeice, *Modern Poetry: A Personal Essay* (Oxford: Oxford University Press, 1938), p. 205.

[4]   James A. Davies, *A Reference Companion to Dylan Thomas* (Westport, CT: Greenwood Press, 1998), p. 189.

[5]   Edna Longley, *Louis MacNeice: A Study* (London: Faber & Faber, 1988), p. 79.

[6]   Letter to E. R. Dodds, 5 February 1940. Quoted in Jon Stallworthy, *Louis MacNeice* (London: Faber & Faber, 1995), p. 270.

[7]   MacNeice, *The Poetry of W. B. Yeats*, p. 18.

[8]   *Selected Literary Criticism of Louis MacNeice*, ed. Alan Heuser (Oxford: Clarendon Press, 1987), p. 162.

[9]   'Life in the moment', *Times Literary Supplement*, 31 March 1961; 'Poet on watch', *Times Literary Supplement*, 27 September 1963. Edna Longley, for example, regards *Autumn Sequel* as an artistic failure. Edna Longley, *Louis MacNeice: A Study*, pp. 115–16.

[10]   'Life in the moment', *Times Literary Supplement*, p. 199.

[11]   Louis MacNeice, *Varieties of Parable* (Cambridge: Cambridge University Press, 1965), p. 3.

[12]   See W. J. McCormack, *From Burke to Beckett: Ascendancy, Tradition and Betrayal in Literary History* (Cork: Cork University Press, 1994), pp. 164–205.

[13]   MacNeice, *Varieties of Parable*, p. 15.

[14]   Dylan Thomas, *Quite Early One Morning* (New York: New Directions Press, 1960), p. 178.

[15]   John Goodby, '"Very profound and very box office": the Later Poems and *Under Milk Wood*', in John Goodby and Chris Wigginton (eds), *Dylan Thomas: New Casebook* (Basingstoke: Palgrave, 2001), p. 203.

Bibliography

Primary texts (Louis MacNeice and Dylan Thomas)

Higgins, F. R. and Louis MacNeice, 'Tendencies in modern poetry', *The Listener*, 27 July 1939.

MacNeice, Louis, *Blind Fireworks* (London: Victor Gollancz, 1929).

—— *Poems* (London: Faber & Faber, 1935).

—— *Poems* (New York: Random House, 1937).

—— *Modern Poetry: A Personal Essay* (Oxford: Oxford University Press, 1938).

—— *The Earth Compels* (London: Faber & Faber, 1938).

—— *Zoo* (London: Michael Joseph, 1938).

—— *Collected Poems, 1925–1940* (London: Random House, 1941).

—— *Plant and Phantom* (London: Faber & Faber, 1941).

—— *The Poetry of W. B. Yeats* (London: Faber & Faber, 1941).

—— *Springboard* (London: Faber & Faber, 1944).

—— *Ten Burnt Offerings* (London: Faber & Faber, 1952).

—— *Solstices* (London: Faber & Faber, 1961).

—— *The Burning Perch* (London: Faber & Faber, 1963).

—— *Varieties of Parable* (Cambridge: Cambridge University Press, 1965).

—— *Collected Poems*, ed. E. R. Dodds (London: Faber & Faber, 1979).

—— *Selected Literary Criticism of Louis MacNeice*, ed. Alan Heuser (Oxford: Clarendon Press, 1987).

—— *Selected Poems*, ed. Michael Longley (London: Faber & Faber, 1988).

—— *The Selected Prose of Louis MacNeice*, ed. Alan Heuser (Oxford: Clarendon Press, 1990).

—— *The Strings Are False: An Unfinished Autobiography*, ed. E. R. Dodds (London: Faber & Faber, 1996).

Thomas, Dylan, 'That sanity be kept', *Sunday Referee*, 3 September 1933.

—— *18 Poems* (London: *Sunday Referee* and the Parton Bookshop, 1934).

—— *Twenty-five Poems* (London: Dent, 1936).

—— *The Map of Love* (London: Dent, 1939).

—— *Deaths and Entrances* (London: Dent, 1946).

—— *Quite Early One Morning* (New York: New Directions Press, 1960).

—— *Early Prose Writings*, ed. Walford Davies (London: Dent, 1971).
—— *The Poems*, ed. Daniel Jones (London: Dent, 1971).
—— *Collected Stories*, ed. Walford Davies (London: Dent, 1983).
—— *The Collected Letters*, ed. Paul Ferris (London: Dent, 1985).
—— *Collected Poems, 1934–1953*, ed. Walford Davies and Ralph Maud (London: Dent, 1988).
—— *The Notebook Poems, 1930–34*, ed. Ralph Maud (London: Dent, 1989).
—— *The Broadcasts*, ed. Ralph Maud (London: Dent, 1991).
—— *The Filmscripts*, ed. John Ackerman (London: Dent, 1995).
—— *Under Milk Wood*, ed. Walford Davies and Ralph Maud (London: Dent, 1995 [1954]).

Primary texts (others)

Auden, W. H., *The English Auden: Poems, Essays and Dramatic Writings, 1927–1937*, ed. Edward Mendelson (London: Faber & Faber, 1937).
—— *Collected Poems*, ed. Edward Mendelson (London: Faber & Faber, 1976).
Eliot, T. S., *The Complete Poems and Plays* (London: Faber & Faber, 1969).
Isherwood, Christopher, *Goodbye to Berlin* (London: Minerva, 1989).
Muldoon, Paul (ed.), *The Faber Book of Contemporary Irish Poetry* (London: Faber & Faber, 1986).
Pound, Ezra, *The Cantos* (London: Faber & Faber, 1998).
—— *The Letters of Ezra Pound: 1907–1941*, ed. D. D. Paige (London: Faber & Faber, 1951).
Skelton, Robin (ed.), *Poetry of the Thirties* (Harmondsworth: Penguin, 1964).
Thomas, R. S., *Collected Poems* (London: Dent, 1983).
Yeats, W. B., *Selected Poems*, ed. A. Norman Jeffares (London: Pan, 1974)

Critical works on Dylan Thomas and Louis MacNeice

BOOKS, BIBLIOGRAPHIES, CONCORDANCES, DEDICATED ISSUES
Ackerman, John, *A Dylan Thomas Companion* (Basingstoke: Macmillan, 1991).
—— *Dylan Thomas: His Life and Work* (Basingstoke: Macmillan, 1991).
—— *Welsh Dylan* (Bridgend: Seren, 1997).
Bold, Alan (ed.), *Dylan Thomas: Craft or Sullen Art* (London: Vision Press, 1990).
Brinnin, John Malcolm, *Dylan Thomas in America* (London: Dent, 1956).
—— (ed.), *A Casebook on Dylan Thomas* (New York: Crowell, 1960).
Brown, Terence, *Louis MacNeice: Sceptical Vision* (Dublin: Gill and Macmillan, 1975).
—— and Alec Reid (eds), *Time Was Away: The World of Louis MacNeice* (Dublin: Dolmen Press, 1974).
Burns, Richard, *Ceri Richards and Dylan Thomas: Keys to Transformation* (London: Enitharmon Press, 1981).

Cleverdon, Douglas, *The Growth of 'Milk Wood'* (London: Dent, 1969).

Cox, C. B. (ed.), *Dylan Thomas: A Collection of Critical Essays* (Englewood Cliffs, NJ: Prentice Hall, 1966).

Coulton, Barbara, *Louis MacNeice in the BBC* (London: Faber & Faber, 1980).

Davies, Aneirin Talfan, *Dylan: Druid of the Broken Body* (London: Dent, 1964).

Davies, James A., 'Dylan Thomas', *Annotated Bibliography of English Studies* (Abingdon: Swets & Zeitlinger, 1997), CD-ROM.

—— *A Reference Companion to Dylan Thomas* (Westport, CT: Greenwood Press, 1998).

Davies, Walford, *Dylan Thomas: An Open Guide* (Milton Keynes: Open University Press, 1986).

—— *Dylan Thomas*, Writers of Wales series (Cardiff: University of Wales Press, 1990).

—— (ed.), *Dylan Thomas: New Critical Essays* (London: Dent, 1972).

Emery, Clark, *The World of Dylan Thomas* (Coral Gables, FL: University of Miami Press, 1962).

Farringdon, Jillian M. and Michael G. Farringdon, *A Concordance and Word-Lists to the Poems of Dylan Thomas* (Oxford: Oxford Microform Publications, 1980).

Ferris, Paul, *Dylan Thomas* (Harmondsworth: Penguin, 1978).

—— *Caitlin: The Life of Caitlin Thomas* (London: Hutchinson, 1993).

Fitzgibbon, Constantine, *The Life of Dylan Thomas* (London: Dent, 1965).

Garlick, Raymond (ed.), *Dock Leaves* 5: 'A Dylan Thomas number', 13 (Spring 1954).

Gaston, Georg, *Dylan Thomas: A Reference Guide* (Boston: G. K. Hall, 1987).

—— ed., *Critical Essays on Dylan Thomas* (Boston: G. K. Hall, 1989).

—— ed., *Critical Essays on Dylan Thomas* (Boston: G. K. Hall, 1989).

Genet, Jacqueline and Wynne Hellegouarch (eds), *Studies on Louis MacNeice* (Caen: Centre de Publications de l'Université de Caen, 1988).

Goodby, John and Chris Wigginton (eds), *Dylan Thomas: New Casebook* (Basingstoke: Palgrave, 2001).

Grindea, Miron (ed.), *Adam: International Review, A Literary Monthly in English and French: Dylan Thomas Memorial Number*, 238 (1953).

Hardy, Barbara, *Dylan Thomas's Poetic Language: The Stream that is Flowing Both Ways* (Cardiff: University of Wales Press, 1987).

Heaney, Seamus, *Dylan the Durable? On Dylan Thomas* (Bennington, VT: Bennington College, 1992).

Holbrook, David, *Llareggub Revisited: Dylan Thomas and the State of Modern Poetry* (London: Bowes & Bowes, 1962).

—— *Dylan Thomas: The Code of Night* (London: Athlone Press, 1972).

Jones, Daniel, *My Friend Dylan Thomas* (London: Dent, 1977).

Jones, T. H., *Dylan Thomas* (Edinburgh: Oliver & Boyd, 1963).

Kershner, R. B., *Dylan Thomas: The Poet and His Critics* (Chicago: American Library Association, 1976).

Kidder, Rushworth Moulton, *Dylan Thomas: The Country of the Spirit* (Princeton, NJ: Princeton University Press, 1973).

Kleinman, H. H., *The Religious Sonnets of Dylan Thomas* (Berkeley: University of California Press, 1963).

Korg, Jacob, *Dylan Thomas* (New York: Twayne, 1965).

Lernout, Geert (ed.), *The Crows Behind the Plough: History and Violence in Anglo-Irish Poetry and Drama* (Amsterdam: Rodopi, 1991).

Longley, Edna, *Louis MacNeice: A Study* (London: Faber & Faber, 1988).

McDonald, Peter, *Louis MacNeice: The Poet in his Contexts* (Oxford: Clarendon Press, 1991).

McKinnon, William T., *Apollo's Blended Dream: A Study of the Poetry of Louis MacNeice* (Oxford: Oxford University Press, 1971).

Marsack, Robyn, *The Cave of Making: The Poetry of Louis MacNeice* (Oxford: Clarendon Press, 1982).

Maud, Ralph, *Entrances to Dylan Thomas's Poetry* (Pittsburgh: University of Pittsburgh Press, 1963).

—— *Dylan Thomas in Print: A Bibliographical History* (with Appendix) (London: Dent, 1970).

Miller, J. Hillis, *Poets of Reality: Six Twentieth-Century Writers* (Cambridge, MA: Harvard University Press, 1966).

Moore, D. B., *The Poetry of Louis MacNeice* (Leicester: Leicester University Press, 1972).

Moynihan, William T., *The Craft and Art of Dylan Thomas* (Ithaca, NY: Cornell University Press, 1968).

Murdy, Louise B., *Sound and Sense in Dylan Thomas's Poetry* (The Hague: Mouton, 1966).

Olson, Elder, *The Poetry of Dylan Thomas* (Chicago: University of Chicago Press, 1954).

O'Neill, Michael and Gareth Reeves (eds), *Auden, MacNeice, Spender: The Thirties Poetry* (Basingstoke: Macmillan, 1991).

Peach, Linden, *The Prose Writing of Dylan Thomas* (Basingstoke: Macmillan, 1988).

Pratt, Annis, *Dylan Thomas's Early Prose: A Study in Creative Mythology* (Pittsburgh: University of Pittsburgh Press, 1970).

Rolph, Alexander J., *Dylan Thomas: A Bibliography* (London: Dent, 1956).

Stallworthy, Jon, *Louis MacNeice* (London: Faber & Faber, 1996).

Stanford, Derek, *Dylan Thomas* (New York: Citadel Press, 1964).

Tedlock, E. W. (ed.), *Dylan Thomas: The Legend and the Poet* (London: William Heinemann, 1960).

Tindall, William York, *A Reader's Guide to Dylan Thomas* (New York: Octagon Books, 1962).

Treece, Henry, *Dylan Thomas: 'Dog Among the Fairies'* (London: Lindsay Drummond, 1949).

Tremlett, George, *Dylan Thomas: In the Mercy of His Means* (London: Constable, 1991).

Williams, Robert Coleman (ed.), A *Concordance to the Collected Poems of Dylan Thomas* (Lincoln: University of Nebraska Press, 1967).

ESSAYS, ARTICLES, REVIEWS, LECTURES

Armitage, C. M., 'MacNeice's prose fiction', *Honest Ulsterman*, 73 (1983).

Connolly, Cyril, 'Comment', *Horizon*, June (1940).

Davies, James A., 'Dylan Thomas's "One Warm Saturday" and Tennyson's *Maud*', *Studies in Short Fiction*, 14 (1977).

—— '"Crying in My Wordy Wilderness"', *Anglo-Welsh Review*, 83 (1986).

—— '"A Picnic in the Orchard": Dylan Thomas's Wales', in *Wales: The Imagined Nation*, ed. Tony Curtis (Bridgend: Poetry Wales Press, 1986).

—— '"Hamlet on his father's coral": Dylan Thomas and paternal influence', in *Welsh Writing in English: A Yearbook of Critical Essays*, 1 (1995).

—— '"A Mental Militarist": Dylan Thomas and the Great War', in *Welsh Writing in English: A Yearbook of Critical Essays*, 2 (1996).

—— 'Questions of identity: Dylan Thomas, the movement, and after', in *Appropriations and Impositions: National, Regional and Sexual Identity in Literature*, ed. Igor Navrátil and Robert B. Pynsent (Bratislava: Nàrodné literáne centrum, 1997).

Davies, Walford, 'Imitation and invention: the use of borrowed material in Dylan Thomas's prose', *Essays in Criticism*, 18 (1968).

Grigson, Geoffrey, 'How much me your verbal acrobatics amaze', in *The Harp of Aeolus and Other Essays* (London: Routledge, 1948).

Hardy, Barbara, 'Region and Nation: R. S. Thomas and Dylan Thomas', in R. P. Draper (ed.), *The Literature of Region and Nation* (Basingstoke: Macmillan, 1989)

Heinemann, Margot, 'Louis MacNeice, John Cornford and Clive Branson: three left-wing poets', in Jon Clark, Margot Heinemann et al. (eds), *Culture and Crisis in Britain in the Thirties* (London: Lawrence and Wishart, 1979).

Holme, Christopher, 'The radio drama of Louis MacNeice', in John Drakakis (ed.), *British Radio Drama* (Cambridge: Cambridge University Press, 1981).

Lahey, Philip A., 'Dylan Thomas: a reappraisal', *Critical Survey*, 5 (1993).

Lewis, Peter Elfed, 'The radio road to Llareggub', in John Drakakis (ed.), *British Radio Drama* (Cambridge: Cambridge University Press, 1981).

Loesche, Katherine T., 'Welsh poetic syntax and the poetry of Dylan Thomas', *Transactions of the Honourable Society of Cymmrodorion* (1979).

—— 'Welsh poetic stanza form and Dylan Thomas's "I dreamed my genesis"', *Transactions of the Honourable Society of Cymmrodorion* (1982).

—— 'An early work on Irish folklore and Dylan Thomas's "A grief ago"', in A. T. E. Matonis and Daniel F. Melia (eds), *Celtic Language, Celtic Culture* (Van Nuys, CA: Ford & Bailie, 1990).

Kennelly, Brendan, 'Louis MacNeice: an Irish outsider', in M. Seskine (ed.), *Irish Writers and Society at Large* (Gerrards Cross: Colin Smythe, 1985).

Kirkham, Michael, 'Louis MacNeice's poetry of ambivalence', *University of Toronto Quarterly*, 56 (1987).

McDonald, Peter, 'The rector's son', *The Honest Ulsterman*, 73 (1983).

McKay, Don, 'Dot, line, and circle: a structural approach to Dylan Thomas's imagery', *Anglo-Welsh Review*, 18 (1969).

—— 'Crafty Dylan and the "Altarwise" sonnets', *University of Toronto Quarterly*, 55 (1986).

Mayhead, Robin, Review of *Collected Poems, 1934–1952*, *Scrutiny*, 19 (1952–53).

Mellors, W. H., 'The bard and the prep school', *Scrutiny*, 9 (1940).

Paulin, Tom, 'The man from no part: Louis MacNeice', and 'In the salt mines', in *Ireland and the English Crisis* (Newcastle upon Tyne: Bloodaxe, 1984).

Porteus, Hugh Gordon, 'Map of Llareggub', *New English Weekly*, 7 September 1939.

Pratt, Terrence M., 'Adventures in the poetry trade: Dylan Thomas and Arthur Rimbaud', *English Language Notes*, 24, 4 (1987).

Read, Herbert, 'The map of love', *Seven*, 6 (1939).

Roberts, Michael, 'The brassy orator', *London Mercury*, 9 October 1939.

Roche, Tony, 'A reading of *Autumn Journal*: the question of Louis MacNeice's Irishness', *Text and Context*, 3 (1988).

Schvey, Henry I., 'Dylan Thomas and surrealism', *Dutch Quarterly Review*, 5 (1975).

Southwark, James G., 'Louis MacNeice', in *Sowing the Spring: Studies in British Poets from Hopkins to MacNeice* (Oxford: Blackwell, 1940).

Stoddard, Eve Walsh, 'The poetics of parable in the later poems of Louis MacNeice', *Concerning Poetry*, 18 (1985).

Volsik, Paul, 'Neo-Romanticism and the poetry of Dylan Thomas', *Études Anglaises*, 42 (1989).

Williams, Raymond, 'Dylan Thomas's play for voices', *Critical Quarterly*, 1 (1959).

Young, Alan, 'Image as structure: Dylan Thomas and poetic meaning', *Critical Quarterly*, 17 (1975).

General critical and theoretical works

BOOKS

Aaron, Jane, Teresa Rees, Sandra Betts and Moira Vincentelli (eds), *Our Sisters' Land* (Cardiff: University of Wales Press, 1994).

Alpers, Paul, *What is Pastoral?* (Chicago: University of Chicago Press, 1996).

Alpert, Michael, *A New History of the Spanish Civil War* (London: Macmillan, 1994).

Althusser, Louis, *Lenin and Philosophy and Other Essays*, trans. B. Brewster (London: NLB, 1971).

Andrews, Elmer (ed.), *Contemporary Irish Poetry* (London: Macmillan, 1992).

Ashcroft, Bill, Gareth Griffiths and Helen Tiffin (eds), *The Post-Colonial Studies Reader* (London: Routledge, 1995).

Baudelaire, Charles, *The Painter of Modern Life and Other Essays*, trans. Jonathan Mayne (London: Phaidon, 1964).

Beevor, Anthony, *The Spanish Civil War* (London: Cassell, 1999).

Benjamin, Walter, *One Way Street and Other Writings*, trans. Edmund Jephcott and Kingsley Shorter (London: NLB, 1979).

Bergonzi, Bernard, *Reading the Thirties: Texts and Contexts* (London: Macmillan, 1978).

Bhabha, Homi K., *The Location of Culture* (London: Routledge, 1994).

Borkenau, Frank, *World Communism* (Ann Arbor: University of Michigan Press, 1962).

Botting, Fred, *Gothic* (London: Routledge, 1996).

Branson, Noreen and Margot Heinemann, *Britain in the Nineteen Thirties* (London: Weidenfeld & Nicolson, 1971).

Breton, André, *Manifestos of Surrealism*, trans. Richard Seaver and Helen R. Lane (Ann Arbor: University of Michigan Press, 1972).

Brown, Terence and Nicholas Grene (eds), *Tradition and Influence in Anglo-Irish Poetry* (Totowa, NJ: Barnes & Noble, 1989).

Bürger, Peter, *Theory of the Avant-Garde*, trans. Michel Shaw (Minneapolis: University of Chicago Press, 1984).

Butler, Judith, *Bodies That Matter: On the Discursive Limits of 'Sex'* (New York and London: Routledge, 1993).

—— *Excitable Speech: A Politics of the Performative* (London: Routledge, 1997).

Caesar, Adrian, *Dividing Lines: Poetry, Class and Ideology in the 1930s* (Manchester: Manchester University Press, 1991).

Callinicos, Alex, *Against Postmodernism: A Marxist Critique* (Cambridge: Polity Press, 1989).

Conran, Anthony, *The Cost of Strangeness* (Llandysul: Gomer Press, 1982).

Conran, Tony, *Frontiers in Anglo-Welsh Poetry* (Cardiff: University of Wales Press, 1997).

Corcoran, Neil, *English Poetry since 1940* (London: Longman, 1993).

Craig, Cairns, *Out of History: Narrative Paradigms in Scottish and British Culture* (Edinburgh: Polygon, 1996).

Crawford, Robert, *Devolving English Literature* (Oxford: Clarendon Press, 1992).

Cunningham, Valentine, *British Writers of the Thirties* (Oxford: Oxford University Press, 1988).

Daiches, David, *Literary Essays* (Edinburgh: Oliver & Boyd, 1956).

—— *The Present Age in British Literature* (Bloomington: Indiana University Press, 1958).

Davie, Donald, *Articulate Energy* (London: Routledge & Kegan Paul, 1955).

Deane, Seamus, *A Short History of Irish Literature* (London: Hutchinson, 1986).

—— *Celtic Revivals: Essays in Modern Irish Literature, 1880–1980* (London: Faber & Faber, 1985).

—— *Strange Country: Modernity and the Irish Nation: Irish Writing Since 1790* (Oxford: Clarendon Press, 1997).

Derrida, Jacques, *Of Grammatology*, trans. Gayatri Chakravorty Spivak (Baltimore, MD: Johns Hopkins University Press, 1976).

—— *Glas*, trans. John P. Leavey, Jr. and Richard Rand (Lincoln: University of Nebraska Press, 1986).

Dowson, Jane (ed.), *Women's Poetry of the 1930s* (London: Routledge, 1996).

Dreyfus, H. L. and P. Rabinow, *Michel Foucault: Beyond Structuralism and Hermeneutics* (New York and London: Harvester Wheatsheaf, 1982).

Eagleton, Terry, *Criticism and Ideology: A Study in Marxist Literary Theory* (London: Verso, 1976).

—— *The Ideology of the Aesthetic* (Oxford: Blackwell, 1990).

Empson, William, *Some Versions of Pastoral* (London: Chatto & Windus, 1935).

—— *Argufying*, ed. John Haffenden (London: Hogarth Press, 1988).

Ferris, Paul, *Caitlin: The Life of Caitlin Thomas* (London: Hutchinson, 1993).

Foucault, Michel, *Madness and Civilisation: A History of Insanity in the Age of Reason*, trans. Richard Howard (London: Tavistock, 1967).

—— *The Order of Things: An Archaeology of the Human Sciences* (London: Tavistock, 1970).

—— *Discipline and Punish* (New York: Random House, 1977).

Freud, Sigmund, *The Standard Edition of the Complete Psychological Works* (London: Hogarth Press and the Institute of Psychoanalysis, 1953).

Garfield, Simon, *Mauve* (London: Faber & Faber, 2001).

Gibbons, Luke, *Transformations in Irish Culture* (Cork: Cork University Press in association with Field Day, 1996).

Gilbert, Sandra and Susan Gubar, *No Man's Land: The Place of the Woman Writer in the Twentieth Century, Vol. 3: Letters to the Front* (New Haven: Yale University Press, 1994).

Graham, Helen and Paul Preston (eds), *The Popular Front in Europe* (London: Macmillan, 1987).

Grigson, Geoffrey, *Poetry of the Present: An Anthology of the Thirties and After* (London: Phoenix House, 1949).

Harris, John, *A Bibliographical Guide to Twenty-four Modern Anglo-Welsh Writers* (Cardiff: University of Wales Press, 1994).

Harvey, John, *The Art of Piety: The Visual Culture of Welsh Nonconformity* (Cardiff: University of Wales Press, 1995).

Heaney, Seamus, *Place and Displacement: Reflections on Some Recent Poetry from Northern Ireland* (Grasmere: Trustees of Dove Cottage, 1984).

—— *The Redress of Poetry: Oxford Lectures* (London: Faber & Faber, 1995).

Hewitt, John, *Ancestral Voices: The Selected Prose of John Hewitt*, ed. Tom Clyde (Belfast: Blackstaff Press, 1987).

Hynes, Samuel, *The Auden Generation: Literature and Politics in England in the 1930s* (London: Bodley Head, 1976).

Inglis, Tom, *Moral Monopoly: The Catholic Church in Modern Irish Society* (Dublin: Gill and Macmillan, 1987).

Johnson, Pamela Hansford, *Important to Me: Personalia* (London: Macmillan, 1974).

Jones, Glyn, *The Dragon Has Two Tongues* (London: Dent, 1968).

Kiberd, Declan, *Inventing Ireland: The Literature of the Modern Nation* (London: Vintage, 1996).

Koestler, Arthur, *The God that Failed: Six Studies in Communism*, ed. Richard Crossman (London: Hamish Hamilton, 1950).

Kristeva, Julia, *Powers of Horror: An Essay on Abjection* (New York: Columbia University Press, 1982).

Levinson, Marjorie, *Keats's Life of Allegory* (Oxford: Blackwell, 1988).

Lewis, Saunders, *Is there an Anglo-Welsh Literature?* (Cardiff: Guild of Graduates of the University of Wales, 1939).

Light, Alison, *Forever England: Femininity, Literature and Conservatism between the Wars* (London: Routledge, 1991).

Lloyd, David, *Anomalous States: Irish Writing and the Post-Colonial Moment* (Dublin: Lilliput Press, 1993).

Longley, Edna, *Poetry in the Wars* (Newcastle upon Tyne: Bloodaxe, 1986).

—— *The Living Stream: Literature and Revisionism in Ireland* (Newcastle upon Tyne: Bloodaxe, 1994).

Lukács, Georg, *The Meaning of Contemporary Realism*, trans. John and Necke Mander (London: Merlin Press, 1963 [1937]).

Lyotard, Jean-François, *The Postmodern Condition: A Report on Knowledge*, Theory and History of Literature, vol. 10 (Minneapolis: University of Minnesota Press, 1984).

McCormack, W. J., *Ascendancy and Tradition in Anglo-Irish Literary History from 1789 to 1939* (Oxford: Clarendon Press, 1985).

—— *The Battle of the Books: Two Decades of Irish Cultural Debate* (Mullingar: Lilliput Press, 1986).

—— *From Burke to Beckett: Ascendancy, Tradition and Betrayal in Literary History* (Cork: Cork University Press, 1994).

McDonald, Peter, *Mistaken Identities: Poetry and Northern Ireland* (Oxford: Clarendon Press, 1997).

Matthews, Steven and Keith Williams (eds), *Rewriting the Thirties: Modernism and After* (London: Longman, 1997).

Maxwell, D. E. S., *Poets of the Thirties* (London: Macmillan, 1969).

Merleau-Ponty, Maurice, *Phenomenology of Perception*, trans. Colin Smith (London: Routledge, 1962).

—— *The Visible and the Invisible*, ed. Claude Lefort, trans. Alphonso Lingis (Illinois: Northwestern University Press, 1968).

Miller, J. Hillis, *Poets of Reality: Six Twentieth-Century Writers* (Cambridge, MA: Harvard University Press, 1966).

Moi, Toril, *Sexual/Textual Politics: Feminist Literary Theory* (London: Routledge, 1991).

Montefiore, Jan, *Feminism and Poetry: Language, Experience, Identity in Women's Writing* (London: Pandora, 1987).

—— *Men and Women Writers of the 1930s: The Dangerous Flood of History* (London: Routledge, 1996).

Morrison, Blake, *The Movement: English Poetry and Fiction of the 1950s* (London: Methuen, 1986).

Musselwhite, David E., *Partings Welded Together: Politics and Desire in the Nineteenth-Century English Novel* (London: Methuen, 1987).

Nicholls, Peter, *Modernisms: A Literary Guide* (Basingstoke: Macmillan, 1995).

Norris, Christopher, *William Empson and the Philosophy of Literary Criticism* (London: Athlone Press, 1978).

—— *The Truth About Postmodernism* (Oxford: Blackwell, 1993).

Orwell, George, *Collected Essays, Journalism and Letters*, 2 (Harmondsworth: Penguin, 1954).

—— *Homage to Catalonia* (Harmondsworth: Penguin, 1974).

Patterson, Annabel, *Pastoral and Ideology: Virgil to Valéry* (Oxford: Clarendon Press, 1988).

Paulin, Tom, *Ireland and the English Crisis* (Newcastle upon Tyne: Bloodaxe, 1984).

Peach, Linden, *Ancestral Lines* (Bridgend: Seren, 1993).

Pearce, Lynne, *Reading Dialogics* (London: Edward Arnold, 1994).

—— *Feminism and the Politics of Reading* (London: Edward Arnold, 1997).

Perloff, Marjorie, *The Futurist Movement: Avant-Garde, Avant Guerre, and the Language of Rupture* (Chicago: University of Chicago Press, 1986).

—— *Radical Artifice: Writing in the Age of Media* (Chicago: University of Chicago Press, 1991).

Punter, David, *The Literature of Terror: A History of Gothic Fictions* (London: Longman, 1980).

Ray, Paul C., *The Surrealist Movement in England* (Ithaca, NY: Cornell University Press, 1971).

Scarfe, Francis, *Auden and After: The Liberation of Poetry 1930–1941* (London: Routledge & Kegan Paul, 1943).

Shohat, Ella and Robert Stam, *Unthinking Eurocentricism: Multiculturalism and the Media* (New York: Routledge, 1994).

Simpson, Louis, *A Revolution in Taste* (New York: Macmillan, 1978).

Sisson, C. H., *English Poetry, 1900–1950: An Assessment* (New York: St Martin's Press, 1971).

Spender, Stephen, *World Within World* (London: Hamish Hamilton and the Book Society, 1951).

Symons, Julian, *The Thirties: A Dream Revolved* (London: Faber & Faber, 1975).

—— *Makers of the New: The Revolution in Literature, 1912–1939* (London: André Deutsch, 1987).

Thomas, M. Wynn, *Corresponding Cultures: The Two Literatures of Wales* (Cardiff: University of Wales Press, 1999).

Tolley, A. T., *The Poetry of the Thirties* (London: Victor Gollancz, 1975).

Trotsky, Leon, *Literature and Revolution* (Ann Arbor: University of Michigan Press, 1960).

Whites, John J., *Literary Futurism: Aspects of the First Avant-Garde* (Oxford: Clarendon Press, 1991).

Wilde, Alan, *Horizons of Assent: Modernism, Postmodernism and the Ironic Imagination* (Baltimore, MD: Johns Hopkins University Press, 1987).

Williams, Gwyn A., *When Was Wales?* (Harmondsworth: Penguin, 1991).

Williams, Raymond, *What I Came to Say* ed. Neil Belton, Francis Mulhern and Jenny Taylor (London: Hutchinson Radius, 1989).

Wills, Clair, *Improprieties: Politics and Sexuality in Northern Irish Poetry* (Oxford: Clarendon Press, 1993).

Young, Alan, *dada and after: extremist modernism and english literature* (Manchester: Manchester University Press, 1981).

ESSAYS, ARTICLES AND REVIEWS

Adamowicz, Elza, 'Monsters in surrealism: hunting the human-headed bombyx', Peter Collier and Judy Davies (eds), *Modernism and The European Unconscious* (Cambridge: Polity Press, 1990).

Adorno, Theodor, 'Looking back on surrealism', in *Notes to Literature*, vol. 1, ed. Rolf Tiedemann, trans. Shierry Weber Nicholsen (New York: Columbia University Press, 1991).

Auden, W. H., 'Poetry, poets and taste', *The Highway* (Workers' Educational Association, December 1936). Reprinted in *The English Auden: Poems, Essays and Dramatic Writings, 1927–1939*, ed. Edward Mendelson (London: Faber & Faber, 1977).

Austin, J. L., 'Performative-constative', in John R. Searle (ed.), *The Philosophy of Language* (Oxford: Oxford University Press, 1971).

Bhabha, Homi K. 'The commitment to theory', *New Formations*, 5 (1988).

—— 'Cultural diversity and cultural dfferences', in Bill Ashcroft, Gareth Griffiths and Helen Tiffin (eds), *The Post-Colonial Studies Reader* (London: Routledge, 1995).

Breton, André, 'Premier manifeste', in *Manifestes du surrealisme* (Paris: Jean-Jacques Pauvert, 1962).

Butler, Judith, 'Performative acts and gender constitution: an essay in phenomenology and feminist theory', in Sue-Ellen Case (ed.), *Performing Feminism: Feminist Critical Theory and Theatre* (Baltimore, MD: Johns Hopkins University Press, 1990).

Derrida, Jacques, 'Traumatism to promise', in *Points: Interviews 1974–1994*, ed. Elizabeth Weber (Stanford: Stanford University Press, 1995).

Donoghue, Denis, 'Confusion in Irish studies', Queen's University of Belfast/ English Society Lecture, Queen's University of Belfast, 5 March 1998.

Eagleton, Terry, 'Capitalism, modernism and postmodernism', in Patricia Waugh (ed.), *Postmodernism: A Reader* (London: Edward Arnold, 1992).

Ellmann, Maud, 'Eliot's abjection', in John Fletcher and Andrew Benjamin (eds), *Abjection, Melancolia and Love: The Work of Julia Kristeva* (London: Routledge, 1990).

Graham, Colin, 'Liminal spaces: post-colonial theories and Irish culture', *Irish Review*, 16 (Autumn/Winter, 1994).

—— 'Post-colonial theory and Kiberd's "Ireland"', *Irish Review*, 19 (Spring/ Summer, 1996).

Hopkins, Chris, '"James Joyce is an Irish Edition of Mr Caradoc Evans": two Celtic naturalists', *Irish Studies Review*, 19 (Autumn, 1995).

Jones, T. Gwynn, 'The modern trend in Welsh poetry', *Western Mail*, 19 July 1939.

Kearney, Richard, 'Myth and motherland', in Field Day Theatre Company (ed.), *Ireland's Field Day* (London: Hutchinson, 1985).

Kennedy, Liam, 'Modern Ireland: post-colonial society or post-colonial pretensions?', *Irish Review*, 13 (Winter 1992/3).

Longley, Edna, 'Signposting the century', *Poetry Review*, 86: 1 (Spring 1996).

Montrose, Louis A., '"Eliza, Queen of shepheardes", and the pastoral of power', *English Literary Renaissance*, 10 (1980).

Park, Katherine and Lorraine J. Daston, 'Unnatural conceptions: the study of monsters in sixteenth- and seventeenth-century France and England', *Past and Present*, 92 (1981).

Roberts, Harri, '"Tower of Babel": Heteroglossia and the (de)construction of meaning in Glyn Jones's *The Valley, The City, The Village* and Niall Griffiths's *Grits*', in *Welsh Writing in English: A Yearbook of Critical Essays*, 7 (2002).

Said, Edward, 'Yeats and decolonization', in Barbara Kruger and Phil Mariani (eds), *Making History*, Discussions in Contemporary Culture, 4, (Seattle: Bay Press, 1989).

Sharpe, Jenny, 'Figures of colonial resistance', *Modern Fiction Studies*, 35 (1989).

Slemon, Stephen, 'Unsettling the Empire: resistance theory for the Second World', *World Literature Written in English*, 30:2 (1990).

Tolley, A. T., 'The Thirties: but whose?', *Poetry Review*, 83: 4 (1993/4).

Wright, Elizabeth, 'The uncanny and surrealism', in Peter Collier and Judy Davies (eds), *Modernism and the European Unconscious* (Cambridge: Polity Press, 1990).

Index

Broadcasts

Prose